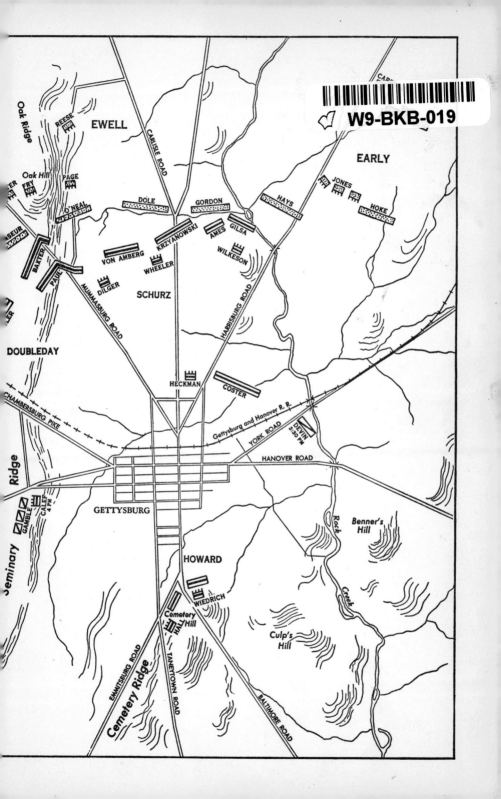

THE GUNS AT GETTYSBURG

Other Books by FAIRFAX DOWNEY

History

SOUND OF THE GUNS
INDIAN-FIGHTING ARMY
DISASTER FIGHTERS
OUR LUSTY FOREFATHERS
HISTORY OF DOGS FOR DEFENSE
HORSES OF DESTINY
DOGS OF DESTINY
CATS OF DESTINY
MASCOTS
GENERAL CROOK, INDIAN FIGHTER

Biography

THE GRANDE TURKE; SULEYMAN THE MAGNIFICENT
BURTON, ARABIAN NIGHTS ADVENTURER
RICHARD HARDING DAVIS: HIS DAY
PORTRAIT OF AN ERA, AS DRAWN BY C. D. GIBSON

Historical Novels, Juveniles

WAR HORSE
DOG OF WAR
JEZEBEL THE JEEP
CAVALRY MOUNT
THE SEVENTH'S STAGHOUND
ARMY MULE
TRAIL OF THE IRON HORSE
A HORSE FOR GENERAL LEE
THE SHINING FILLY

Humor and Light Verse

A COMIC HISTORY OF YALE
FATHER'S FIRST TWO YEARS
WHEN WE WERE RATHER OLDER
YOUNG ENOUGH TO KNOW BETTER
LAUGHING VERSE (edited)

THE GUNS AT GETTYSBURG

By FAIRFAX DOWNEY

DAVID McKAY COMPANY, INC.

New York

Material from *The Glory Road*, by Bruce Catton, Copyright 1952 by Bruce Catton,
reprinted by permission of Doubleday and Company, Inc.

MANUFACTURED IN THE UNITED STATES OF AMERICA

VAN REES PRESS • NEW YORK

To the memory of a great artilleryman

GENERAL HENRY JACKSON HUNT

Chief of Artillery, Army of the Potomac

Foreword and Acknowledgments

My *Sound of the Guns, the Story of American Artillery from the Ancient and Honorable Company to the Atom Cannon and Guided Missile,* because of its scope could allot only part of a chapter to the guns at Gettysburg. It had not long been written before I was impelled to turn to another book entirely devoted to the heroic and critical parts played by the gunners of the Union and the Confederacy on those three July days of 1863.

Artillery in the famous battle had been largely neglected, it seemed to me, as it had to a battery officer who fought there. "Gettysburg," wrote Lieutenant Colonel Tully McCrea,* "has been discussed from every point of view except that of the artillery, yet every account of the battle refers to the effectiveness of the arm. Scarcely any of them omit to mention the distinguished part which it performed, but how this was brought about, and wherein the management of the batteries differed from that of Chancellorsville or other preceding battles, has been passed by as a mere tactical or administrative detail, overshadowed by the magnitude of the conflict as a whole."

There are such notable exceptions as the treatment of the Confederate artillery in Wise's *The Long Arm of Lee,* which assigns four chapters to Gettysburg and contains excellent material on the gunners of the South. Colonel Wise's work was inspired by the same inattention to the arm which animated my book. "The reports of the various commanders engaged in the war are generally vague on

* *Journal of the Military Institution of the United States,* V. 22 (1898), p. 528.

matters pertaining to the artillery," he observes in his preface. "... The result is that he who enters into an investigation of more than the most casual character finds himself involved in a game of historical dominoes, with many of the pieces lacking. ... More often than not, the corps, division, and brigade returns include the artillery personnel in the strength of the infantry, and rarely are the names of batteries, or the number of guns engaged, specified. Over such details is merely thrown the cloak of the mysterious word 'artillery,' as if that should suffice for the curious." While *The Long Arm of Lee* pays due tribute to the command and service of the Union cannon at Gettysburg, its preoccupation is of course with the opposing artillery.

Other exceptions to the general disregard of the guns at Gettysburg are the articles in *Battles and Leaders of the Civil War* by General Hunt, the Union Chief of Artillery, along with Freeman's *Lee's Lieutenants* and Catton's *Glory Road*. All three narratives, however, present full-scale pictures of the combat. The cannon that confronted each other from Cemetery and Seminary ridges are of necessity accorded proportionate consideration, their role in the battle more briefly noted than in the following pages, concentrated on the artillery action.

Besides the works already mentioned, chief sources for this book were the *Official Records of the Rebellion*, the invaluable battery histories, and various other eyewitness accounts.

Although this book was written from the artillery viewpoint by an artilleryman with service in both World Wars, it is not intended to detract from the glory that belongs to the infantry. The author's grandfather, Major George Mason Downey, an infantry officer, won two brevets for gallantry in action in the Peach Orchard. On the Pennsylvania field the infantry still maintained its proud title of Queen of Battles, finally gaining or holding ground and achieving the ultimate decision. Artillery, by its own statement and acceptance of its mission, remained a supporting arm. Yet Gettysburg may be said to have heralded a day when the crown would pass to fire power. It was the Union cannon that broke all but the spearhead of

Pickett's assault, the last great charge in the old tradition. Thenceforth, slowly but inevitably, fire power, however delivered—on the ground, by airplane or guided missile—would complete its usurpation and reign as King of Battles.

As I did for *Sound of the Guns,* I offer my heartfelt thanks to my friend, Colonel Harry C. Larter, Jr., Artillery, U.S.A., Retired, for his painstaking criticism of the manuscript of this book. His invaluable suggestions included such detailed minutiae as the two basil leather pads carried by drivers to protect harness sores.

Others to whom I am deeply grateful include:

Dr. Frederick Tilberg, Historian, Gettysburg National Military Park, for a tour of the battlefield and a bibliography of battery histories that guided my research;

Bruce Catton, who approved this work at its outset as a worthwhile undertaking and whose books are an inspiration to any Civil War historian;

Colonel Jennings C. Wise for counsel and permission to quote from *The Long Arm of Lee;*

General C. A. Baehr, veteran artilleryman and thorough student of Gettysburg, for his study of the artillery's participation in the battle and invaluable aid on the preparation of maps;

Major Charles West for criticism, encouragement, and supervision of illustrations;

Dr. James C. Hazlett, expert on the ordnance employed at Gettysburg and a member of a branch of the family of the commander of Hazlett's Battery;

Lieutenant Colonel William A. Knowlton for useful references;

Harold L. Peterson and Robert L. Miller of the Company of Military Collectors & Historians for enactment in uniform of a color film showing the firing of a Civil War cannon.

Libraries that rendered most helpful and courteous service include those of Dartmouth College, the New York Public, Yale and Harvard universities, the U.S. Military Academy, the Artillery and

Guided Missile Center at Fort Sill, Oklahoma, and the University Club, New York.

All my gratitude, as for previous books, is due my wife, Mildred Adams Downey, for criticism and typing; to Kennett L. Rawson, editor, David McKay Company, Inc., and Mrs. Douglas Ryan of its staff; my agent, Oliver G. Swan, of Paul R. Reynolds & Son.

FAIRFAX DOWNEY

West Springfield, New Hampshire

Contents

xi

Illustrations

following page 112

Illustrations in the Text

THE GUNS AT GETTYSBURG

CHAPTER 1

Guns and Men

The guns still stand at Gettysburg.

They stand on the very ground where they flamed and thundered through three days of crucial battle.[1] Muzzles still point toward the foe they faced in July, 1863. As defiant of time as of shells that burst around them, they will soon have withstood the passage of a century.

These are the cannon of the Union and the Confederacy. Field-pieces of light and horse artillery. Smoothbore Napoleons, 3-inch rifles, Parrotts, howitzers, breech-loading Whitworths.[2] Stacked beside the sturdy carriages on which their iron or bronze barrels rest are small heaps of their ammunition: round shot, shell and shrapnel, canister of deadly, short-range blasts. Wheeled chests that carried those missiles loom to the rear. Nearby are sometimes ranked poled limbers. Teams hitched to them galloped into action, drawing the rumbling guns and caissons through the little Pennsylvania town where roads and the threads of history met—rushing them down from the ridges into an arena of wheatfields and peach orchards—struggling up the steep and rocky slopes of Little Round Top.

Rifle, revolver, saber, and shot-torn banners—the Stars and Stripes and the Stars and Bars—they are cased in capitols and museums. But under the open sky, upon the field where the smoke of battle wreathed them, the guns still stand at Gettysburg.

Along tree-fringed turnpike and lane, over broad acres, hard by the dark fastness of Devil's Den, beside the stone wall of The Angle, the monuments rise—statues of bronze and shafts of granite and marble. Their plaques and inscriptions bear names of men and

3

regiments that ring with valor. The guns also have their emblems of stone and their tablets.[3] These cannon belonged to a Virginia battalion, those to a Massachusetts, an Ohio, or a Regular battery. Here they fought to the finish—rolled back toward the Potomac in retreat and pursuit—battled through the remainder of the war— returned at last in peace to commemorate the glory here won. Often they speak more eloquently, these silent guns, than the words graven on the pedestals and columns rising around them.

They mark a midpoint between the crude cannon of the past and the complex mechanisms of the twentieth century which would win for artillery its reputation as the greatest killer on the battle- field. Compared to the mighty atomic cannon, they wear an aspect of antiques. Yet these Gettysburg guns, for all their simplicity, were deadly engines of destruction, and a special aura clings to them. They represent the 272 pieces, mustered by the Army of Northern Virginia, and the 362, brought to the field by the Army of the Potomac,[4] to take part in an ever-memorable conflict that proved to be the turning point of the Civil War, the high-water mark of the Confederacy. They poured forth a hail of shells, some 55,000 rounds,[5] stupendous for the time.[6] In the artillery duel of the second day alone they delivered the heaviest volume of fire ever heard in this hemisphere. They fought at ranges that narrowed from miles to yards and down to point-blank volleys. No other war has witnessed more desperate close combat around the guns. To one young cannoneer in the heat of battle they "became things of life —not implements but comrades." [7]

Metal against mortality, the guns at Gettysburg have survived the men who served them.[8] Gone now are all the gunners in blue or gray. Some lie near where they fell, under white stones in the military cemetery. Others, who lived to fight on, only to die in later battles, or to complete their spans in years of peace, have one and all answered the last roll call. By records they and their com- rades in arms left they can be summoned back from Valhalla to man their guns again.

Chiefs of artillery and field officers. Battery commanders and

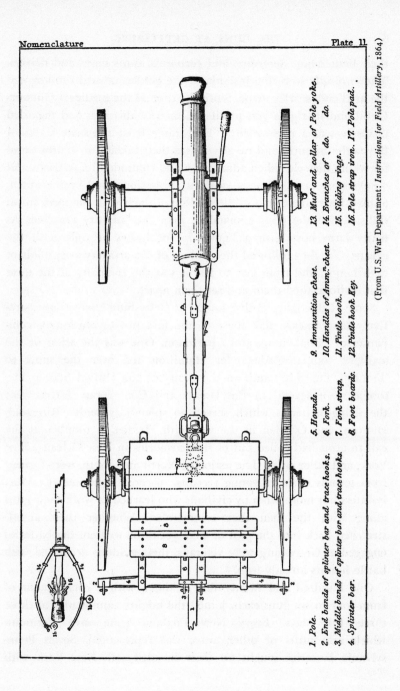

(From U.S. War Department: *Instructions for Field Artillery*, 1864)

1. Pole.
2. End bands of splinter bar and trace hooks.
3. Middle bands of splinter bar and trace hooks.
4. Splinter bar.
5. Hounds.
6. Fork.
7. Fork strap.
8. Foot boards.
9. Ammunition chest.
10. Handles of Amm.ⁿ chest.
11. Pintle hook.
12. Pintle hook Key.
13. Muff and collar of Pole yoke.
14. Branches of   do.   do.
15. Sliding rings.
16. Pole strap iron. 17. Pole pad.

their lieutenants. Sergeants and corporals, cannoneers and drivers. They proudly wore the insignia of the golden crossed cannon and the artillery's scarlet stripe. Since the time of the medieval Gunners Guild and its rights and privileges, men of this arm had regarded themselves as a *corps d'élite*. They came from the same walks of life as the infantry and cavalry it was their mission to support and for whom they cherished admiration and comradeship. Artisans and shopkeepers, farmers and woodsmen, professional and business men, a small leavening of old soldiers. More of them with the mechanical skills, which the guns demanded, than the infantry enrolled. As many farm boys with a knowledge of horses as rode with the cavalry. Yet they followed the guidons of the artillery as symbols of high honor, and from first to last it was the company of the guns that distinguished them and set them apart.

Some of the batteries that fought at Gettysburg claimed comparatively long lineage like those of the first pre-Revolutionary companies of Philadelphia and Charleston. One was the scion of the artillery company Alexander Hamilton led over the snow to Trenton, the oldest unit in the Army of the United States. The forebears of several in the Union and Confederate forces were the flying batteries which served so splendidly under Ringgold, Duncan, and O'Brien in the war with Mexico. A number at the call to arms had rolled out of state armories in New Orleans, New York, and other cities. The majority, North and South, were formed from groups of eager young recruits, officered sometimes by West Pointers but more often by civilians who learned to work their guns along with the men they commanded. Whether their annals stretched back into the past or were yet to be written, the batteries engaged at Gettysburg were veterans, their guidons decorated with battle honors already won.

One hundred and twenty-nine of them, with a complement of from four to six guns each, joined the mighty cannonades of those three July days. Every New England state save Vermont, which sent units of other arms, was represented. Seven Pennsylvania batteries fought on their invaded soil. New York with nineteen far surpassed the quota of any other state. Only the Regulars with 25 outnumbered it. Maryland, holding to the Union but with loyalties divided, contributed one. So did Michigan and West Virginia, severed from her parent state and sometimes as in Maryland's case pitting kinsmen against each other. Four were of Ohio artillery, two of New Jersey.[9]

Seventeen battalions, commanded by such valiant and able gunner officers as Alexander and Pegram, rumbled up from the South. Their batteries, seldom numbered or lettered, bore the names of leaders or places of origin, titles made illustrious on the field of battle—the Rockbridge Artillery, the Richmond Howitzers, the Washington Artillery of New Orleans. The majority pridefully claimed Virginia as their native state, but Louisiana seconded her, and artillerymen from North and South Carolina, Georgia, Mississippi, Maryland, and Alabama contended here for a cause destined to be lost. They engaged the enemy with fewer pieces, a lighter weight of metal, with more limited and often inferior ammunition. Against as heavy odds elsewhere they had won victory, victory which on this field thrice narrowly slipped their grasp.

Clatter of cavalry, tramp of infantry, rumbling of artillery. Converging on the little town of the crossroads and its natural amphitheater formed by eastern and western ridges, 97,000 men who wore Union blue and 75,000 in Confederate gray marched to engage in the greatest battle ever fought on the American continent.

CHAPTER 2

The First Day of Battle

MORNING

•◦•

Battery A, 2nd U.S. Artillery
Pegram's Battalion, C.S.A.
Richmond Battery
Fredericksburg Battery
Richmond Letcher Battery
Pee Dee (S.C.) Artillery
Richmond Purcell Battery

•◦•

A little southwest of the town of Gettysburg Calef's Battery, A of the 2nd U.S. Artillery, was encamped. Its guns stood in position along the Baltimore Road, ready to rake it or limber up and move out in a hurry. In the half light of dawn its horses had been watered, fed, and groomed, and its men had eaten breakfast. Drivers harnessed and hitched, and cannoneers saddled their mounts. The rising sun of that first day of July, 1863, promised to be hot. It gleamed on the roofs of houses and barns and shimmered on the wheatfields.

Stamping of many more hoofs, snorting, and voices swelled the sounds from the artillery lines. All around them Buford's cavalry division, supported by the battery, was stirring. Its troops also had attended to their animals and themselves, saddled up, and led out. Major General John Buford was an officer who demanded strict field discipline and readiness for action in or out of the presence of the enemy, and there was no doubt that Rebel forces were somewhere in the vicinity. The division had shadowed them all the way from the mountaintops of the Blue Ridge, keeping in such close touch that it clashed frequently with Gray horsemen.

For Lee's army, flushed with the victories of Fredericksburg and Chancellorsville, had crossed the Potomac and was invading the North. It was pushing into Pennsylvania, driving for Harrisburg to destroy the bridge across the Susquehanna River and disable the Pennsylvania Railroad, link with the West. After that, Lee had told his staff, he could turn his attention to Philadelphia, Baltimore, or Washington. To counter his thrust the Union Army, now under General George Gordon Meade, was making forced marches up from the South, paralleling the advance of the enemy. But the Blue columns were trailing, and nothing but hastily called out militia stood between the Army of Northern Virginia and the Pennsylvania capital. Here was presage of disaster. One more Southern triumph could overwhelmingly strengthen the Northern peace party, might, even yet, assure foreign intervention, and end the war with independence for the Confederate States of America.

To Buford, ordered to reconnoiter the Gettysburg area, it seemed as queer as it was uncomfortable to have the Rebels north of the Army of the Potomac. But there they most certainly were. They had had enough cavalry to brush him out of their path but not to screen their advance effectively or override him. Buford did not know that Lee had allowed General J. E. B. Stuart with the bulk of the Gray horse to go riding around the Union rear.

Doubling Buford's certainty of the enemy's whereabouts was the fact that his pickets had spotted some of the Johnnies two days earlier on a ridge only a mile west of town. They saw the Yankee scouts and withdrew. Likely they'd be back from that direction or perhaps the northeast. Roads converged on Gettysburg like spokes on the hub of a wheel, and all of them to the north had to be watched. Couriers galloped the southern ones with Buford's reports. They returned with word that two corps of Meade's slowly concentrating army were close enough to come to the support of the cavalry if trouble developed.

In Battery A's park sergeants ran their eyes over its 3-inch Ordnance rifles, trim guns mounted on lightweight carriages, for horse artillery must move rapidly to keep up with cavalry. Those rifled pieces could throw a shell 4,000 yards but that was extreme range and seldom used. Guns with Buford's horse were usually close up behind the front line or in it, covering his dismounted troopers. Might as well have been supporting infantry, A Battery said, and drew plenty of canister when it replenished its caissons from the ammunition train. Buford was one of the new type of cavalry commanders. While he could deliver a whooping charge if need be, mostly his men fought on foot. If they had to pull out, horse holders galloped up with their mounts as the artillery's did with their cannoneers' horses. Riflemen and gunners got away fast. By the time the enemy came up, they were out of the saddle and opening fire from a new position.

Along the line of the battery's carriages chains rasped as limber pole props were let down to take weight off the necks of wheel pairs. Drivers smoothed back the manes of their horses beneath collars as they had the hair under saddle blankets. In case of trouble each driver carried two basil leather pads—tanned sheepskin with the wool still on—to put under a collar and relieve pressure on a sore neck. Such injuries must be guarded against more than ever, with the animals as worn and gaunt as they were. No wonder. Only three weeks ago the battery had been supporting Buford's command in Pleasonton's hell-for-leather cavalry clash with Stuart at Brandy Station, Virginia. It had been a long, hard march to Gettysburg and a fighting one, the guns unlimbered now and again to beat off Confederate cavalry charges. Caisson corporals checked ammunition. The chests at least were full, which was more than could be said of the battery's strength. Calef had only one officer instead of the four authorized; two of his three sections—two guns to a section—were commanded by sergeants. Still there were men enough to serve the pieces and horses enough to pull them, the twelve caissons, and the traveling forge and battery wagon containing stores for shoeing and repairs.[11] Battery A was ready for action, and John Haskell Calef, U.S. Military Academy, Class of 1858, so reported to the brigade commander.

Calef was still a lieutenant, though he was later to win a brevet for gallantry in the battle that lay ahead.[12] Promotion was slow as molasses in the Regulars, slow as it had always been, wartime regardless.[13] Usually only a transfer to the Volunteers assured quick steps up. Many a West Pointer, notably a number of former artillerymen, led a brigade, or division of state troops.[14] They were lost to their old arm, and replacements were hard to come by. Competent artillery officers were scarce; behind the best of them lay the long training essential for specialists. Yet whatever a man's rank, there was no more dashing a command in the army than a battery of horse artillery, and furthermore Calef's was a Regular battery.

Old Regulars they called themselves with pride. There had not been many of them at the beginning of the war—Congress kept the U.S. Army small in peacetime—and it was under strength at that. There were considerably fewer now after two years of casualties. New enlistments were scanty. A man got no bounty for joining up with the Regulars. Thinned ranks had been filled with Volunteers.[15] After a while the recruits called themselves Regulars, too, which was all right with the old-timers if the youngsters tried to live up to the name.

None of the former civilians standing to horse that July morning had been allowed to forget that they had the honor to be members of Battery A, 2nd U.S. Artillery—Regulars by the grace of God, or words to that effect. They were reminded that A was one of the first batteries to roll into Washington in 1861 and the first horse artillery to be revived since the Mexican War. It had fought right on through from First Bull Run. Like any outfit worth its salt it boasted distinctions and differences. There was, for instance, the special claim it staked to Taps during the Yorktown campaign. True, a brigadier, Dan Butterfield, had composed the call, but

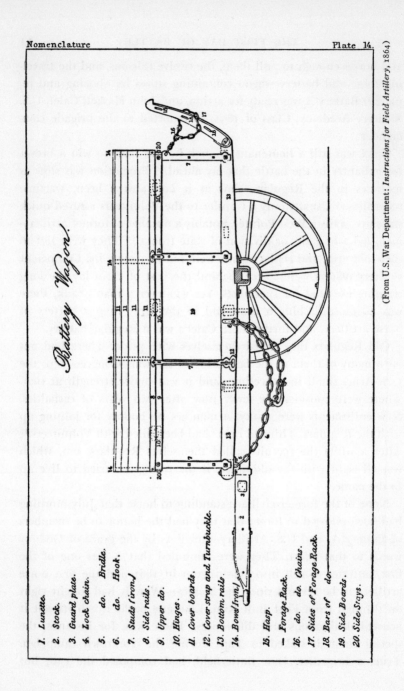

Battery Wagon.

1. Lunette.
2. Stock.
3. Guard plate.
4. Lock chain.
5. do.   Bridle.
6. do.   Hook.
7. Studs (iron.)
8. Side rails.
9. Upper do.
10. Hinges.
11. Cover boards.
12. Cover strap and Turnbuckle.
13. Bottom rails.
14. Bows (iron.)
15. Hasp.
— Forage Rack.
16. do.   do.   Chains.
17. Sides of Forage Rack.
18. Bars of   do.
19. Side Boards.
20. Side Stays.

(From U.S. War Department: Instructions for Field Artillery, 1864.)

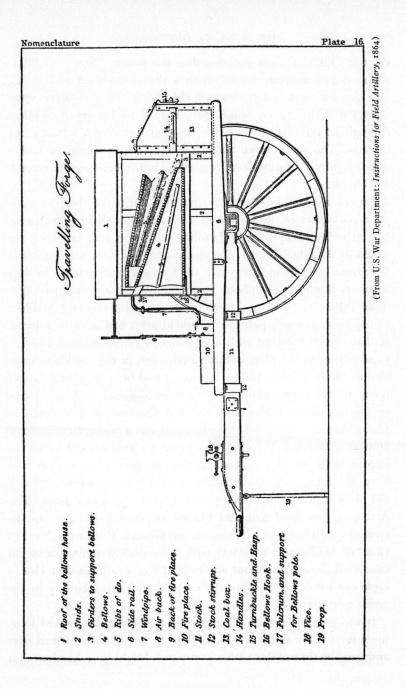

Travelling Forge.

1   Roof or the bellows house.
2   Studs.
3   Girders to support bellows.
4   Bellows.
5   Ribs of du.
6   Side rail.
7   Windpipe.
8   Air back.
9   Back of fire place.
10 Fire place.
11 Stock.
12 Stock stirrups.
13 Coal box.
14 Handles.
15 Turnbuckle and Hasp.
16 Bellows Hook.
17 Fulcrum, and support
    for Bellows pole.
18 Vice.
19 Prop.

(From U.S. War Department: *Instructions for Field Artillery*, 1864)

Captain Tidball, then commanding the battery, first ordered it sounded at a military burial when a cannoneer died of wounds, and the enemy was too close to risk firing the customary three volleys over his grave. Since then, thanks to Battery A, buglers throughout the army blew those poignant notes for a soldier's last bivouac. The Seven Days, notably Malvern Hill, Antietam, and a dozen cavalry skirmishes had tempered A's iron before it rode north to Gettysburg.

An organization with service stretching back into the past owns priceless traditions. Embodied in a motto, referred to in a line or two of orders, they may be familiar only to a few, but they are generally if vaguely sensed. *Forsan et haec olim meminisse juvabit*— Perchance even these things will rejoice men to remember in days to come. Bounden to uphold long-established honor, soldiers fight more gallantly. So it was, *noblesse oblige,* with the 2nd Artillery whose heritage was a rich one. Winfield Scott had been its colonel. Its batteries had served with distinction at Chippewa and Lundy's Lane in the War of 1812, in bitter campaigns in the Florida swamps against the Seminoles, and in Mexico. A had been Duncan's Battery then, and the army had never seen a more able one. Its feats of arms in the storming of Monterey and the Convent of San Pablo at Churubusco deserved to be cherished. It was a young lieutenant of Duncan's, Henry J. Hunt, who galloped his gun straight up to the citadel walls of Mexico City. Although almost every man and horse was hit as he unlimbered, he and other survivors manhandled the piece forward, muzzle to muzzle with a Mexican cannon. The American gun fired first and blasted the enemy weapon and its crew to bits. That young lieutenant was General Hunt now, Meade's Chief of Artillery. If an officer with more than 300 guns under his command should single out any unit, it was a safe bet that Hunt's eagle eye would be bent on the conduct of his old battery in the battle to come.

It was getting on toward eight o'clock. Cannoneers looked longingly toward the town. A fellow ought to be allowed to stroll over and pass the time of day with a pretty girl. Might get a handout that would be welcome after months of army grub. Pennsylvania girls would be a pleasant change from the spitfires down South, who glared and flounced indoors when a handsome Yankee artillery outfit rolled by. Plainly, though, there was no chance of anybody being let loose. Battery A had followed the old army custom of hurrying up to wait and like as not would keep on doing more of the same all day.

Then it happened. To the northwest, somewhere out along the Chambersburg Pike, scattering shots cracked, faint but unmistakable. All the horses' ears pricked up as if they had been pulled by a single string. Men stiffened and took their posts, eyes on the battery commander. There was an answering rattle of rounds, closer, fired in quick succession. Must be one of the new Spencer repeating carbines Buford's troopers had been armed with recently.

An interval. Pounding of hoofs at a gallop. That would be some of the pickets coming back to report. Probably their corporal had stayed behind, ridden up for a closer look, and loosed off those rapid shots from his Spencer at the Johnnies. Battery A, standing to horse, needed no more than Calef's upswept arm. Mount. Hook on the guns. Cannoneers swung into saddles, each squad forming up behind its piece. The battery was in column on the road when orders to roll came from the brigade commander.

It clattered through town behind the Blue squadrons. People stared from doorways. They'd better be getting down into their cellars—there was going to be plenty of shooting hereabouts. Veering left on to the Chambersburg Pike, Calef, told to select his own position, shouted, his voice half lost in the tumult of hoofs and wheels: "Forward, into Battery!" His bugler sounded.

IN BATTERY

The battery fanned out from column into line, slowing to a halt. Out in front pioneers began tearing down fences in the field of fire.

Before Calef could give the command for action front, a horseman galloped up. Here was Buford himself, a general who knew just where he wanted his artillery. One section to the right of the pike, another to the left, the third still farther to the left, he directed. The battery would hold the center of the line of dismounted cavalry. Calef saluted, giving the order.

Smartly the sections took their designated places. Cannoneers, turning their mounts over to horse holders, swarmed around the carriages, unlimbering guns—flung open ammunition chests, and ran forward to muzzles with shells—rammed them home and stood clear. Gunners peered over sights along the barrels.

Musketry crackled. Gray skirmish lines were sweeping across the fields now. Blue pickets, retiring before them, filtered back into the main line. Calef nodded to his bugler. Brassy notes, urgent, imperative, cut through the racket. Commence firing!

COMMENCE FIRING

Lieutenant John W. Roder trained one of his section guns on a group of mounted men three quarters of a mile away. He jerked the lanyard. The first artillery shot in the Battle of Gettysburg boomed, fired by Battery A, 2nd U.S. Artillery.[16]

Yonder on the ridge to the west dust clouds swirled. That was Rebel artillery going into position.

If ever an officer looked less like a hell-roaring artilleryman, it was the Confederate major leading those dust-kicking batteries across the ridge. William Johnson Pegram was beardless and mustacheless in a war where whiskers were virtually insignia of rank. Sometimes a perky little bow tie peeped incongruously above the collar of his gray tunic. His Southern courtliness, combined with modesty and innate shyness, lent him a deferential air everywhere but on the battlefield. Thick-lensed spectacles over extremely nearsighted eyes completed the aspect of a schoolteacher in uniform. But when the war cut short his student days at the University of Virginia, it was the art of artillery that Willie Pegram taught and practiced after a brief tour in the infantry. That art owned no abler exponent. Since the death of the gallant Pelham, paladin of horse artillerymen, no Gray gunner was rated higher than William Johnson Pegram.

They said—and the praise made him blush painfully—that he habitually fought his guns at close quarters because those weak eyes of his couldn't see a dozen yards, and he refused to open fire until he had the enemy in plain view. When he went forward to reconnoiter positions, word would run along infantry columns he passed: "There's going to be a fight. Here comes that damn little man with the 'specs'!" At Mechanicsville, commanding one of the batteries comprising his battalion today, he had held his ground for hours under a terrific infantry fusillade and the concentrated fire of five six-gun batteries. By nightfall 50 of his 90 cannoneers were casualties, half his horses killed, and four of his six guns knocked out. He took the surviving pieces back into action next day. Supporting Stonewall Jackson's "foot cavalry" at Cedar Mountain, Pegram sighted a strong column marching on the flank of his guns. In the failing light neither he nor officers with better sight could identify it as friend or foe.

Pegram at once turned his battery over to his lieutenant, saying: "McGraw, I shall ride up close to these fellows; keep a sharp lookout, and if you see me wave my hat, open all the guns." In a moment he was galloping toward the column now within a hundred yards, reined in his horse close to the silently-moving mass, turned, and waved his hat. Another moment and he rode at full speed into the line of guns where old Stonewall sat on his sorrel watching the column. Pegram cried out in great glee: "Pitch in, men; General Jackson is looking at you!" The enemy was broken in a few minutes by his rapid fire, but speedily put three batteries into position and returned it. For 2 hours this single battery fought 18 guns of the enemy, and it was not until 10 o'clock that his heated and disabled Napoleons were silenced.[17]

He sought shyly to avoid the compliments he earned by his feats of arms. To escape them he seldom went into Richmond when home on leave. He preferred, as the grandiloquent quotations, beloved by oratory of the day, put it, "the iron-throated plaudits of his guns," "the fiery pang of shells." Once to steady his artillerymen under close attack he had called out, "Men, whenever the enemy takes a gun from my battery, look for my dead body in front of it." And in the last bitter days of the war at Five Forks, the only time he ever lost a gun, he would keep his word.

Major Pegram, though he sat firm in his saddle, looked pale today. On the sick list but refusing evacuation, he had ridden the last 90 miles of the march in an ambulance to be able to take over his command on this field of battle.

The battalion he led was one of 17 with the Confederate Army. Their superior organization could well be envied by the understaffed Federals.[18] Each battalion had a field officer in addition to its commander, and a complete commissioned staff. Failures of such readily-wielded striking forces in the forthcoming battle must be laid to the corps which controlled them and to deficiencies in equipment. They were still short of horses despite those requisitioned on the northward march. Pegram had nine Napoleons, eight rifles, and two howitzers, well below the normal complement for his five batteries. Yet the *esprit de corps* of this splendid artillery was never higher.

Odds Pegram had faced on other fields were about to be reversed this morning. As the brigades of Archer and Davis, Heth's Division, A. P. Hill's Corps, charged down the slopes and plunged through Willoughby Run, Pegram's 19 guns unlimbered and prepared for action against Calef's six.

It has been said that a lack of shoes dictated the battleground. The Confederates that withdrew June 29 when they saw Buford's scouts had been in search of much-needed footgear, reputed to be stocked in Gettysburg. These coming on now could well use them, too, with the exception of one organization. Crenshaw's Battery, Pegram's Battalion, wore good boots. In an army that hard campaigning and dwindling supply had left threadbare and ragged, these gunners sported uniforms of fine English cloth. No thanks in either case to the Quartermaster General, C.S.A., but to Captain Crenshaw.

When that Richmond wholesale merchant formed the battery in March, 1862, and was elected its commander, he had equipped it out of his own pocket with handsome uniforms, overcoats, blankets, shoes, and even underclothes. He had advanced money to the government for the purchase of its horses and its guns: two 10-pounder Parrotts, a pair of 12-pound brass howitzers, and two 6-pounder brass guns, and so brought it into the field far earlier than would have been the case with ordinary issue. His men, "the jolliest, most rollicking, fun-loving crowd of youngsters between 16 and 25" —clerks, salesmen, carpenters, business executives, and farmers— made a fine-looking artillery outfit. They fought as well as they looked at Gaines's Mill, Second Manassas, and Sharpsburg, valiantly led by Crenshaw. Then to his keen regret he was taken from his beloved battery to serve as a purchasing agent in Europe for the Confederate Government.[19]

Fredericksburg, where the new captain was killed. Chancellorsville. By then the battery looked as tattered as the rest of the army. But William G. Crenshaw had not forgotten it. In Europe on his own account he bought a uniform and a pair of boots for each batteryman and shipped them back. A Federal cruiser gobbled up the blockade runner carrying them. Crenshaw duplicated his gift, and this time it got through. It was again a fine-looking lot of artillerymen that marched north to Gettysburg. What if the Northern girls didn't appreciate it? They made uncomplimentary remarks as the battery rolled by, but the men laughed them off. They envied the remark of one of Hood's Texans; its story was going around the army. When he sighted a Chambersburg matron, her ample bosom adorned with a sizable U.S. flag, scowling from her doorway, the Texan had driven her into outraged retreat. "Take care, madam," he called out. "Hood's boys are great at storming breastworks when the Yankee colors is on them." [20]

Lieutenant A. B. Johnston led the battery into action that first day of July. It was still called Crenshaw's and would be to the end of the war and thereafter. The memory of his valor and generosity was indelible. His name was proudly borne by the battery through forty-eight battles and many skirmishes.

Crenshaw's Battery went into position on Herr Ridge. It opened fire shortly after Calef's guns began thundering—so soon that it would always dispute the honor of the first shot.

The Purcell Battery had been Pegram's first artillery command and it was dear to his heart. Captain Joseph McGraw led it today. A big, tough man with the stamp of Ireland on him, he had been a teamster. He rose through the ranks to a commission, becoming Pegram's most trusted officer and finally a lieutenant colonel. Later in the war he was severely wounded and suffered the amputation of an arm, refusing an anesthetic and never uttering a sound; as soon afterward as possible he reported back for duty. The battery was named for John Purcell of Richmond, who had equipped it with uniforms, blankets, and so on at his own expense as Crenshaw had done. Such was the fervor of patriotism at the outset of the war that many a unit—batteries, companies, and even regiments—was armed and uniformed by individuals or through popular subscription. It was not enough for the ladies of a city or township to present stands of colors, or for a friend to give the colonel or the captain a charger. The considerable expense of all or part of the accouterments and supplies required was privately assumed by devoted citizens, South or North, unwilling to wait for slow provision by the state.[21]

The battery's most elegant member was not with it today, but he was not far away, having been detached to serve as a captain on Longstreet's staff. F. W. Dawson, affectionately called "The

Britisher," had volunteered in England. A dress suit, Inverness cape, and a bowie knife, made to order by a surgical instrument firm, graced his luggage when he crossed the Atlantic on a blockade runner. He served briefly in the Confederate Navy but left it to join Pegram and the Purcell, where he was wounded and promoted to first lieutenant.[22]

These hard-fighting artillerymen had been engaged in every battle of the Seven Days where they lost 59 out of 80 men, with only enough at the end to man a single gun. Recruited up and constantly whittled down again, this one battery, hailed by Pegram himself as "the coolest and most desperate men he ever saw in a tight place," in four years of warfare lost 200 killed or wounded.

Its guns chimed in with those of the Pee Dee Artillery of South Carolina and with the fire of the Fredericksburg Battery. Despite the Confederate victory in the battle named for their town, the Fredericksburg men still had a score to even at Gettysburg. They had not forgotten the shelling and burning of their homes and their sacking by Federal troops in the manner of medieval warfare. In the Richmond Letcher Battery, named for Virginia's wartime governor, shells were flung at the enemy less vindictively. A big Irishman, Martin Douglas, was Number 4 on one of the Letcher guns, his duty to pull the lanyard. Every time he jerked it, sending a projectile hurtling to burst on the foe, he would cross himself and mutter a prayer, "Lord, be marsiful to their poor souls." [23]

Puffs of smoke from those five batteries of Pegram's, blossoming along the hillside, and the Gray infantry lines sweeping forward were in clear view for Buford in the vantage point he had taken after posting Calef's guns. In the tower of the Lutheran Theological Seminary, crowning the ridge named for it, the panorama of the battlefield, both for this opening phase and those that would develop, was presented to him. The General nodded with satisfaction. Here was a strong defensive position. His lines could fall back on the ridge from which he was watching. If they were forced from it and on back through Gettysburg, yonder to the south of the town lay another good position in the shape of a fishhook. Holding

Cemetery Ridge there, the Union Army could anchor its right flank
on Culp's and Cemetery hills and its left on those wooded knobs,
Little Round Top and Round Top. All depended on whether the
army could arrive in time, urgently summoned by the couriers he
had sent galloping to Reynolds' I Corps.

Buford's satisfaction vanished in apprehension. His lines were
spread very thin. Brigades of one or two Rebel divisions, with
probably the rest of a corps behind them, were flooding along both
sides of the Chambersburg Pike toward his left and center. His right
would have to be extended and reinforced to meet an attack that
might be launched along the Mummasburg Road. Buford swiveled
around and gazed still farther right where the Carlisle and Harrisburg roads were brown shafts, menacing from the north. Blue
troops and plenty of them would be needed to fend off a Rebel
corps coming from that direction, as well it might.

The General turned back toward the fight in hand. His dismounted troopers were doing him proud, staving off the weight of
numbers flung against them. Calef's Battery, holding its ground as
sturdily, was in hot action.

Up on the slopes Pegram's guns redoubled their fire. Too bad
General Heth had not ordered his and McIntosh's battalions to
open before he sent brigades charging in. They could have pounded
apart those Blue lines and cleared the way for the assault. Some
generals were prone to forget their artillery and what it could do for
them. As it was, Pegram had loosed off without having been given
a definite objective.[24] However, nobody needed to point out his
present primary target to him. He concentrated 12 of his pieces on
that lone Union battery and pounded it.

It became "extremely warm" thereabouts, Calef remembered.
Buford, observing that his artillery was about to be blown off the
field if it stayed where it was, sent an aide galloping with orders
for each section to withdraw by piece. The cavalry was being forced
to retire as well, and the unsupported guns would be lost in a
jiffy.

Over in First Sergeant Newman's section four horses were down.

Calef rushed up a caisson limber to help him pull out, but Newman managed it himself, dragging one gun with the surviving pair of the team. The Rebel infantry was so close, the sergeant apologized to his commander, that he had been unable to save the harness from the dead horses. A little later he slipped back and salvaged two sets out of four. Remounts would be easier to obtain than harness for them, and Calef's Battery must keep rolling.

The other battered sections also broke free. As Calef took the opportunity to replenish his ammunition chests, another order came from Buford: flush that lot of Rebels out of the ditch over there. Lieutenant Roder galloped one of his guns into battery. Gray riflemen converged on it shouting, "There's a piece. Let's take it!" They very nearly did. A bullet in the leg knocked over the corporal about to load, but a private snatched the round of canister from his hands and rammed it down to the breech. The gun slammed, blasting back its would-be captors. Roder, enfilading the ditch, raked its length, filling it to the rims with mangled bodies.

Pegram's guns, moved forward, barked louder and faster. Calef, by Buford's citation, had "held his own gloriously, worked his guns deliberately with great judgment and skill, and with wonderful effect upon the enemy." [25] General Hunt would hear of it, too, as they hoped he would, and declare that "Calef's battery, engaging double the number of its own guns, was served with an efficiency worthy of its former reputation as 'Duncan's battery' in the Mexican War." [26] But Battery A, 2nd U.S. Artillery, had been just about put out of action for the time being, and the cavalrymen's line was bent to the breaking point. With their artillery they had stood against the enemy's large odds and heavier weight of metal for two vital hours.

Ten o'clock. Tramp of marching feet and rumble of wheels. Colors flaunting red, white, and blue in the sunlight. Drums thumping and fifes shrilling "The Campbells Are Coming." Reynolds' I Corps, with Howard's XI to follow, had arrived in time.

Buford from his belfry tower saw Reynolds galloping ahead of his command and clattered down the stairs to meet him. "There's the devil to pay!" the cavalryman called, and outlined the situation.

Reynolds hurried off a despatch to Meade, reporting contact with the enemy. "I will fight inch by inch," he wrote, "and if driven into the town I will barricade the streets and hold him back as long as possible." [27]

The fresh Blue infantry veered west of Gettysburg and toward Seminary Ridge. Now the unbalanced scales of battle swung to equipoise and commenced to tilt the other way.

By the clash of two corps the armies had been committed to combat. Lee, finally learning of the close approach of the Federals, had been forced to turn aside from his objective and meet them. Meade's troops were inevitably drawn away from his selected defensive position along Pipe Creek, fifteen miles away, toward the widening whirlpool of conflict at Gettysburg.

CHAPTER 3

The First Day of Battle

BEFORE AND AFTER NOON

·•·

2nd Maine Battery
McIntosh's Battalion, C.S.A.
  Danville (Va.) Battery
  Hardaway (Ala.) Battery
  2nd Rockbridge Battery
  Virginia Battery (Johnson)
Batteries L and E, 1st New York Light Artillery
Battery B, 1st Pennsylvania Light Artillery
5th Maine Battery
Battery B, 4th U.S. Artillery

·•·

Major General John F. Reynolds, leading his Union I Corps into action, was an old artilleryman of the Mexican War, veteran of the bloody street fighting at Monterey and the glorious day at Buena Vista. He had five batteries, one of them commanded by a captain of the same name as his. All of them were good. Artillery odds were nevertheless against him. Calef's guns, 2nd U.S. Artillery, had been blown off the field by Pegram's battalion, and on its left McIntosh's guns were booming, with two more battalions of Hill's III Corps, C.S.A., coming forward.

But Reynolds' first concern was not his cannon but to throw in his infantry to take over the line from Buford's tired Blue troopers. He went about it with the competence of one of the Union's best generals. The command of the Army of the Potomac might have been his today. He had once refused it, believing he would not be given a free hand, and it went to Meade. Men would later speculate on that turn of events. If Reynolds had held the top post, he might well, they thought, have destroyed Lee's army in retreat after the battle, an opportunity Meade failed to seize. If— Military history abounds in that pregnant preposition, and the Battle of Gettysburg possesses an inordinate share. If Stonewall Jackson had not been mortally wounded at Chancellorsville— If Lee had not permitted Jeb Stuart to go riding off with the bulk of the cavalry on that long circuit—[28] If Ewell had pressed his attack on the afternoon of the first day— If Warren had not been watching on Little Round Top— If Longstreet had not delayed on the third day— However, the potentialities in regard to Reynolds were about to be ended as he rode toward the firing line. A Confederate sharpshooter had found a first-rate position in an old stone barn, and the muzzle of his rifle was searching for a good target such as an officer on horseback.

North and south of the Chambersburg Pike, also called the Cashtown Road, Reynolds flung his infantry into the fight. There marched the famous Iron Brigade, "a command of Michigan, Wisconsin, and Indiana soldiers who deserved their name." [29] They wore their black slouch hats like the badge of honor they were, honor won by superb gallantry in past combats and to be earned again today at fearful cost. Shortly the Southerners would sight that headgear, distinctive among prevailing forage caps, and shout a tribute: "Here are those damned black-hat fellers again . . . 'Tain't no militia—that's the Army of the Potomac!"

Now as musketry crackled, and the Gray guns barked louder, one of Reynolds' batteries galloped forward. It was high time. The Blue line was gunless. Calef's battered artillery had gone limping to the rear, one piece pulled by its sole surviving pair, a battery badly punished but gathering itself to return if there were need of it— and there would be.

The relieving unit was the 2nd Battery, 1st Maine Light Artillery. When it was organized in 1861, a one-legged former West Pointer, Davis Tilson, subsequently a general, had trained it well. The man who rode at its head today was Captain James A. Hall, marked since Fredericksburg for extraordinary coolness in action. In that battle he had steadied supporting infantry by his complete disregard of heavy enemy cannonading. Sitting his horse beside his firing battery, he nonchalantly carried on a shouted conversation—only bellowed words could be heard in the racket—with two colonels.

While the soldiers hugged the ground and watched admiringly, a rebel shell came whistling in between Captain Hall and the two colonels, narrowly missing the colonels and going on to crash into a caisson in the rear, exploding it with an earth-rocking crash. Captain Hall looked faintly annoyed. Very deliberately he dismounted, walked over to one of his guns, painstakingly sighted it at the rebel battery which had fired the shot. Satisfied, he stepped back and waved his hand at the gun crew. The gun was fired and landed a direct hit, dismounting a rebel gun amid a cloud of torn earth and flying splinters. The battery commander walked back to his horse, mounted, and resumed the interrupted conversation as if nothing had happened.[30]

Now Hall galloped up and unlimbered 400 yards beyond Seminary Hill. Instantly a dozen Rebel guns concentrated on this tempting target. The Maine gunners stayed where they were and blazed back, driving two opposing pieces to shelter behind a barn. But the Blue infantry was being overlapped and it was ordered to pull back. Shortly Hall found himself isolated on the ridge, with an enemy column charging in fast on his right flank. While his left section continued the artillery duel, he swung his right and center guns to meet the assault. Sixty yards—canister range. Four muzzles belched murderous charges into the attacking column. Broken, it reeled back but re-formed again, this time with skirmishers thrown out ahead. The men in gray and butternut brown raced forward, dropped prone, and began to pick off Maine cannoneers and horses. There was no stopping them. Canister, which had slaughtered massed men, swept between and above the skirmishers like a scythe over stubble. "Artillery against skirmishers," an infantry observer noted, "is like shooting mosquitoes with a rifle." [31]

Artillery Horse in Action

(From *How the Battle Was Fought*, by James F. Long)

The 2nd Maine Battery had to pull out or be overwhelmed. It retired by sections, four of its guns firing to cover the retreat of the other two; then the next pair withdrawing in turn. Seventy-five yards to the rear a section would unlimber and open again. But Rebel bullets were fast killing off the horses. Some of the poor beasts were hit because they were in the way of flying lead; others were deliberately dropped. Even in the heat of battle it came hard to a rifleman, who loved animals, to shoot a horse. It was almost like cutting down a noncombatant, a different matter from a soldier's blazing away at an enemy doing his best to kill him. Yet a team crippled meant a gun immobilized, a gun open to capture, one that could be turned against the foe.

Soon one of the Maine cannon was entirely dehorsed, and the artillerymen had to fasten prolonge ropes to its carriage and haul it back by hand. That was too slow, with skirmishers closing in so rapidly. On the next move manpower would never make it. Hall was about to dash forward himself in an effort to save the piece when his division commander ordered him to abandon it and station the rest of his battery near the town to stave off pursuit.

Hall obeyed the latter part of the order but he could not endure giving up that gun. State of Mainers can be stubborn men, and it was a disgrace for a battery commander to lose a gun, as deep a humiliation as the capture of an infantry regiment's colors. He sent a sergeant and five men back to recover the fieldpiece. All were wounded or taken prisoner. Then the battery, ordered back into the line again, was led by a staff officer through an unfinished railroad cut and for 1,200 yards, without being able to turn about, it was raked by enemy artillery. At last, fighting off skirmishers, it escaped from that trap and managed on the way out to retrieve the lost gun and most of the harness from the dead horses. Then the half-crippled 2nd Maine was ordered out of the fight and put its three undisabled cannon in position near the cemetery.

On I Corps' left the conflict was going better for the Union. The valiant Iron Brigade hit the Southerners hard, rocked them back, outflanked them. Reynolds, one of the foremost of the war's frontline generals, rode forward into the smoke of battle, looming above it on his charger. It was then that the Rebel sharpshooter in the old stone barn found his target. His rifle spoke, and Reynolds toppled from his horse, a bullet through his head. Furiously the Iron Brigade renewed its onslaught, capturing Confederate General Archer and hundreds of his men. North of the turnpike the Blue ranks, reinforced, caught the contagion of victory and surged forward, also taking prisoners by the hundred.

Down from the hills to the northwest flowed more Gray infantry, Pender's Division of Hill's Corps coming to the support of Heth's broken lines. General Lee, whose presence had been enough to turn the tide in many a fray, was now on the field, too. Battle had been joined. Let it be pressed. Another of his corps, Ewell's, was marching toward Gettysburg from the north and should soon be in position to strike the Federal right.

With the Confederate foot rumbled two more gunner battalions under the able Colonel Reuben Lindsay Walker, Hill's Corps Chief of Artillery. Before long their cannonading would augment Pegram's and that of David McIntosh.

Major McIntosh's Battalion included an unusually-armed unit, the Alabama Battery commanded by Captain W. B. Hurt. Among its pieces were two breech-loading Whitworths, one of the three makes of cannon imported from England by the Confederacy and the only such guns on this battlefield. The day of breech-loaders was just dawning; it would be some years still before they superseded muzzle-loaders. Hurt's men were keen about their weapons and their long-reaching, accurate fire. For any cannoneer it was a blessing to be able to fling open a breechblock and slide in a round instead of running to the muzzle and turning his back to the enemy to load. At 5 degrees of elevation Whitworths could hurl a 12-pound bolt 2,800 yards. A handicap was their ammunition supply since their hexagonal bores required specially-shaped projectiles.[32] But the Alabamans' caissons were full today, and at long range they scoured the Federals in the railroad cut and bombarded them in the woods with shells that screeched terrifyingly in flight.

Captain Berryman Z. Price's Danville Battery and Captain Marmaduke Johnson's Virginia Battery swelled the Whitworths' fire, joined by a third Virginia unit, the 2nd Rockbridge. From the beginning of the war the Rockbridge Artillery had stood among the élite. In the tradition of Southern chivalry they wore a lady's favor, for they had been mustered in as the McDowell Guard in honor of Miss Lillie McDowell of Lexington, Virginia, who would later be married to a Rockbridge major. She had presented the artillerymen with a pair of fine horses, harness, an ambulance, and considerable clothing and other equipment. She also had paid a young fellow under military age a bounty to serve with the battery as her personal representative. From the outset he had proved worthy of her trust, although he was not at his post with the guns today. Only a few days previously he had been captured while on hazardous detached service.

McIntosh's and Pegram's fire, slow at first, grew in intensity as if in response to the verses of the Southern poet, who asked, "Why lingers the light artillery?" and answered:

> The gunner cries with a tug and a jerk;
> The limbers fly, and we bend to our work;
> The handspike in, and implements out—
> We wait for the word, and it comes with a shout—
> "Load!" [33]

The Gray guns pounded the Union infantry whenever it appeared in mass, at the same time counterbatterying the Blue artillery, which "returned shell for shell, though the Confederates believed they had the better of the duel." [34] While they could not yet be certain of dominance, they and the skirmishers had driven both Calef's and Hall's batteries to retreat, and mercilessly pummeled the latter when it returned through the railroad cut. But the Union battle lines still held or surged forward, and large batches of prisoners in gray could be seen being herded to the rear.

Ground gained and held, casualties inflicted and prisoners taken —these were measures of victory. And its instrument was the infantry, as the artillerymen of both sides were well aware. This was a war of the shoulder rifle whose Minié ball could kill at 1,000 yards.

"Sharpshooters used telescopic sights with deadly effect. Ordinary marksmen at the usual battle ranges of two hundred or three hundred yards often cut down gun crews with 'minnie balls' before the artillery was able to fire more than a few rounds." [35]

Certainly artillery was formidable both at long range and in the close infighting of this war from which gunners did not shrink. Cannon could plow bloody furrows through the ranks of foot troops with solid shot—could mow them down with bursting shell and shrapnel. Canister, tin cans containing iron or lead balls packed in sawdust, and the similar but less frequently used grapeshot were like "the murderous blasts of a giant sawed-off shotgun." In single, double, and even triple charges their frightful devastation at short range and point-blank anticipated that wrought by the later-day machine gun.[36] Napoleon's principle of massed artillery fire had been magnificently exemplified by Hunt's batteries on Malvern Hill and to some extent in other battles. Gettysburg would see it delivered by Alexander and Hunt again. But not until World War I would the artillery establish, and continue to maintain, its reputation as the greatest killer on the battlefield.

Meanwhile the infantry reigned without peer as Queen of Battles. Pegram's and McIntosh's battalions, for all their superiority in numbers and organization, had not alone knocked out the two opposing Union batteries. It was finally the Confederate skirmishers, picking off cannoneers and horses, who had forced them to withdraw.

Up into the Blue line galloped another I Corps battery. Captain G. H. Reynolds rode at the head of Battery L, 1st New York Light Artillery,[37] organized at Rochester in 1861, his six 3-inch rifled guns rumbling behind their jouncing carriages, cannoneers clinging desperately to their seats on the chests. Colonel Charles S. Wainwright, I Corps Chief of Artillery, directed L to take position between the town and the Seminary, then to move still farther forward. It was too hot there. Rebel cannon swept the New York guns with deadly crossfire from the right. Captain Reynolds clutched his forehead and reeled, struck by a shell fragment that would cost him an eye. They carried him back to a hospital in the town, and Lieutenant George Breck took over. Gray infantry was storming in on the battery's left now, while its own infantry masked its fire, and it was compelled to give ground. It opened again, with its bugler pitching in to help out a depleted gun crew.

Not for long could Battery L make a stand. Under shellfire and a hail of bullets its infantry support melted away, and the guns were left exposed to the full weight of the attack. Limber to the rear. Pull out fast.

But it could not pull out fast. The Chambersburg Pike ahead of it was jammed with a mass of retreating foot troops, neither to be threaded nor skirted. Battery L was forced to move at an agonizing walk. Close behind it rose the Rebel yell. Bullets whistled past. At last the pike emptied and was clear. The infantry had swung off it to take cover in the railroad cut, that ready-made trench. Breck signaled his bugler. "Trot"—and never was the call more welcome— blared above the din. It came too late. Lead was thudding into the carriages and the bodies of the horses at the battery's rear. The off wheeler of the last piece screamed and went down. His driver cut him out of the traces. Then three more of the team collapsed, threshing about in a welter of blood and tangled harness, and a lieutenant's mount also was killed. There was no saving the gun now. They had to let it go. Yet, as General Hunt was to declare, there were occasions when a gun could be lost with honor, and Battery L's loss after its gallant stand was such an instance. And the record of the 1st New York was to be cleared by the recapture of the piece later in the battle.

More Confederate troops, wave on wave, were sweeping down from the northwest. Hill's Corps was twice the strength of Reynolds', now commanded by General Abner Doubleday. On that reputed founder of the game of baseball a third strike was about to be called. Casualties in the Iron Brigade and the 147th New York Infantry, which had held its ground, isolated, nearly to the point of annihilation, had been appalling.

The Union I Corps had need of all its guns. Now its three remaining batteries were about to enter the battle.

On the march toward Gettysburg a sergeant of Battery B, 1st Pennsylvania Light Artillery, riding past a group of other I Corps gunners, had halted his mount.

"Boys," he called to members of Battery B, 4th U.S. Artillery, "don't forget this is free soil. We are now about half a mile north of the Keystone State line."

His own home, he told them, was only about ten or twelve miles away, in the direction of Hanovertown, and added: "You are Wisconsin, Indiana, Michigan, and New York boys, and maybe you don't know how a Pennsylvanian feels when he may have to fight tomorrow in his mother's dooryard!"

They looked at him soberly, and one answered for the rest.

"We'll stand by you until hell freezes over and then fight on the ice!" [38]

"WE'LL STAND BY YOU UNTIL HELL FREEZES!"

(From *The Cannoneer*, by Augustus Buell)

The morrow had arrived, and the sergeant and his battery pushed forward to the defense of their state. B had been well trained by its original commander, Henry T. Danforth, now the regiment's lieutenant colonel. He had served in Bragg's flying battery in the Mexican War and preserved the tradition of General Zachary Taylor's famous order to Bragg on the battlefield of Buena Vista: "Double shot your guns and give 'em hell!" [39] The present battery commander, Captain James H. Cooper, followed it when he put his guns in position on the left of a Pennsylvania infantry regiment. He opened fire and had silenced a Rebel battery when a second began to rake him from the right. He changed front and engaged it. Then Gray infantry poured down from the crest and through the woods along his former front. Cooper shifted again to spray them with bursts of shell and shrapnel and, as the range closed, with canister.

Captain Greenleaf T. Stevens' 5th Maine Battery joined in. A large part of its personnel were husky Kennebec lumbermen, and they swung trails as if they were levering a big pine stick with a cant hook. Heavy going was nothing to drivers who had handled logging teams in snow, slush, or mud. Today there were fewer of the artillerymen from the northmost state. The battery had suffered so severely at Chancellorsville that it had had to be re-equipped and its thinned ranks filled with infantrymen. Even with green cannoneers the 5th Maine now was acquitting itself well, and it was as hard pressed as the Pennsylvanians. It beat off one attack, but its guns had no time to cool before crews were compelled to pivot them to meet another onslaught driving in on their exposed right flank.

Battery B, 4th U.S. Artillery, was also on the field, fulfilling its pledge to stand by fellow artillerymen from Pennsylvania—and Maine as well. One of the most famous batteries in the army, its regimental roots stretched back to the Revolution. Around the guidon of B, wrote its historian, "twine the triple laurels of 1812, the Mexican War, and the Struggle for the Union." [40] On its record stood a feat of arms that ranks as one of the epics of the field artillery—its supremely gallant stand at the Battle of Buena Vista in Mexico. There, under heavy cannonading and volleys of musketry from charging enemy, Lieutenant John Paul Jones O'Brien without infantry support had fought the guns he called his

"Bulldogs," bearing the brunt of Santa Anna's attack. Pressed back, he retreated but only by the distance his pieces recoiled after each discharge, then blasted away again with double canister. Finally, with only two guns left in action and all the horses killed, the battery fired a last round into assailants only yards from the muzzles. The wounded O'Brien and his few surviving gunners limped to the rear. They lost their guns but saved the day by holding off the foe till Bragg's Battery galloped to the rescue, and American infantry rallied.[41]

John Gibbon, now leading a division in Hancock's II Corps, had taken command of the battery in 1861 when it rolled into Washington much depleted in strength after long service in the West. He had filled its ranks with men from Volunteer regiments, who offered themselves when he appealed for recruits for the battery that had defended the gorge at Buena Vista. In spite of the Volunteer belief that discipline in a Regular outfit was strict and duty tough, he obtained 150 of the "finest material for soldiers I ever saw." To stimulate their pride Gibbon ordered six small national flags made and inscribed with the names of the states from which the Volunteers came; they were fastened to the battery's pieces. Cannoneers were told the guns belonged to their states and that it was up to them to defend them.[42] Both they and he lived up to it. In the cornfield at Antietam, when the battery was losing men fast but doggedly holding its ground, Gibbon, then a brigadier, had ridden up, vaulted from his saddle, and helped man an almost crewless gun, taking the place of both the gunner and Number 3.

Today the battery was commanded by James Stewart whom Gibbon had called "the best First Sergeant I ever saw in the service." Here indeed was an accolade, a good top sergeant being the most constant measure of any outfit's efficiency, its most indispensable man, however well officered. Stewart was promoted sergeant major at the special request of the Army of the Potomac's Chief of Artillery, General Hunt, and then commissioned. Some noncoms cannot jump the gap between the ranks and the leadership and responsibilities required of an officer. Stewart could. He was a captain and one of the best when he brought B to Gettysburg.

B was armed with bronze 12-pounder, smoothbore, muzzle-loading Napoleons, the gun-howitzer developed in the reign of the French emperor, Napoleon III, and named for him. The U.S. 1857 model became the foremost fieldpiece of the Civil War. While it could throw a projectile 1,610 yards, it of course lacked the accuracy of rifled guns. Ordinarily it was used at short ranges, with canister a favorite charge. To man Napoleons was a test of a battery's mettle. It often meant hand-to-hand combat, with enemy charging the guns, overrunning them, and battling to capture them. For close defense B, like other units, had been issued sabers. Average artillerymen soon discarded those cumbersome, useless weapons dangling from their belts. In the early days of the war the route of a battery's march was marked by sabers stuck in the mud for Ordnance to pick up and pass on to the cavalry if it wanted them, which it usually did not, preferring its own issue with less blade curve and better handguard. B's were carried in its battery wagon, Stewart being an old Regular with strong respect for property accountability; he did not intend to have an inspector report them missing and find them as debits on his pay roll. Officers and noncoms continued to carry sabers, more as badges of authority than anything else; Stewart, according to regulations, flourished his for signaling orders. The revolver was the ideal artillery small arm, but few were supplied the rank and file and those mostly to horse artillery. In default of anything better artillerymen wielded handspikes and rammer staffs, threw stones or used their fists, when they struggled with the enemy in their gun positions.[43]

Stewart's Battery was to come close to that eventuality this noon as it took position, three guns to the right of the railroad cut under "The Old Man," three to the left under Lieutenant James Davison, sited to sweep the Chambersburg Pike. The day was growing hotter. Cannoneers, many no more than nineteen years old, and not a few even younger, stripped off jackets and rolled up sleeves,

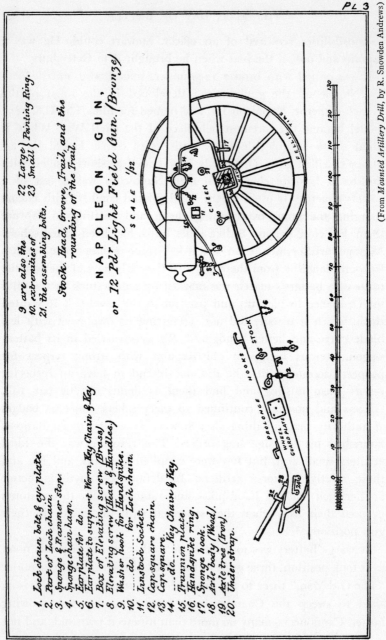

PL 3

1. Lock chain bolt & eye plate.
2. Part of Lock chain.
3. Sponge & Rammer stop.
4. Sponge chain hasp.
5. Ear plate for do.
6. Ear plate to support Worm, Key Chain & Key.
7. Box of Elevating screw (Brass)
8. Elevating screw (Head & Handles)
9. Washer hook for Handspike.
10. .... do .... for Lock chain.
11. Linstock Socket.
12. Cap-square chain.
13. Cap square.
14. .... do .... Key Chain & Key.
15. Trunnion plate.
16. Handspike ring.
17. Sponge hook.
18. Axle body (Wood).
19. Axle tree (Iron).
20. Under strap.

9 are also the
10. extremities of   22 Large } Painting Ring.
21. the assembling bolts.   23 Small }

Stock, Head, Groove, Trail, and the
rounding of the Trail.

NAPOLEON GUN,
or 12 Pd[r] Light Field Gun. (Bronze)

SCALE ¹/32

Evans & Cogswell, lith. Columbia, S.C.

(From Mounted Artillery Drill, by R. Snowden Andrews)

watching the panorama of conflict to their front. The weight of the
enemy's attack was commencing to overpower the Blue infantry.
Other I Corps batteries to the fore were limbering and falling
back. B, sighting tips of color staffs coming up over a little ridge,
then the point of bayonets, and finally the Rebels themselves,
knew its turn had come. Davison shouted sharp orders: "Load—
canister—double!" Rammer heads thumped, and section chiefs
reported ready. The lieutenant's command was instant. "Ready—
by piece—fire!"

Viciously each Napoleon spat its content of spreading balls of
iron, then flamed again and again. The attacking line reeled,
wilted, and dropped prone. But other regiments were closing in on
the half-battery's left and pouring in heavy fire. Davison was hit
twice, one bullet shattering an ankle. While one of his men held
him up, he ordered action left. Cannoneers, several of them with
bloody heads, swung the pieces around as on a hinge. They raked
the full length of the Rebel line with double charges of canister.
Yet the maneuver had exposed the half-battery's right to the Gray
riflemen first repulsed, and these were up again and sweeping the
position with volley after volley of crossfire. Union infantry crawled
up on the railroad embankment to answer them, and from across
the cut the guns of Stewart's half-battery were flashing like a solid
streak of chain lightning.

Rebel bullets whittled down the crews. Gun shields and aprons
were far in the future, and there was no cover except that afforded
by the felloes and spokes of the wheels of the Napoleons. A
cannoneer standing between them and the barrel to prime or stop
the vent had slight, momentary protection. Orderly Sergeant John
Mitchell, who would one day succeed to the command of the battery,
moved calmly from gun to gun, changing men about to keep them
manned, as one artilleryman after another was hit and fell—stooping
over a wounded man to help him to his feet to serve his piece
again—ordering the badly injured who could still walk to stagger
to the rear. Davison hobbled about, cheering his men on, praising

them and shouting, "Feed it to 'em, God damn 'em! Feed it to 'em!"
A cannoneer vividly remembered that desperate fight.

The very guns became things of life—not implements, but
comrades. Every man was doing the work of two or three.
At our gun at the finish there was only the Corporal, No. 1
and No. 3, with two drivers fetching ammunition. The water
in Pat's bucket was like ink. His face and hands were smeared
all over with burnt powder. The thumbstall of No. 3 was
burned to a crisp by the hot vent-field. Between the black of
the burnt powder and the crimson streaks from his bloody
head, Packard looked like a demon from below! Up and down
the line men reeling and falling; splinters flying from wheels
and axles where the bullets hit; in rear, horses tearing and
plunging, mad with wounds or terror; drivers yelling, shells
bursting, shot shrieking overhead, howling about our ears
or throwing up great clouds of dust where they struck; the
musketry crashing on three sides of us; bullets hissing,
humming and whistling everywhere; cannon roaring; all
crash on crash and peal on peal, smoke, dust, splinters, blood,
wreck and carnage indescribable; but the brass guns of Old
B still bellowed and not a man or boy flinched or faltered!
Every man's shirt soaked with sweat and many of them
sopped with blood from wounds not severe enough to make
such bulldogs "let go"—bareheaded, sleeves rolled up, faces
blackened—oh! if such a picture could be spread on the
canvas of life! Out in front of us an undulating field, filled
almost as far as the eye could reach with a long, low, gray
line creeping toward us, fairly fringed with flame![44]

The Gray line, unstoppable, crept closer. Davison was down now,
weak from loss of blood. Sergeant Mitchell took over, signaling up
the limbers. Seeing them coming, Rebel riflemen redoubled their
fire. Drivers, horses, and more cannoneers were hit, as they hooked
on the guns. Mitchell ordered Cannoneer "Cub" Buell up into the

saddle of a wounded swing driver. A horse of the lead pair dropped. They cut him out of the harness and drove back toward the town.

Just after the withdrawal Captain Stewart rode into the vacated position. Confederates swarming into it called on him to surrender. He wheeled his horse and galloped away, blazing back over its haunches with his revolver. Two bullets from a volley sent after him ripped through his blouse. Suddenly his road of escape was blocked by more enemy troops, closing in and surrounding him. He spurred through the cordon, put his charger at a fence, and soared over it splendidly. At the height of the leap a shell fragment struck him in the thigh. He kept his saddle but grew so nauseated from the shock he had to dismount and drink water from a field furrow. That revived him sufficiently to rejoin his battery on its retreat to the town. With its rearmost gun, half-crippled but patched up, he fought off pursuers with double canister at 100 yards. At last he led B, as directed, to a position on Cemetery Hill. The battery had lost 36 men out of 90-odd present for duty. Nearly half its horses had been killed or wounded. One of its caissons had been blown up and three others abandoned, wheels or axletrees smashed. But it had all its guns and it was still able and willing to fight. The Buena Vista Battery had upheld its valiant tradition.

The courageous stands made by the I Corps batteries, outgunned and exposed to attack by infantry, had held up the Gray advance, inflicted heavy casualties, and helped cover the retreat of their own foot troops. Their severe losses and near sacrifice were due to a tragic misunderstanding by the corps Chief of Artillery, Colonel Wainwright, who had ordered them into the positions they took instead of their subsequent ones on Cemetery Hill. "Having heard incidentally some directions given to General Doubleday about holding Cemetery Hill," he stated in his report, "and not knowing that there was such a place, while the seminary was called indiscriminately 'Cemetery' and 'Seminary,' I supposed the latter was meant." [45]

But it was massive reinforcement of one side or the other that would decide the issue of these early hours of the first day of battle—

the trite but true dictum of getting there first with the most men. Summoned by hard-riding couriers and marching to the sound of the guns, General O. O. Howard's XI Union Corps was advancing rapidly from the south, while General Richard S. Ewell's II Corps, C.S.A., was about to swoop down from the north.

Meade's army, unlike Lee's, used its eyes—its cavalry. Buford's alert pickets, watching the northern roads, promptly reported the approach of fresh Confederate forces. As Howard arrived with his corps and assumed command as the senior officer on the field, he extended the right of his line to meet the ominous new threat. The foremost division of Ewell's Corps, that of Rodes, prepared to assault in the vicinity of the present Peace Memorial. Heth, with the weight of Pender's Division behind him, was about to renew his assault on the Union left. Meanwhile another of Ewell's divisions, Early's, was surging down the Harrisburg Road, bound to strike the Federal right flank like a battering ram.

The stage was set for a Union debacle, for another great Southern victory, even without Longstreet's still absent corps. Meade's five remaining corps could not reach the scene in sufficient strength in time to blunt a bold thrust that could have won the Battle of Gettysburg that day.

CHAPTER 4

The First Day of Battle

AFTERNOON AND NIGHT

•••

Carter's Battalion, C.S.A.
    Jeff Davis (Ala.) Artillery
    King William (Va.) Artillery
    Morris (Va.) Artillery
    Orange (Va.) Artillery
Battery I, 1st New York Light Artillery
13th New York Battery
Battery I, 1st Ohio Light Artillery
Battery K, 1st Ohio Light Artillery
Battery G, 4th U.S. Artillery
Garnett's Battalion, C.S.A.
    Donaldsonville (La.) Artillery
    Huger (Va.) Artillery
    Pittsylvania (Va.) Artillery
    Norfolk Light Artillery Blues
Poague's Battalion, C.S.A.
    Albemarle (Va.) Artillery
    Charlotte (N.C.) Artillery
    Madison (Miss.) Artillery
    Warrenton (Va.) Battery
Lane's Battalion, C.S.A.
    Companies A, B, and C, Sumter (Ga.) Battalion

Jones's Battalion, C.S.A.
Charlottesville (Va.) Artillery
Courtney (Va.) Artillery
Louisiana Guard Artillery
Staunton (Va.) Artillery

A general in gray rode along Seminary Ridge with his staff, reconnoitering the ground and determining the best positions for his batteries. He rather strongly resembled Robert E. Lee and was not infrequently mistaken for him, as in the case of the private who, beginning to cheer the officer he thought was the Commander in Chief, subsided and corrected himself:

" 'Tain't Marse Robert. It's 'Old Artillery.' "

General William Nelson Pendleton,[46] Chief of Artillery of the Army of Northern Virginia, was a West Pointer who had resigned his commission to enter the ministry. When Virginia seceded, he donned uniform again at the age of fifty-one as a captain of the Rockbridge Artillery. Over his regimentals he still figuratively wore the surplice and with other clergyman officers of the Confederate Army carried on the tradition of the fighting bishops of the medieval wars. Regular chaplains yielded camp pulpits when Pendleton was in the vicinity; he missed no opportunity to conduct services. It would have been in character for him to have followed the precedent of a famous artillerist, King Gustavus Adolphus of Sweden, who led his kneeling army in prayer before the Battle of Lützen. Indeed the story was told of Pendleton that during the Valley Campaign he stood among his guns, directed upon the enemy, devoutly raised a hand in benediction, and shouted above the din of conflict:

"May the Lord have mercy on their poor souls." The upraised hand swept downward. "Fire!" [47]

In some battles Pendleton had failed to make the best use of his reserve artillery or even to bring it into action at all. He was by no means the peer of his opposite number, Hunt, the Federal artillery chief, and he lacked the gunner genius of his subordinate, Colonel E. Porter Alexander. Yet his services as an organizer had been considerable and continued to be so throughout the war. He had done much toward endowing "The Long Arm of Lee" with striking power and reach.

Confederate field artillery before it marched to Gettysburg—at Sharpsburg (Antietam) and elsewhere—had won the right to that title. Its "distinguished reputation . . . rested not upon its comparative efficiency with the same branch of the Federal Army, for all recognized the superiority of the latter, in organization, drill, discipline, matériel, and equipment. It was but the direct result of the personal character of its officers and men, who, except in courage, were overweighed in all that made for the force of their blows," [48] In not a few cases both senior and junior officers declined promotion which would transfer them from the service of the guns.

Lieutenant Colonel Thomas H. Carter, leading an artillery battalion of Ewell's Corps into the mounting conflict at Gettysburg, was content to remain with the gunners' arm. A handsome man with military mustache and imperial, he mirrored the Southern cavalier he was. It was under dour old Major Jackson, the future Stonewall, professor of artillery and military tactics at Virginia Military Institute, that Carter, like others, had learned his gunnery and learned it well. He put it into practice as he brought his battalion on to the field from the northwest. On what was then the Confederate left he placed Page's Morris Artillery, named for Lieutenant Edward Morris, who had helped organize it, and Reese's Jeff Davis Artillery, gunners from Alabama. Oak Hill was the exposed but commanding position he chose for Fry's Orange Artillery and for the King William Battery under his own half-brother, Captain William P. Carter.

It is better not to serve with a brother in the same unit, another Confederate artilleryman advised. Worry over each other distracts brothers from duty, worry from which they are spared, at least during the heat of battle, if they are separated. The two Carters disregarded such apprehensions. In fact, the battalion commander, avoiding any suspicion of favoritism, sent his half-brother's battery into the hottest spots. During the artillery fire fight that now began to rage, the King William men were hard hit but held their ground with reckless daring.

Gray guns on Oak Hill shot it out, shell for shell, with two Federal batteries which had moved up to oppose them. A gap in the Union line had opened at that point, and these newly-arrived cannon were its only barrier. One was firing Napoleons, the other rifles. The smoothbores were advanced, closing the range. Though they were taken under crossfire by other Rebel artillery as well as by frontal bombardment, they swept the hill with metal, knocking out pieces of their adversaries.

These two new hard-fighting units belonged to the XI Corps, brought up by General Howard and put in on the right of the I Corps, now Doubleday's. Howard's line, prolonged to meet the threat of Ewell's Confederates from the north, had stretched so thin that the gap had opened which the pair of batteries was now defending. While precious minutes ticked by, these twelve guns stood as a dike against a rising gray sea.

But the fortunes of war had a way of running against the XI Corps—"those damned Dutchmen" as the rest of the Army of the Potomac scornfully and inaccurately called its largely German-American personnel. Its generals bore such names as Schurz, Steinwehr, and Schimmelfennig. Rolls read like those of the Hessian regiments we fought in the Revolution, or of the German armies we were to meet in two world wars. Prejudice against men of foreign birth or extraction ran strong in a nation only a few generations removed from the same status. It was little affected by the fact that the soldiers of the XI Corps were citizens who had emigrated from their native land to escape military conscription but nevertheless had readily volunteered to defend their adopted country. Patriotism notwithstanding, they had been fervently damned since Chancellorsville when Stonewall Jackson's brilliant surprise flanking attack rolled over and routed them. One of the XI's artillery captains had given timely warning, disregarded by both corps and army headquarters; then vainly done his utmost to stave off the Confederate onslaught with his battery. A single valiant feat of arms could not palliate wholesale disaster. The Dutchmen advancing to Gettysburg "still carried Chancellorsville on their shoulders."

Redemption was not to be won today. The cards were once more stacked against the XI. It was its fate to arrive in support of the hard-pressed I Corps at the moment when Hill's Gray lines were being reinforced and Ewell's columns from the north were moving in to strike the Union right. Before more of Meade's troops could come up, the XI, beaten back and in part overrun, would once more know such desperate hours as it had suffered in May in the Virginia wilderness.

The XI Corps cannon, mentioned as stoppering the gap between Howard and Doubleday, were manned by Ohioans and New Yorkers.

Battery I, 1st Ohio Artillery, was commanded by Captain Hubert Dilger, who at the outbreak of the war had resigned from the Prussian Army's horse artillery and hastened to the United States to fight for the Union. "Leatherbreeches" they called him because he was too veteran a horseman to wear issue cloth that wore through after days in the saddle. A top battery commander with the best unit in the corps, it was he who had given that disregarded alarm at Chancellorsville and stood off Jackson's artillery and infantry, first with all six of his guns, then with a single piece to cover the others' retreat. His horse was hit and fell on him. "Leatherbreeches" dragged himself clear and hobbled off, enemy riflemen close on his heels. As he was about to be captured, his orderly rode back, took him up behind on his mount, and the two escaped. Dilger and his battery fought on, making one stand after another in front of shattered, fleeing Blue divisions. It was one of the greatest field artillery rearguard actions in history and one of the least known.[49] Nevertheless Hubert Dilger was still a captain and would remain in that rank for the duration of the war, though repeatedly recommended for promotion. The stigma of being a "damned Dutchman" was a heavy handicap.

Dilger unlimbered his six Napoleons in the gap and opened at 1,000 yards on enemy artillery. Then Captain William Wheeler's 13th New York Battery rushed up and went into action alongside the Ohioans. Dilger stepped over. Would his fellow battery commander kindly cover him while he advanced? The range was long for smoothbores. Captain Wheeler obliged, redoubling the fire of his four 3-inch rifles. The Ohio gun teams trotted forward, only to be halted by a deep ditch. Dilger dismounted his cannoneers and ordered them to fill it with fence rails which they did under a hail of shells. Forthwith teams pulled the carriages across, and the Napoleons blazed again at a range reduced by several hundred yards. The two Union batteries then engaged in their spirited duel with the Rebel artillery on Oak Hill. Though one of the New York guns was dismounted, five of the enemy's were put out of action.

Slowly, then faster, Confederate pressure forced back the arc of the defense until it bent and began to break. Shellfire and bullets flailed the Blue guns and infantry. Wheeler retired, not limbering yet but dragging back his guns by prolonges so that they could maintain a steady fire during retreat. A solid shot broke the axle of one of his pieces. Survivors of its crew lashed the barrel under a limber, but it broke loose and they lost it. When Dilger pulled out, his battery was caught in a jetsam of infantry, ambulances, and wagons that jammed into the town. "Leatherbreeches," in rearguard action again, stationed a section in the street near the public square and held off pursuit for a time. But the unfortunate XI Corps paid a heavy toll in killed, wounded, and prisoners, its remnants streaming back to Cemetery Hill.

Along with Dilger's and Wheeler's, the three other batteries of the XI were striving to cover its retreat.

Captain Michael Wiedrich's Battery I, 1st New York, came into action with the mouths of cannoneers and drivers red-smudged. On their way to Gettysburg they had picked and eaten luscious, ripe cherries from trees while they were rolling past, and there had been little time for a man to wipe his lips.[50] At the sound of the guns the battery took up the trot, then a gallop. Unlimbered, its 3-inch Rodmans, sturdy cannon because of the casting method devised by their inventor for whom they were named, began to boom.

They were joined by the four 12-pounders of Battery K, 1st Ohio, Captain Lewis Heckman. Soon these were hard pressed to hold their ground. Gray skirmishers closed in. They hit K from the flanks and stormed it frontally between discharges. The shrill Rebel yell rose among the smoking pieces. One gun was captured, then another, as the artillerymen fell, shot and clubbed by muskets. Survivors, desperately fighting off their assailants, managed to limber and save their last two guns. But the battery was so badly crippled when it reached Cemetery Hill that it was sent to the rear, unable to take part in the rest of the battle.

Meanwhile the fifth artillery unit of XI Corps was making a memorable stand. North of the town and near Rock Creek was a small hillock that could be described as an outwork of the cemetery bastion. It was held by Barlow's small division, supported by Battery G, 4th U.S. Artillery. The battery commander was First Lieutenant Bayard Wilkeson, a nineteen-year-old New Yorker. Two brevets for gallantry in action already stood on his record, and now he was about to win a third, giving him the honorary rank of lieutenant colonel. For this fine young officer the first day of July marked the end of the road, as for so many others. The story of his valiant passing is one of Gettysburg's most dramatic and poignant episodes.

At the moment the lieutenant was putting his guns into position, his father, Samuel Wilkeson, correspondent for the *New York Times*, was at Meade's headquarters, en route to cover the battle. He would not reach the field in time to be an eyewitness of the first day's conflict. Details of the personal tragedy he was to report came to him from his son's comrades in arms.

An attempt to hold that little knoll, occupied by infantry and Wilkeson's guns, was perhaps a forlorn hope. But it was a vantage point, with the land lying flat around it, and the menace to the Federal right was grave. Any time that could be gained while the defenses of Cemetery Hill were organized was of high value. For a space they did hold it, obstinately and bloodily, against the Rebel foot that ringed it, lapping up around its base, and the sweeping fire of two batteries. Wilkeson, erect on his charger, rode from gun to gun, directing raking volleys that blasted back the assailing division. Battery G's Regulars spared him quick glances of loyal admiration. It steadied men to look up and see their commander calmly disregarding everything the enemy could throw. Cannoneers, with the saving grace of hot action that gave them no time to think of themselves, bent over their pieces again. They worked their four smoothbores as fast as they could swab, load, and fire.

Some say it was a sharpshooter that got Lieutenant Wilkeson in his sights. It is also related that a Confederate brigadier, finding it impossible to capture the hillock unless those Yankee guns were silenced or driven off, ordered his two batteries to concentrate on the mounted officer.[51] In any event, the artilleryman and his horse were a first-rate target and aiming point. Under a storm of metal they crumpled to the ground. All Wilkeson's men could do for him in that critical moment was bind up his grave wound, carry him to the county almshouse nearby, and run back to their guns.

Confederate artillery had the exact range and were pinpointing all Battery G's smoothbores. Lieutenant Eugene A. Bancroft, now in command, shifted his sections and fought on. But another attacking column was about to strike the knoll from the right and rear. Defending infantry, their leader, General Barlow, desperately wounded, fell back. Bancroft limbered and pulled out with all speed to save his guns.

DRIVERS MOUNT

CANNONEERS MOUNT

That night Wilkeson, lying at the point of death, asked for water. When a canteen was brought, a badly injured man beside him begged, "For God's sake give me some!" The canteen, handed over untouched, was drained to the last drop. Wilkeson smiled at the other, turned slightly, and expired.[52] So died an artilleryman whom General Hunt was to honor in his report as "a young officer of great gallantry." [53]

On the front page of the *New York Times* of July 6, 1863, blazoned with headlines on the Battle of Gettysburg, stands a dispatch from Samuel Wilkeson, dated two days earlier from Headquarters, Army of the Potomac—an account running a column and a half. It cannot be wondered at that the bereaved father could not altogether preserve the detachment of a reporter in the light of the stunning news he was given when he arrived. The dispatch begins:

> Who can write the history of a battle whose eyes are immovably fastened upon a central figure of transcendently absorbing interest—the dead body of an oldest born, crushed by a shell in a position where a battery should never have been sent, and abandoned to death in a building where surgeons dared not to stay?

The correspondent, continuing with such details of the battle as he had "the heart for," ended with a moving paragraph.

> My pen is heavy. Oh, you dead, who at Gettysburg have baptised with your blood the second birth of Freedom in America, how you are to be envied! I rise from a grave whose wet clay I have passionately kissed, and I look up to see Christ spanning this battle-field with his feet and reaching

fraternal and lovingly up to heaven. His right hand opens
the gate of Paradise—with his left he beckons to these
mutilated, bloody, swollen forms to ascend.

Many other eyes those July days saw "the glory of the coming of
the Lord" with exaltation and dimmed with tears when word came
of the fallen at Gettysburg.

The retreat of G of the 4th U.S. and the rest of the artillery of
the XI and I Corps to Cemetery Hill staged a macabre spectacle.
Batteries whirling in through the graveyard gate. Carriages crashing
into the tombstones and bowling them over.[54] Cannoneers digging
emplacements in the burial mounds, pits that would serve for the
bodies of some of them. Here by fate's choice of a battlefield more
dead would be marshaled under white crosses than many generations of the little country town could have interred.

Earthworks rose in front of the guns. One of the XI Corps German
generals, Steinwehr, a Prussian professional, saw to that. Batteries
need no longer shoot it out in the open, as so many of them had
all day. They prepared for action again in posts assigned them by
their corps artillery chiefs, positions commanding the town and
the approaches from the northwest. Most of them had been roughly
handled. Losses were severe in personnel—some units had to be
pieced out by infantrymen—and many horses had been killed, yet
only a few of their guns and caissons had been knocked out or lost.
This remained a formidable array of artillery and it was ready to
resist to the last, supporting and defended by the weary but equally
resolute infantry that held the bastion with it.

The Union line hereupon commenced to assume the fishhook
shape which would constitute Meade's defensive position throughout the remainder of the battle. First to form was the beginning
of the hook's curve, running through Cemetery Hill. Thence it
was to circle on a little later to traverse Culp's Hill, with the barb
pointed at Spangler's Spring. The fishhook's shank was to run from
Cemetery Hill almost due south along Cemetery Ridge to a terminus

at Little Round Top. Blue corps, marching to the battlefield, presently would man that stem. It was the hook curve which must withstand an expected all-out assault late this afternoon. If it snapped, that would be the end of the fight named for the cross-roads town. There would be another conflict somewhere, since the bulk of the Northern army had not been engaged. But beneath the two Bull Runs, Fredericksburg, and Chancellorsville history would have inscribed another Southern victory—Gettysburg.

Token of help that was coming, whether in time or not, was the arrival of General Hancock, sent on ahead of his II Corps by General Meade to take command on the field. Hancock, a fighter, inspired confidence by his presence, and his first act was a vital contribution to the defense. He ordered a division to occupy Culp's Hill, which in enemy hands would render Cemetery Hill untenable. Now the fishhook was barbed.

Meanwhile the enveloping Confederate attack was swinging forward like the stroke of a gigantic sickle. From Seminary Ridge and the north it had swept through the town of Gettysburg, wielded to mow down the defenses of the hills in its path. General Lee directed Ewell "to press those people," to storm and capture Cemetery Hill, "if practicable." About four o'clock the arc of the whole line advanced to the assault.

Most of the divisional and reserve artillery of two corps was now in action or in position. Pegram and McIntosh had been joined by the rest of the guns of Hill's III Corps. Lieutenant Colonel John J. Garnett's Battalion: the Donaldsonville, Huger, Pittsylvania, and Norfolk Blues Artillery. Major William T. Poague's Battalion: the Albemarle, Charlotte, and Madison Artillery, and the Virginia Battery from Warrenton. Poague, a fine gunner officer, had once commanded the Rockbridge Artillery whose first armament consisted of four 6-pounder smoothbores, christened Matthew, Mark, Luke, and John "because they spoke a powerful language." Many a V.M.I. cadet had trained on those apostolic cannon, which as the war progressed were replaced by heavier pieces and relegated to the defenses of Richmond. Captured when the capital fell, they were subsequently returned to the Virginia military school. On their retirement in 1913 to be placed around the statue of Stonewall Jackson, it was their old commander that led them there, riding, as gray as the uniform he had worn with honor, at the head of the column.

On the field also was Major John Lane's group: Companies A, B, and C of the Sumter, Georgia, Battalion. Augmenting the fire of Carter's guns were more cannon of Ewell's II Corps. Lieutenant Colonel Hilary P. Jones's Battalion: the Charlottesville, Courtney, and Staunton Artillery, and that of the Louisiana Guard. Batteries from six Southern states were paving the way for their infantry and dealing with enemy guns. Losses in the Confederate forces, inflicted by stout opposition, had been heavy, but the Union had suffered as severely. Save for the last bastion, the field had been carried by the troops in gray.

Before the Federals had concentrated on Cemetery Hill and organized its defenses, while they were still falling back on that eminence in retreat that at points was close to rout, when Barlow's Division and Wilkeson's guns were being driven from the outwork knoll—then, with the battle tide at flood, was the moment.

General Ewell delayed. He waited for Johnson's Division and Latimer's, Dance's, and Nelson's battalions of artillery. They would not arrive until nearly sunset. Irresolute, the Confederate corps commander sat his charger, sat his saddle somewhat awkwardly, for a battle wound had cost him a leg and he wore a peg one. A good record lay behind "Old Baldy." There was no question of his courage. This was a command decision that confronted him. Lee had not directly ordered him to attack but to do so "if practicable." Finally Ewell decided against it. One of his brigadiers vainly begged to be allowed to drive home the assault. Another is said to have flung down his sword at Ewell's feet and refused to serve longer under such a general. In frustration poised columns longed for Stonewall Jackson. "Old Jack," they never doubted, would have rolled up that Union flank as he had at Chancellorsville.

Impetus slowed, stalled, was lost. In the fatal interval Cemetery Hill, bristling with entrenched riflemen and emplaced cannon, was converted into one of those field fortresses against which, time and time again in the war, assault waves had broken bloodily. Hancock had ordered the seizure of commanding Culp's Hill. His II Corps, along with the III, was coming onto the field by forced marches.

By five-thirty it was too late to launch a successful attack. A rare opportunity had vanished.[55] The sound of battle diminished and died away.

They gathered the wounded from shell-harrowed fields. In churches, schools, homes, and barns—improvised hospitals—surgeons carried on their bloody business. Burial details hastily covered some of the many dead. Here and there a man wandered about, searching for a missing comrade. Soldiers sank into the sleep of exhaustion except for sentinels, prodding themselves awake until their reliefs came. In the artillery lines officers and noncoms saw to the replenishment of the ammunition chests. Drivers, some of them mourning favorite horses that had been killed, watered and fed replacements or surviving pairs. Picketed or tied to carriage wheels or trees, the animals, limbs trembling from weariness, lay down one by one or slept standing, with that ability horses possess of locking their leg joints.

Troops, in the military phrase, rested on their arms. They were fought out, and a night attack was as unlikely as combat on the morrow was certain. Only the groaning of the wounded, the sounds of changing the guard, and the stirrings of the restless broke the silence of the night. For a while the summer air hung heavy with lingering fumes of powder smoke and the stench of blood and sweat.

It was after midnight when General Meade, accompanied by General Hunt, reached the battlefield. In contrast to some of his predecessors Meade, a former artilleryman, placed firm reliance on his Chief of Artillery, and that confidence was to be amply repaid in the two days ahead. Inspect the guns on Cemetery Hill,

Meade ordered, and Hunt rode off to check the positions as best he could in the darkness.

A remarkable man, Henry Hunt, one of the great gunner generals, cast in the mold of Henry Knox of the Revolution. As a young officer in the war with Mexico he had earned his right to wear the crossed-cannon insignia with honor in that muzzle-to-muzzle duel on the threshold of the Halls of Montezuma—had won his spurs as a battery commander at First Bull Run—had displayed his genius as an artillerist in the massing of guns that conquered at Malvern Hill, and on Stafford Heights at Fredericksburg helped stave off disaster. His eyes, ordinarily pensive, could be piercing. There was decision in the firmness of his lips and the set of his bearded jaw. Prompt in action, outspoken, he was definite on the employment of the artillery he handled so competently and the role it should play in battle.[56] Overruled he might be, as was to happen on a moment during the crisis of the third day, but he would not let it pass ungainsaid.

An eerie stillness lay on the battlefield, unshattered by shots fired by nervous sentries or the sudden roar of a gun. Sleep brought oblivion from memories of the deaths and wounds of the day past, from the menace of the morrow. Hunt let his charger pick its way carefully through the darkness around the defenses of Cemetery Hill. Now and again he spoke briefly with a battery commander, roused by his coming—perhaps a little longer with one he knew well, such as Stewart. A few words were enough. The guns were well placed. These artillerymen had fought hard and well. Let them have their rest. They must turn to at dawn.

Hunt had ordered the reserve artillery and the ammunition train forward, and they were moving up through the sultry night. The emergency pool of guns, on which Hunt would draw in critical moments, was strong and dependable. It consisted of one Regular and two Volunteer brigades, which with the train were under the command of Brigadier General Robert O. Tyler. A guard of 500 heavy artillerymen, armed as infantry, was assigned to each brigade to protect transport and perform camp duties, by order of the artillery chief. Another of Hunt's innovations was the detail by every battery of a mounted orderly to brigade headquarters for liaison.

The ammunition train carried an average of 270 rounds for every gun. Moreover, Hunt on his own initiative had organized a special ammunition column, provided with twenty rounds extra for every piece in the army to meet sudden deficiencies his experience had taught him were certain to arise. Therefore he was ready with reassurance when the worried Meade informed him that notwithstanding his orders one corps had left its whole ammunition train behind and that others, particularly the I and XI, whose expenditures had been heavy, were reporting shortages. There would be "enough ammunition for the battle," Hunt answered, "but none for idle cannonades, the besetting sin of some of our commanders." [57]

Such was the measure of a great artilleryman, who foresaw the need of every cannon and shell he could muster before this battle started.

CHAPTER 5

The Second Day of Battle

DEVIL'S DEN AND THE PEACH ORCHARD

•••

Eshleman's Battalion, C.S.A.
    1st, 2nd, 3rd, and 4th Companies,
        Washington (La.) Artillery
Alexander's Battalion, C.S.A.
    Ashland (Va.) Artillery
    Bedford (Va.) Artillery
    Brooks (S.C.) Artillery
    Madison (La.) Light Artillery
    Virginia (Parker's) Battery
    Virginia (Taylor's) Battery
Cabell's Battalion, C.S.A.
    Battery A, 1st North Carolina Artillery
    Pulaski (Ga.) Artillery
    1st Company, Richmond Howitzers
Dearing's Battalion, C.S.A.
    Fauquier (Va.) Artillery
    Hampden (Va.) Artillery
    Richmond Fayette Artillery
    Virginia Battery (Blount's)
Henry's Battalion, C.S.A.
    Branch (N.C.) Artillery
    German (S.C.) Artillery

Palmetto (S.C.) Artillery
Rowan (N.C.) Artillery

5th Massachusetts Battery
9th Massachusetts Battery
15th New York Battery
Batteries C and F, 1st Pennsylvania
  Light Artillery
Battery B, New Jersey Light Artillery
2nd Battery, Connecticut Light Artillery
Battery D, 1st New York Light Artillery
4th New York Battery
Battery E, 1st Rhode Island
  Light Artillery
Battery K, 4th U.S. Artillery
Battery C, 4th U.S. Artillery
Battery C, 5th U.S. Artillery
Batteries F and K, 3rd U.S. Artillery
Battery G, 1st New York Artillery
Batteries F and G, 1st Pennsylvania
  Light Artillery
6th Maine Battery
Battery I, 5th U.S. Artillery
Battery C, 1st Massachusetts Artillery

Under the luminous moon of the night of July 1 the artillery of Longstreet's I Corps left their camp at Greenwood, Pennsylvania, and rolled toward Gettysburg. All along the columns, from sergeants to corporals, from cannoneers to drivers, word spread through the army grapevine, which often carries truth as well as rumor. Hill and Ewell had hit the enemy hard and driven him all the past day. Probably the bluebellies—"those people," as Marse Robert called them in his quietly courteous way—were now hanging on to a defensive position, and extra guns would be needed to blast them out of it. In any event there would be plenty of them to be dealt with in the morning. Their ranks could be shattered, their flanks turned, their armies hurled back in battle, but Yankees kept coming in seemingly inexhaustible numbers. After a while it grew a bit discouraging, and the war dragged out endlessly. Yet the Army of Northern Virginia was deep in Union territory now, and maybe this was the last campaign.

The road was "a ribbon of moonlight" across the unscarred Pennsylvania countryside. Right good farming land, ran comments passed back from lead driver to swing and on to the man on the near pole horse. Harness leather creaked, and trace chains jangled. Above the rhythmic clump of hoofs an occasional axle groaned in complaint. Slap on some grease from the tar bucket at the next halt, a sergeant made note. A tired driver, lounging in his saddle, heard from an officer riding past: "Sit up or get down and walk. You'll wear a sore on that nag's back." Up ahead a captain listened to the sounds of horses, gun carriages, and caissons behind him and looked back over his shoulder with the pride a commander feels when he leads an able and trusted battery into battle.

Field artillery on the march makes its own music, music that returns for years afterward to fill the dreams of veterans. In those gunner columns converging on Gettysburg the concordance of sounds seemed somehow to furnish an obbligato to the martial strains of "La Marseillaise" in the case of one battalion. For to Major Benjamin F. Eshleman's Washington Artillery of New Orleans, largely of Gallic descent, France's anthem was the perfect accompaniment, as stirring as the lively strains of "Dixie." Perhaps some of the Louisiana artillerymen hummed the tune or that of their own camp song, "The Cannoneer," written by First Sergeant A. G. Knight of the 2nd Company to the air of "The Happy Land of Canaan" and enumerating the duties of every man in a gun squad.

We will sing of the boys who make the loudest noise,
And from fighting you can scarcely restrain them. *Aha!*

They have "guns," "howitzers," "rifles," and other sorts of
  trifles
To send soldiers past the "Happy land of Canaan." [58]

The oldest military organization in Louisiana, the Washington
Artillery, was first mustered in 1838. It had served as a battery in
Texas seven years later and briefly as infantry in the Mexican War.
Its crest was a tiger head superimposed on crossed cannon, and be-
neath it the motto, "Try us." Tried it had been from the early
combats of the Civil War onward and not found wanting.

Equipped by public contributions, its battalion of four companies (a fifth would subsequently be organized) had been ordered
to Virginia in 1861. They arrived resplendently uniformed—scarlet-
crowned French kepis—blue jackets and trousers decked with scarlet
piping—white gaiters—plenty of gold braid on the officers' sleeves.
"Bandbox soldiers," other troops called them. For a time the
battalion lived high. Its German commissary sergeant was a first-
rate forager. He was accompanied by his wife, dressed as a
vivandière, those French Army women auxiliaries who marched
with their regiments, a small cask of wine or brandy slung over a
shoulder. While the worthy *frau* could not pass as the image of
Ouida's lithesome *vivandière* in *Under Two Flags*, she reflected the
best traditions of her post, enduring hard campaigning and nursing
the sick and wounded. A famous chef from a New Orleans restaurant
regaled the Washingtons' repasts—they could not be described as an
army mess—with delicacies until transport grew short, and the pots
and pans of his art were pitched in the ditches; thereupon he
resigned in disgust and went home with his pet fox. However, he
was replaced by a galaxy of Negro cooks, headed by French-speaking
François. These were augmented by body-servants, who acted as
barbers, blacked boots, groomed the horses, and foraged. In battle
they made tracks to the rear, returning to their duties when the
shooting stopped.

After First Manassas (Bull Run) the battalion toasted the capture
of Yankee guns with champagne, looted from the hampers of

picnicking spectators. Before long it was reduced to hardtack and sherry, then to parched corn and branch water.

The Louisiana gunners carried on with the war which they referred to as "a little difference between the Washington Artillery and U.S." Songs rose around their campfires, and they never neglected to celebrate Mardi Gras.

A heritage of their French blood was that superb *panache*, which distinguished the élite troops of Napoleon Bonaparte. One member put in words the emotion that animated the Washington Artillery when its four batteries "advanced in full armor into action."

> As we stretch out upon the road, the Colonel orders, "Battalion, trot, march!" The drivers swing their strong whips, and the teams break into a brisk trot, and away we go, with the carriages rumbling, the harness rattling, and the iron hoofs of the horses striking fire from the flint road.
>
> What a glorious sight it is! See the sixteen guns! What beauties! The finest in the world—rifles and Napoleons taken from the enemy at Manassas and Seven Pines. Sixteen caissons—thirty-two carriages in all—nearly 300 men and 200 horses. What a sight to gladden a soldier's eye! In front of all rides the Colonel on his black stallion, "Rebel." A pace behind rides the adjutant; then the chief bugler, and the guidon-bearer, carrying the little scarlet banner with its blue cross, the gift of Constance Carey, fashioned from her own gown. Just behind come the batteries, the captains riding in front of each.[59]

On Marye's Hill at Fredericksburg the Washingtons had lost six of their prized guns when supporting infantry was overrun. But the Yankees lost the battle, and the spirit of the men from Louisiana soon revived. Issued new weapons, they fought on. Now, long since having ceased to be "bandbox soldiers," they marched through the night toward Gettysburg.

Twenty-six more guns lengthened the train that wound over

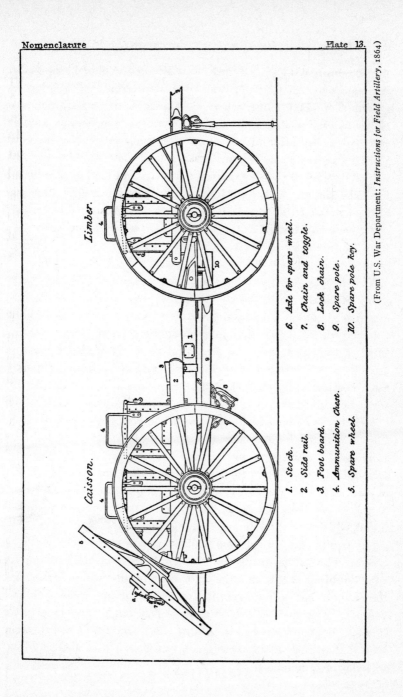

Limber.

Caisson.

1. Stock.
2. Side rail.
3. Foot board.
4. Ammunition Chest.
5. Spare wheel.

6. Axle for spare wheel.
7. Chain and toggle.
8. Lock chain.
9. Spare pole.
10. Spare pole key.

(From U.S. War Department: *Instructions for Field Artillery*, 1864)

the moonlit road—the strong battalion of Colonel E. Porter Alexander, completing the reserve of artillery of the I Corps. A graduate of West Point, where he subsequently commanded the Corps of Cadets, Alexander was a veteran of the Indian wars in Oregon. An engineer turned gunner, he rates as the South's most brilliant artillerist, as Pelham had been its most dashing. He had helped develop the wig-wag system with flags and torches, invaluable for field communications. Many a Confederate battery owed its efficiency to his training. The two most colorful ones he led that night were handsome Captain George V. Moody's Madison Battery from Louisiana and Captain William W. Parker's "Boy Company" from Virginia.

The former, mostly Irishmen called "Tips," probably because many originally hailed from Tipperary, were a tough, belligerent lot, as ready to fight among themselves as take on the enemy. While fists served to settle intra-battery arguments, the "Tips" carried butcher knives strapped to their belts. Those were for defense against savage cows and ferocious hogs along the route of march. Such beasts allegedly attacked the Madison artillerymen and paid for it by ending up as steaks or fried pork.

Strictly disciplined in contrast were the young Virginians of the "Boy Company," not a few of them in their early teens. "The robbing of the cradle, if not the grave, was begun early in the war." Disobedience of orders meant being strapped to the spare wheel of a caisson. But Captain Parker could be as gentle upon occasion as he was severe. He was a doctor and served as surgeon to his own command, which was allowed an ambulance; it carried a medicine chest, camp equipment, stores, two violins and a guitar, hens, and a rooster. The battery could count on fresh eggs and milk as well. A cow, doubling as a pack animal for cooking utensils, accompanied the column, her mileage running well into the hundreds. Sick and wounded youngsters of the battery received tender care from their surgeon-commander or his Negro body-servant. Officers were known to swing out of their saddles and turn over their mounts to footsore cannoneers.

The lads, far from being coddled, stood the test of battle. "There is something awfully solemn in the shriek of a coming shell," one of them wrote. " 'Hark from the tombs a doleful sound!'—'Awake, my soul, stretch every nerve!'—'My thoughts on dreadful subjects roll, damnation of the dead!'—with a liberal mixture of 'I'm coming, old Black Joe!'—seem, to the nervous ear, to commingle in one horribly solemn melody, and no wonder people get 'converted' on the battlefield." [60]

Some of the company's cannon and 40 of its men had been captured at Chancellorsville, but the latter had been recovered by exchange and were ready for action again.

About one mile west of Seminary Ridge the reserve artillery halted, made park, and watered and fed its horses.

Simultaneously the divisional guns of the Confederate I Corps had been advancing to Gettysburg. Any artilleryman would have spared a glance of admiration for the fine condition of the pieces, horses, and equipment of the Rowan, North Carolina, Battery of Henry's Battalion. Captain James Reilly insisted they always be given the best of care. Touch the harness and it felt soft and supple; it had been treated with neat's-foot oil, obtained from cattle hoofs discarded at the commissary pens. Stirrup straps or traces of dried, cracked leather might break in other outfits, but no such accidents occurred when Reilly's Battery galloped into action.

In another battery of the same battalion an observer would have noted the German looks of most of the officers, cannoneers, and drivers. Change them from uniform into farm clothes and they could have passed for the Pennsylvania "Dutch" of this countryside in which they were about to fight. Or put them in blue instead of gray and they would match gunners of the Federal XI Corps. But no one derided Captain William K. Bachman's men as "damned Dutchmen." Tolerance of those of foreign birth or descent was far more prevalent in the South than in the North, and these were respected citizens or residents of Charleston, whose German community had uniformed and equipped them. Their roll was almost solidly Teutonic. Some had taken part in the siege of Fort Sumter. Adding to the battery's international flavor was the fact that a Cuban veteran of the struggle for independence from Spain, Colonel Ambrosio José Gonzales, was Chief of Artillery for the Department of South Carolina.

Cabell's Battalion included the 1st Company, Richmond Howitzers, under Captain H. H. Carlton. Their armament might comprise more guns than howitzers, but their title had remained fixed since their organization by George W. Randolph, later Secretary of War. He had served as a midshipman in the old navy and at the outbreak of the war attempted to convert naval boat howitzers into field artillery. Although the scheme was dropped in favor of other types of ordnance, the name clung to this and other companies subsequently formed. Behind them all lay a long and distinguished battle record. A famous mascot, the little dog "Stonewall," belonged to the Howitzers. He was a regular dog of war, accompanying his company into battle and capering around among the thundering guns, barking shrilly. When the battery changed position, a cannoneer would pick "Stonewall" up and drop him into a compartment of an ammunition chest to be lifted out when the guns unlimbered and opened fire again. Even at Chancellorsville, while the Howitzers were being pounded with heavy shelling by enemy artillery, the mascot never deserted his comrades, and his barks mingled with cheers for that victory.

The divisional guns, reaching Gettysburg about seven o'clock on the morning of July 2, were placed, along with the reserve battalions, under the command of Colonel Alexander. That officer, summoned by General Longstreet, reported to him and General Lee on Seminary Ridge where he was told that the I Corps would assault the Union left. He thereupon commenced a long and careful reconnaissance and posted his batteries, keeping them out of sight of the Federal signal station on Little Round Top.

From the ridge concealed cannon peered eastward toward the shank of the fishhook of the Blue line. Yonder lay their routes of advance and fields of fire. They were confronted by a jumbled mass of rocks called Devil's Den, a bad place for artillery but a fine one for sharpshooters. Beyond, north of Big Round Top, rose that smaller eminence, Little Round Top. Thickly wooded, it could not be observed whether it was empty or occupied. Farther north was better ground for artillery: a peach orchard, then a wheatfield. Thence the line of the Confederate I Corps guns was prolonged by that of the III and then by that of the II, which ringed the fishhook's curve at Cemetery and Culp's hills. It was there that Lee had directed Ewell to launch a diversionary attack when he heard the sound of Longstreet's assault and carry it through if it went well, yet only forty-eight of the corps' eighty-odd guns were in position. If Ewell were to "press those people," as he had failed to do yesterday, he would need all the artillery power at his command.

On the second day the battlefield of Gettysburg, bordered by ridges, more markedly assumes the aspect of a huge amphitheater, a stage where the batteries of this history "have their entrances and their exits." For the most part the morning was quiet, a lull before dramatic action. To the north a few Gray columns appeared, were shelled, and withdrew as if they had missed their cue. Elsewhere masses of infantry and battalions of artillery gathered in the wings and waited poised.

It was a hot day, oppressively so. Sweltering Union corps, entire or in part, organized their lines. Rear elements were still en route, having made the wearing night marches demanded by Meade's rapid concentration. The I and XI Corps, as has been noted, held the right. XII and II reinforced them on Culp's and Cemetery hills. III prolonged the line to Little Round Top, and V was placed in reserve near the Rock Creek crossing of the Baltimore Pike. VI was coming up. Cavalry guarded the flanks. The reserve artillery and ammunition trains were parked in a central position on a cross-road from the Baltimore Pike to the Taneytown Road.

General Sickles of III Corps stood on Cemetery Ridge and scanned the Peach Orchard that lay athwart his front. A hot-blooded, impetuous man, Dan Sickles, past master of politics, which had paved his way to high command. It seemed to him that the ground down there, once in enemy hands, would gravely threaten his present position. If he pushed a salient into the orchard and put guns on the hillocks through and around it, he judged that his troops would be better disposed for either defense or attack. Would General Meade approve such a move, he inquired at headquarters.

Meade sent Hunt to estimate the situation. Such a salient offered advantages, the artillery chief declared, but it was risky and would dangerously lengthen the line. He would grant no permission to advance on his own authority; it was a matter for the commanding general to decide. Meanwhile, he suggested, make a reconnaissance. As Hunt rode away, Sickles sent infantry forward, and soon a brisk fire fight opened when skirmishers ran into solid ranks of Rebels in the woods beyond the orchard.

So the enemy were already there, mustered to assault. Sickles waited no longer for orders from Meade. As he saw it, the left flank was critically menaced, and it was his duty to protect it. "He took his whole corps forward, a mile-long line of battle with waving flags and rumbling batteries rolling west in the afternoon sunlight." [61] When Meade in angry amazement rode toward the racket of mounting conflict, he found the troops of his quick-triggered subordinate half a mile out in front of the rest of the army. Sickles, asking whether he should withdraw to his original line, was answered by the crash of Longstreet's cannonade. Meade reined tight his restive horse and turned a wrathful, lined face toward his corps commander. Sometimes disrespectful mutters branded George Gordon Meade "the damned old goggle-eyed snapping-turtle." He snapped now, jerking out words in the gun thunder. It was too late to pull back, he told Sickles. Stay where you are and fight it out.

In the Peach Orchard bursting shells bloomed like malignant, scarlet blossoms, fragments of metal splintered the trees, and men watered their roots with blood.

That thundering bombardment, which was the prelude to Longstreet's assault, grew in intensity. The fire of 18 guns of Alexander's

Battalion, the same number from Cabell's, and Henry's 10 was augmented until 54 guns were pouring an avalanche of shells on Sickles' advanced battle line from the crest of the rocky slope where they were stationed. Shoving the pieces back uphill into battery after recoil was exhausting work in that scorching heat. It told on even Moody's tough "Tips," and the Irishmen had to call on infantrymen to help them manhandle their big 24's. Out of the eight doughboys lending a hand two were killed and three wounded before nightfall.

For the batteries of the Union III Corps were taking the punishment inflicted on them and giving it back. Unsilenced, they returned an accurate, effective fire that dismounted two of the cannon on the crest. Flame spurted from muzzles ranked through the Wheat Field, the Peach Orchard, and on into the rocky fastnesses of Devil's Den. Yet the preponderant weight of metal of enemy guns and volleys of Gray riflemen commenced to crush them. Battery E, 1st Rhode Island Light Artillery, under Lieutenant John K. Bucklyn, was suffering casualties that would account for one third of its men and nearly half its horses. Scarcely had the battery clerk volunteered to fill in at a depleted gun squad, when a shell severed his head from his body. A section sergeant, hit in the forehead by a spent ball, reeled in his saddle. He felt the lump, then moved his hand around to the back of his skull to find the hole where the bullet would have emerged. There was no hole, so he rode back to his post. Another sergeant rigged a sling for his crippled left arm and carried on. Bucklyn, a third horse shot from under him, was pierced through one lung by a Minié ball and, choking with blood, was carried to the rear. Battery E was so badly cut up that it was out of action for the rest of the battle.

Captain George B. Winslow's Battery D, 1st New York, prided itself on its marksmanship. In the Peninsula Campaign it had sunk the trail of one of its guns, used 30-second fuses, and forced a Confederate observation balloon, made of silk from dresses given by Richmond women, to descend hastily. It had driven back a piece of enemy railroad artillery and then wrecked its supporting battery.

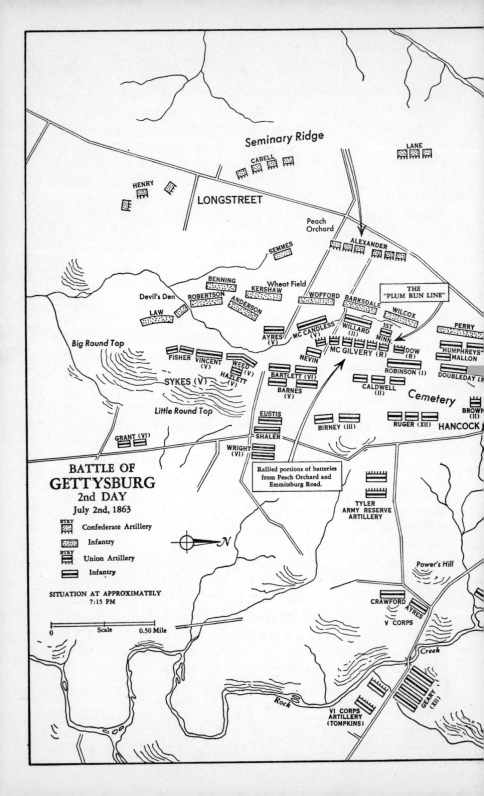

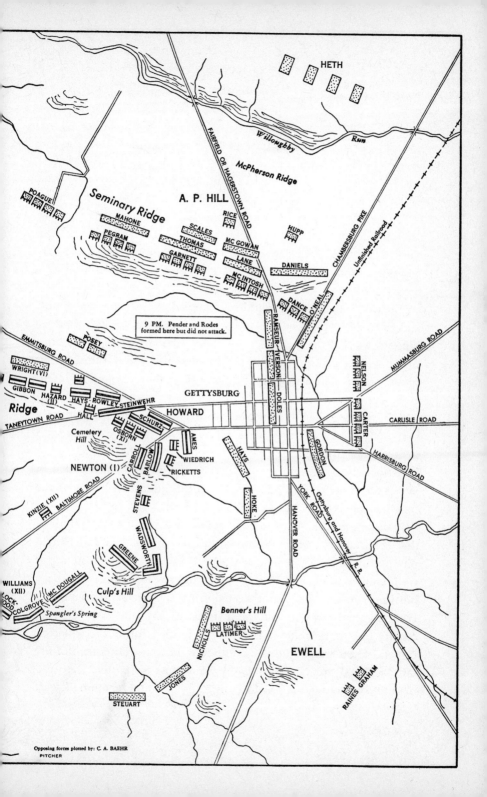

HETH

Willoughby Run

FAIRFIELD OR HAGERSTOWN ROAD

McPherson Ridge

POAGUE

Seminary Ridge

A. P. HILL

CHAMBERSBURG PIKE

Unfinished Railroad

MAHONE

RICE

SCALES

HUPP

PEGRAM

THOMAS

MC GOWAN

GARNETT

LANE

DANIELS

MC INTOSH

DANCE

RAMSEUR

O. NEAL

9 PM. Pender and Rodes
formed here but did not attack.

IVERSON

EMMITSBURG ROAD

POSEY

NELSON

MUMMASBURG ROAD

WRIGHT (VI)

DOLES

CARTER

GIBBON

HAZARD (II)

HAYS

ROWLEY

STEINWEHR

GETTYSBURG

CARLISLE ROAD

Ridge

HALL

HOWARD

TANEYTOWN ROAD

SCHURZ

HARRISBURG ROAD

Cemetery
Hill

OSBORN
(XI)

AMES

HAYS

GORDON

CARROLL

BARLOW

WIEDRICH

YORK ROAD

NEWTON (I)

RICKETTS

HOKE

HANOVER ROAD

Gettysburg and Hanover R. R.

KINZIE (XII)

BALTIMORE ROAD

STEVENS

WADSWORTH

WILLIAMS
(XII)

GREENE

MC DOUGALL

LOCK-
WOOD

COLGROVE

Culp's Hill

Spangler's Spring

Benner's Hill

NICHOLS

LATIMER

EWELL

JONES

STEUART

RAINES GRAHAM

Opposing forces plotted by: C. A. BAEHR
PITCHER

Now the New York gunners hurled solid shot over the heads of their own infantry and held their ground until they met the same fate as the Massachusetts men. Pounded by Rebel artillery and enveloped by sharpshooters, Battery D was forced to retreat, retiring piece by piece.

On the extreme Union left 10-pounder Parrotts boomed steadily. Those sturdy rifled cannon, strengthened by iron hoops shrunken around their breeches—the point of maximum strain—were the invention of Captain Robert Parker Parrott, once an officer of the 3rd Artillery and now head of the West Point gun foundry. Captain James E. Smith's 4th New York Battery, manning them, had been named "The Parrott Battery" when it was organized. A member, on the understanding he would be commissioned second lieutenant, had obtained the prized pieces through his uncle, Captain Parrott himself. Each of the six guns, supplied with 200 rounds of ammunition apiece, received extra-special treatment at the foundry, being tested repeatedly on the target range under the eye of the lieutenant's Uncle Robert. Satisfied, he caused each weapon to be stamped with his name. The 4th New York, ordered to Washington, proudly prepared to take delivery there of its Parrotts only to learn with immense chagrin that they had been issued to another outfit.

Ultimately, however, the battery was equipped with Parrotts, and it was those rifles it put in position this afternoon in one of the toughest spots on the battlefield—Devil's Den.

It was impossible for gun carriages to be driven to the summit of that creviced mass of boulders. Smith's men unhooked and hauled pieces and ammunition chests up by hand. Cannoneers on ropes, trail handles, axles, and wheel spokes, they sweated it out under the burning sun and its heat reflected from the rocks. Manhandling guns up that rocky ascent was a notable feat, and soon another mighty one of the kind was to be performed in another quarter. General Hunt walked up and admired the commanding field of fire but predicted that Smith probably would lose his battery. Extricating those guns under the forthcoming attack would be more difficult and far more hazardous than had been putting them where they were.

The stage was set for another of those sacrifices of Union batteries that too frequently characterize the Battle of Gettysburg—sacrifices to which dire emergencies or mistakes and misjudgments doomed them. On the first day an artillery chief's confusion of "Seminary" with "Cemetery" had contributed to the destruction. Now it was Sickles' unauthorized advance that imperiled the 4th New York and the III Corps and Reserve batteries. Yet infantry regiments were spent freely, and the oblation of cannon and their crews was not offered in vain. For priceless minutes and hours they helped hold the line.

Up on the brow of the Den with a deep ravine to their rear, four of Captain Smith's Parrotts blazed away, doing deadly execution. The third section, off on more accessible ground to a flank, chimed in. At 300 yards they pounded the Gray assault waves. Never stopping to sponge barrels, risking premature explosion of powder charges, they poured in volley after volley of canister. Three times they saw oncoming ranks shredded and their battle flags go down. But enemy sharpshooters were infiltrating Devil's Den and making it live up to its name, dropping the gunners. Blue infantry masked the third section's enfilading fire, and its guns fell silent.

Thrice the 4th New York might have withdrawn but stood its ground, isolated, suspended between the lines. Now it was too late to retreat. One disabled piece they did succeeed in pulling out as they fought off Hood's Texans flooding into the position. At last surviving artillerymen scrambled down the slope, and the three remaining guns were lost.[62] At least the captured pieces could not at once be turned against their former owners, for the crews carried off the rammer staffs and other implements.

Toward the left of the Peach Orchard Battery B, 1st New Jersey Artillery, Captain A. Judson Clark, moved into position. These were Newark men, 70 per cent native-born, the rest "naturalized soldiers equally devoted to their adopted country as its own sons." They had a leavening of veterans: two from the Mexican War, two each from the British and German armies, and one from the French. As the battery in double column approached the Emmitsburg Road, enemy guns at a range of 1,400 yards took it under heavy fire. "Right reverse, trot," Captain Clark ordered—then "Action front!" Down went the trails, and the six Parrotts began to boom.

General Sickles loomed through the smoke. "Hold this position," he directed the battery commander, "while you have a shot in your limbers or a man to work your guns."

The combat was to reach just such a finale for the New Jersey artillery.

How a battery endures ordeal by fire has seldom been more vividly and minutely described than by the "wild Irish boy," Michael Hanifen, whom B was to choose as its historian.

About 4 o'clock [he wrote] a spherical case shot [shrapnel] exploded to the right of the first caisson, filling flanks of the leader and shoulders of the off pole horse with bullets. A fragment of shell disemboweled the nigh pole horse; another took off his foreleg. I was holding him by the bridle; the team started to run, made a fine "left about," dragging horse and me fifty yards to the rear. Pole horse fell dead as soon as they stopped. Banks, Williams, Vandine, and I replaced the pole which was broken,[63] divested the dead horse of harness, and our farrier, Fairchild, brought up some spare horses to re-place similar losses. We put harness on a pair and pulled the caisson to its place in line. The drivers were called upon to carry ammunition to replenish limber chests of guns, and No. 8 to issue ammunition and cut out fuse, as we were firing more rapidly than No. 6 could issue it and cut fuse. Smalley and Morris were wounded. The latter, although having a painful wound, stuck to his gun until ammunition was exhausted, and rode out on trail. Colyer and Tierney and McGowen were wounded. Costello also, and their places at guns were filled by drivers. Timm, gunner, and Riley, No. 5, had hold of a handspike to direct line of fire of gun, at

Smith's position. A shell plunged into ground under the trail and exploded under their feet. The trail flopped up and threw them twenty feet in the air; they fell together; Riley was underneath, both covered with blood and dirt. Timm scrambled to his feet, wiped the dirt out of his eyes, and asked Riley if he was hurt. He said, "By Jiminy, I didn't think they could touch me without taking a limb, and now, d——'em, they have taken half the meat I did have." The shell had sheared all the flesh from Riley's right hip clear to the bone. Bauer, No. 1, received a painful wound in knee. Bonnell, No. 4, was knocked insensible by the concussion. Bauer was ordered to the hospital. Sergt. Clairville called on the drivers to take place of those wounded, as they took vacant positions. Riley stood still like one dazed. Lieut. Simms yelled at him, "Riley, why the bloody h——l don't you roll that gun by hand to the front?" Riley turned his wounded hip and thigh to the Lieutenant's view and said, "Lieutenant, if your hip was shot off like that, what the bloody h——l would you do?" He was ordered to go to the hospital, and went away on one foot and two hands like a lame dog. Caleb Harrison took the place of the injured No. 1. The sponge bucket was broken and its contents spilled. He cursed the Rebels. The spare bucket was put in place, and what little water was in our canteens emptied into it, after which he sponged and rammed home the shell, and the fire of the gun was directed to our opponent and Bonnell pulled the lanyard. We all said, "Take that for Riley." I was sent with seven or eight canteens to the spring near the Trostle house to fill them. As I passed the supporting regiment a shell exploded over the line, killing or wounding seven or eight men. The canteens filled, I faced to the south. A grand but terrible picture met my view. On the road, near by, the Fifth Corps was marching to the left. Our left and front was a sheet of flame. The air was dotted with little balloons of white smoke, showing where shells had burst, and sent their deadly passengers to the fighting lines below. From Longstreet's right, all along to our right as far as one could see, the enemy's artillery was actively engaged, as shown by the white steam-like clouds of smoke arising from their battery positions. To the left I could see the enemy driving our men up the sides of the Little Round Top, and was rejoiced to see them driven back again. The Fifth Corps, which was miles away when the battle began, were hurried to the front to reinforce us. When I got back to the guns all hands had a refreshing drink of water. Some of the men said, "My God, but that is good, this is hotter than h——l here." (92 degrees in the shade that day at Gettysburg). Ames' Battery left the Peach Orchard, and the infantry supporting us were marched into it. Hart's Battery also pulled out, and Watson's Battery I, Fifth United States, took position vacated by Ames. At this time, 5.30, enemy commenced moving down our front and right in heavy columns, from 600 to 800 yards distant. Under cover of a heavy artillery fire they presented a slight flank to us. The fire of the entire line was directed on them, and its effect seemed to be to make them double quick into the Rose woods, where the enemy were pushing our troops back into the wheatfield. Our ammunition was running very low. Orderly Sergeant Galbraith was sent to the rear after John Cronk, whose six-mule team was loaded with extra ammunition. About 6 o'clock Cronk came up on a dead run. Under orders, we were ready to jump into his wagon and unload the boxes of ammunition. How he sang oaths to those mules to keep them quiet under that fire, where a hundred shells were exploding every minute, and the crackle of his whip was like a sharp skirmish fire! He was a hero. A shot in that load would have sent Cronk, Banks, Bush, Buffum, and a few others where peace forever holds her court. In returning from gun to caisson a shell exploded over me. The concussion threw me to the ground, and for a short time I was unconscious. Martin Donohue was bending over me when I became conscious, tears from his eyes falling on my face, and as I bathed my eye-lids he inserted the nozzle of his canteen between my lips, and said, "Mike, shure you're not kilt entirely, for 'tis I would be lonesome without you." When I returned to the gun, which I did slowly, I was somewhat benumbed from shock. The query was, "Were you hit hard?" "No." "Bully boy! Hurry up the ammunition lively now, and we will give them h——l yet. You see the devils are gaining ground on our left." There was a break in our line 500 yards to the left. A crippled battery was leaving the Peach Orchard on the right. A brigade of the enemy, with six battleflags, moved across our front and formed line near the Rose house. They advanced against us under a galling fire. We had been throwing shell and shrapnel into them, but have nothing left but canister. They broke back and reformed at 450 yards. Timm, under Clairville's direction, tried a round of canister at leading regiment, the colors fell, making a beautiful gap in their line, which was closed up, and on they came. Capt. Clark passed from gun to gun, animating and encouraging the men, as cool and calm as if it was a battery drill. Old Bill had a stick in his hand in which he cut a notch for every shot fired, grumbled at slightest error, telling us to keep cool and keep our shirts on. We were getting too wild, and might lose Old Betsey, No. 1 gun. As I handed the next two canisters to Elias Campbell, each containing 76 balls,[64] he said, "This is the stuff to feed them; 'tis good for them; feed it to their bellies, Timm; mow them down, Timm." And Timm aimed to hit them in the middle of their anatomy, and they fell like grass before a mower's scythe. Harrison, who had sponged after every shot and rammed every load since Bauer was hurt, said, "D—— them, we are paying off for Riley now." During this time the front of the Battery was almost a sheet of flame; the men at the guns fairly flew to their work. The guns themselves seemed full of life; dogs of war, nearly red hot; how they roared and thundered! Shells of the enemy's guns were shrieking overhead, or throwing up clouds of dust and dirt where they exploded, bullets were zipping from front and flank. Sergt. McChesney and Bob Stuart were wounded badly, but still staid to work their guns. Splinters were flying from gun carriages and wheels. Horses were being killed and wounded, and taken out of harness, as they fell, by their drivers. At every gun were wounded men, many too slight for hospital. They staid until the last shot was fired, and then rode out on guns. Every one's shirt was soaked with sweat, some with blood. All were grimed with powder smoke, and not a man but kept to his work. Heroes, every one. Our canister fire was too much for the charging column. It threw it into great confusion, and all who were not killed and wounded changed direction to right when about 200 yards distant, and disappeared, seeking shelter behind slope of a hill on our left, near the wheatfield, which had become a veritable crater of a volcano, a very whirlwind of battle. Rebel yells and Yankee cheers alternated rapidly, as either side gained an advantage or reinforcement. There was an incessant roar of musketry and artillery, a rapid movement of troops. Now blue, now gray, as they emerged from the woods and rocks, and charged recklessly into each other's ranks, with yells and shouts and cheers, which were heard above the sound of musketry and artillery. The wheatfield was reaped with the harvest of death. In our front were over 120 dead from three South Carolina regiments. At the Rose house and barn were 200 more. The last round of canister was fired; the last three had been three canisters to one cartridge. The Captain gave the orders to limber up and go to the rear. Phillips' Battery had gone. The infantry on our flanks had fallen back. The enemy (Barksdale's Brigade) were half way through the Peach Orchard on our right flank, as the wheels of the limber struck the trail of gun the lead team was hit. Higgins jumped out of the saddle and cut the traces, and the gun drove off with four horses. A Rebel yelled, "Halt, you

Yankee sons of ——; we want those guns!" Ennis yelled back, "Go to he——l! We want to use them yet awhile." At that moment the remnant of the Sixty-third Pennsylvania, who were lying in sunken road, rose up and poured a volley into their faces, causing them to halt. Had their guns been loaded, a volley would have killed and wounded nearly all our horses and men. Two cannoniers rode out on axle, holding on as best they could. Harrison placed his hand on the gun to support himself. It burned all the skin from palm and fingers. Edson Shephard was hit in left breast, the ball encircling body, leaving a blue welt, and coming out of breastbone three inches from place of entrance. Just as we started a single gun of the enemy came into position in J. Wentz's yard and fired a round of canister. It killed six horses on No. 4 caisson and four on No. 3, wounding Richard Price, Hiram Grover and John Truby. Joseph Baker also was wounded. This obliged us to leave one caisson and one caisson body on the field. Henry C. Buffum and Daniel W. Laws stopped to assist Price to the hospital. They were taken prisoners; Buffum died at Andersonville July 11, 1864—starved to death. Henry E. Davis took shelter behind a boulder and was captured. Then enemy was driven back. Price was taken to Rock Creek hospital; both legs and one arm were amputated. He died August 22d, his songs cheering comrades to the last. Before [the gunners in the] Wentz [yard] could reload we were out of canister range. His fire no doubt was directed on Bigelow, and the cause of Bigelow's heavy loss. In passing to the rear we passed the left flank of Seventh New Jersey, 200 yards to our rear. We fell back through the Trostle lane, out of the vortex of fire that whirled around the Peach Orchard. We halted for some time on the ridge near the Trostle house. Some batteries went into position on our left. The Seventh New Jersey came back and formed line on our right. They had lost 114 out of 331 men.

Wheaton's Brigade of the Sixth Corps formed line in our

rear. They had marched from Westminster, 35 miles, since midnight. The sun set while we were there, 7:34. Our losses were two killed, sixteen seriously and several slightly wounded, three taken prisoners, twenty-three horses killed, and twenty-four wounded. Gen. Hunt informed the writer and several other members of the Battery, at Gettysburg, July 2, 1886, that the returns to him showed that Battery B had fired 1,342 rounds of ammunition July 2, 1863, and that no battery in the United States service had fired that amount in a single day during the war. Clairville's notches on his stick show that right gun fired 241 rounds. We opened the battle on the second day. The appearance of our front after the battle was over showed we made them pay dearly for ground gained, and gave time for reinforcements to reach the front.[65]

At the rear, Captain Clark called what was left of his battery to attention. "Boys," he said, "those of us who survive this war will have reason to be proud of this day's work." His voice lowered, and he spoke with deep reverence. "I ask you all to return thanks to God that He brought us safely out of this day's battle."

General Hunt had been drawing battery after battery from his reserve and flinging them into the conflict. Guns, more guns in a moment of critical need. That was the purpose of this invaluable reservoir of cannon. Bugles sounded, and at trot or gallop the batteries plunged into the fray around the Peach Orchard to confront the long line of enemy guns south of the Emmitsburg Road.

Forward rode Colonel McGilvery of Maine, leading three units of his brigade: Bigelow's 9th Massachusetts (four 12-pounders), Phillips' 5th Massachusetts (six 3-inch rifles), Hart's 15th New York (four 12-pounders). On their heels came Thompson's C and F combined, Pennsylvania Artillery (six 3-inchers) and Sterling's 2nd Battery, Connecticut Artillery, armed with two howitzers and four James, 3.67-inch rifles converted from smoothbores. Brigadier General Tyler, chief of the Reserve, in person brought three 12-pounder outfits: Thomas' C, 4th U.S., Weir's C, 5th U.S., and Turnbull's combined F and K, 3rd U.S.

Still more would shortly be committed: Ames' G of the 1st New York, Ricketts' F and G, 1st Pennsylvania, Dow's 6th Maine. One of Sickles' staff officers, to Hunt's annoyance, drew two batteries—Watson's I, 5th U.S., and Walcott's C, 1st Massachusetts, from V Corps, which had greater need of them. Here, it seemed, as was said of the great array of ordnance mustered by Henry VIII, were "cannon enough to conquer Hell." Yet they were not enough for conquest—barely enough for defense. Flashes of hellfire were rippling along the line of Confederate artillery. They pounded their adversaries, front and salient flanks, with blasts of counterbattery that drove them from position and compelled them to relieve each other. Somehow the line still held against the crescendo of Longstreet's assault.

Hunt, having inspected Smith's guns at Devil's Den, strode off to seek infantry to defend the exposed battery. A brigadier with a lieutenant general's command, he was handicapped by a staff of only four: his adjutant, aide, one orderly, and a flag-bearer. With them he must maintain communication with every part of the battlefield and with the Commander in Chief. All four men were absent on errands when Hunt left the brow of the Den and approached the ravine between it and the Round Tops beyond which he had left his horse. It was there he met with his most trying and dangerous experience in the entire battle, one for which he would have gladly exchanged the shelling to which he was often exposed.

A herd of horned cattle had been cut off and cornered in the ravine by Rebel artillery fire. With a shriek a shell plunged into the body of one, exploded, and tore it to pieces. Other projectiles smashed down, killing and wounding more of the frantic animals, wild with terror. Bellowing, they stampeded, rushing about in their confines in attempts to escape from the storm of iron hail. Hunt had to cross that ravine. A long detour on foot would delay him from reaching points where he was vitally needed. He took a deep breath, scrambled down into the gully, and threaded his way through the panic-stricken mass of cattle. "Luckily," he wrote, "the poor beasts were as much frightened as I was, but their rage was subdued by terror, and they were good enough to let me pass through scot-free but 'badly demoralized.'" [66] He found his horse safe, mounted, and rode off.

Meanwhile his embattled artillerymen, though in desperate straits, were doing him honor.

A dark, heroic destiny led the 9th Massachusetts Battery to the Peach Orchard that second day of July. It is hard to consider it otherwise in the light of the fact that the battery would not have marched to Gettysburg at all except for a strange chance. Orders originally had not scheduled it to accompany the Army of the Potomac from Virginia. When a Pennsylvania artillery unit of the Reserve delayed to pick up a general officer's personal baggage for transportation in its battery wagon, General Hunt heard of it and erupted. Guns under his command moved when and where they were told without fooling around doing favors for high rank. He left the too-obliging Pennsylvanians behind and replaced them with the 9th Massachusetts.[67]

These Bay State gunners had been organized by an artillery officer on leave from the Italian Army. His broken English failing him, he issued orders through a lieutenant who spoke French, reminiscent of Von Steuben in the Revolution. He had his men taught saber fencing and urged they be armed with carbines. Owing to his language difficulty and other causes he resigned, and his place was taken by Captain John Bigelow.

John Bigelow ranks high in the valiant company of battery commanders. His left arm, shattered at Malvern Hill, had healed, and he had returned to duty some time before the march to Gettysburg. He would well remember and vividly set down events of this field where he and his men fought a sacrifice action whose story is one of the battle's epics.[68]

At dawn, July 2, the 9th Massachusetts made a 15-mile march from Taneytown, Maryland, with the rest of Lieutenant Colonel

Freeman McGilvery's 1st Volunteer Brigade of the Reserve Artillery. It moved fast toward the battle ahead over a road so rough and rocky that a badly-packed ammunition chest of another battery blew up and a cannoneer was killed.[69] Parking in rear of Cemetery Hill to await orders, the artillerymen watched smoke puffs of exploding shells dot the sky. As shelter against the glaring sun, they stretched canvas; even in its shade the temperature was 87 degrees. Gunners checked the ammunition, and horses were watered and fed.

It was midafternoon when the artillery chief of the hard-pressed III Corps rode up, asking for more guns. McGilvery barked orders, and a bugler blew Assembly and To Horse. The men of the 9th ran to their teams and carriages, mounted up, and moved out at a lively trot. They halted under shellfire near the Trostle house. Eardrums tingled to crashing infantry volleys and the deep-toned booming of corps cannon striving to repel the furious Confederate assaults.

Bigelow's drawn saber swept forward—jerked up and down, increasing the gait. At full gallop the battery dashed for the crest of a ridge, 400 yards distant. Trails of its six 12-pounders were dropped in rear of the Peach Orchard angle, and instantly the fire of Rebel sharpshooters and two batteries scorched the exposed position. One man was killed and several wounded before the 9th could fire a shot. It stood to its guns, and soon its own billowing powder smoke cloaked it as it engaged enemy cannon 1,400 yards down the Emmitsburg Road. The four Napoleons were well aimed and ably served. Counterbattery fire against them grew wilder—slackened when two Gray limber chests were hit and blew up with flaming roars—then ceased. Bigelow swung his guns to pound advancing infantry, shifting one section from the left to the right flank for a better field of fire. Fuses accurately cut, the shell and shrapnel burst with admirable precision, doing terrible execution. One exploded beneath a mounted officer about to lead a charge. Ranks behind him faltered and broke as he and his horse crumpled. One shell killed and disabled 30 of the 35 men in a company, and a Georgia regiment lost one third of its strength. More than 120 bodies were later counted in that quarter of the field. After the war a Confederate officer grimly told Bigelow, "Visit my Georgia home, and I'll show you enough graves and one-armed and one-legged men to satisfy you for a lifetime." [70]

The 9th was about to pay toll for the destruction it had wrought. With volleys of canister it enfiladed and broke a Gray battle line making for the woods on its left, but sharpshooters among the trees began to cut down gunners and horses. Undefended by infantry, the battery stood in imminent peril of being overrun.

Colonel McGilvery rode up and confirmed its plight. "All of Sickles' men have withdrawn," he said. "You're alone on the field, without supports of any kind. Limber up and get out."

Bigelow answered: "If I attempt to do that, the sharpshooters on my left front will shoot us all down. I'll have to retire by prolonge and firing."

His chief nodded assent. Cannoneers uncoiled the ropes from hooks on the gun trails and fastened them to lunettes of pieces and pintles of limber chests. With part of the crews dragging the carriages to the rear and the rest loading and firing the pieces as they rolled, the 9th retreated toward the Trostle house. Guns boomed, bucked back in recoil, resumed their slow, retrograde movement. The left section fended off skirmishers with canister while the other two plowed furrows in attacking waves with solid shot. But whistling lead was cutting down artillerymen for every yard they moved and dropping teams waiting in the rear. At one gun a cannoneer was hit as he was about to fire. A second man, then a third, were shot as they grasped the lanyard. At last a fourth succeeded in getting off the round. Lieutenant Erickson, a bullet through his lungs and frothing blood at the mouth but refusing to leave his post, was drilled through the head. Casualties mounted toward their fearful total of one officer killed, one mortally and one severely wounded out of four present; six out of seven sergeants killed or wounded; 28 of 60 cannoneers down; 80 of the battery's 88 horses killed or disabled. At length they made it to the stone wall near Trostle's. They cut dead horses out of their harness and prepared to limber and gallop clear of the closing cordon.

Escape was not yet for the all-but-crippled 9th. Here was McGilvery again, calling for a last-ditch stand. "There's a gap of 1,500 yards behind you," he told Bigelow, "and no reserves. You must hold your position at all hazards until I can find some infantry and artillery to fill the hole."

This was it. Bigelow gave his orders. Unlimber. Take what ammunition's left from the chests and stack it beside the guns for rapid fire. Load to the muzzle. Let 'em have it.

The six Napoleons flamed. They held off the frontal attack, but the Rebels lapped both flanks. Now boulders masked the fire of two of the Blue guns. Pull out, Bigelow ordered. One piece upset, was righted amid a shower of bullets, and dragged off. The other smashed straight through the stone wall and won free.

As the battery commander directed the fire of his four remaining guns, Bugler Reed at his side reined his mount back on its haunches. Six Gray riflemen were taking deliberate aim at them. Bigelow and his horse each stopped two bullets. The captain toppled from his saddle, and the bugler dismounted and raised the wounded officer's head.

> I then [wrote Bigelow] saw the Confederates swarming in our right flank, some standing on the limber chests and firing at the gunners, who were still serving their pieces; the horses were all down; overhead the air was alive with missiles from batteries, which the enemy had now placed on the Emmitsburg Road, and, glancing anxiously to the rear, I saw the longed-for batteries just coming into position on high ground, 500 yards away. I then gave orders for the small remnant of the four gun detachments to fall back. My battery had delayed the enemy 30 precious minutes, from 6 to 6:30 o'clock P.M., and its sacrifice had not been in vain.[71]

Bugler Reed, crouching beside his battery commander, heard chivalrous officers of the 21st Mississippi shouting to their men not to fire at the fallen captain again. Lieutenant Whitaker of the 9th, reeling in his saddle from a mortal wound, rode up. Selflessly he put his whisky flask to Bigelow's lips, and they hoisted him up on a horse. Reed, guiding both animals with his left hand, supported the captain with his right arm. Shell, canister slugs, and bullets hummed past them. With steady nerve that would win him a Medal of Honor, never hastening the pace by a step, the bugler walked the horses 300 yards back through the cheering cannoneers of the 6th Maine Battery and on to a hospital.

Confederate Colonel Alexander's 54 guns, in action 500 yards west of Peach Orchard, thundered mightily to demolish the defense of the salient. Against expectation, almost against reason in light of their exposed position, Blue regiments and batteries had opposed the dogged, costly resistance, which has been described in the case of the latter, through the hours of that sweltering afternoon. Yet the Southern assault, gathering momentum and sweeping down on the orchard and through Devil's Den, would not be denied the prize proffered by the ill-judged advance whereby Sickles had placed his corps in jeopardy.

Suddenly Confederate cannon ceased fire. Then they spoke again —three sharp reports. That was a summons for McLaws' Division to attack. They clambered over a stone wall and ran forward. Their rush carried them across the front of their own artillery, masking its fire. Now was Alexander's moment of "artillerist's heaven," a moment for which he never regretted foregoing the command of a brigade of infantry that had been offered him. Placing himself at the head of the six batteries of his own battalion, he ordered them limbered to the front. Then he rose in his stirrups and signaled the charge.

"Perhaps no more superb feat of artillery drill on the battlefield was ever witnessed ... for 500 yards the foaming horses dashed forward, under whip and spur, the guns in perfect alignment, and the carriages fairly bounding over the fields. Every officer and noncommissioned officer rode at his post, and not a team swerved from the line except those which were struck down by a blizzard of Federal shell." [72] Some of the cannoneers clung to seats on the chests, others sprinted beside the whirling wheels. On galloped the battalion until a second signal stayed its onrush, and teams swung around in the beautiful maneuver of action front. Twenty-four gun muzzles gaped at the enemy. Trails cleared pintle hooks, and crews flung themselves upon their pieces. From the ranked line burst a long sheet of smoke and crimson flame.

That crashing cannonade and the infantry masses that flooded in after it and around it rolled up the enemy lines like a tattered blue carpet. Here and there reinforcements stemmed the advance for a time. Then they, too, were torn apart and disintegrated. Sickles' efforts to hold his salient ended when a round shot bowled him and his charger over. One leg shorn off, the rash but brave general was carried to the rear, calmly puffing away on a cigar.

Union batteries formed like phalanxes, one section firing to the front, the other two blazing away, facing right and left. Their ammunition was running low, their cannoneers were being picked off, and their limber horses cut down. Captain Charles A. Phillips of the 5th Massachusetts Battery had planted his guidon to the flank of his gun line when he first took position. That small replica of the Stars and Stripes fluttered gallantly above the battle smoke, its folds stirred by the windy passage of incoming shells. Phillips' ears rang to the *whoosh* of exploding shrapnel, scattering its balls like a shower of hailstones. Those missiles were dropping his horses one by one. He watched his drivers stripping harness from the struggling or heavily inert bodies, a difficult task in any case and doubly so under heavy fire. Soon teams would be so reduced that there would not be animals enough to pull the battery out. The captain called up his limbers and got five of his guns away. The sixth, completely dehorsed, was in imminent danger of capture by Rebels storming in on both flanks and now within pistol shot. A prolonge was toggled to the lunette (ring) at the end of the trail. Phillips, leading his mount with one hand, grasped the end of the rope with the other and swung it over his shoulder. A wounded lieutenant and four men tailed on, and they dragged the piece out of the jaws of the vise closing on it.

Captain James Thompson's Pennsylvania Battery lost a gun, all its team killed while it was retiring. Three of Smith's Parrotts had been swallowed up at Devil's Den. Bigelow's Battery, as has been related, was virtually finished as a fighting unit when it made its valiant stand to plug the wide gap in the line.

The new line McGilvery formed while Bigelow bought him time contained, besides surviving guns from the Peach Orchard, several fresh batteries including Dow's 6th Maine and Watson's I, 5th U.S. With shell and canister they strove to stave off the Confederate onslaught until infantry could come up in support. Every artilleryman sensed that it would be a near thing—touch-and-go whether riflemen came to their aid or the enemy attack overwhelmed them. On the left flank Regulars of the 5th were unable to weather the blasts of lead that flattened gun crews and teams. They fell back, carrying wounded Captain Watson, and abandoning their six 12-pounders. Over the trophies the shrill Rebel yell rose in triumph.

Forward rushed rescuing infantry at the double. Second Lieutenant Samuel Peeples of the 5th U.S. Artillery waved on a panting column, the 39th New York, and pointed to his battery's lost guns. He picked up a fallen soldier's bayoneted rifle and shouted for a charge. Cheering, the New Yorkers followed him. They swarmed over the captured cannon. There was a brief, fierce melee—point-blank fire, muffled by bodies—flashing steel and slugging butts. The six smoothbores, wrested free, were rolled back into the Union lines. Battered remnants of the III Corps filtered out through the hotly engaged II.

Concurrently on the extreme left of the Army of the Potomac a crisis was building up to its climax. Hood's Confederate division had swamped Devil's Den and was swinging down on the wooded slopes of Round Top and Little Round Top. If the latter were occupied, all the Federal defenses along Cemetery Ridge, taken in the flank, would topple like dominoes, and that would be the end of the Battle of Gettysburg.

CHAPTER 6

The Second Day of Battle

LITTLE ROUND TOP
CEMETERY AND CULP'S HILLS

Battery D, 5th U.S. Artillery
Battery L, 1st Ohio Artillery
Battery C, 1st New York Artillery

Latimer's Battalion, C.S.A.
   1st Maryland Battery
   Alleghany (Va.) Battery
   4th Maryland or Chesapeake Battery
   Lee (Va.) Battery
Dance's Battalion, 1st Virginia Artillery
   2nd Company, Richmond Howitzers
   3rd Company, Richmond Howitzers
   Powhatan (Va.) Artillery
   1st Rockbridge Artillery
   Salem (Va.) Artillery
Nelson's Battalion, C.S.A.
   Amherst (Va.) Artillery
   Fluvanna (Va.) Artillery
   Georgia Regular Artillery

Battery M, 1st New York Artillery
Battery E, 1st Pennsylvania Artillery

Battery F, 4th U.S. Artillery

Battery K, 5th U.S. Artillery

Battery H, 1st U.S. Artillery

5th New York Battery

Battery C, West Virginia Artillery

Battery H, 1st Ohio Artillery

1st New Hampshire Battery

Little Round Top, with its spreading panorama of the battle-field, is the most memorable spot for many who visit Gettysburg National Military Park. The Peach Orchard and the Wheat Field present a peaceful aspect, the scars of war long ago erased, though the guns and monuments seem to people them again with surging ranks beneath tossing flags. Those dark, ominous crevices of Devil's Den which still send a shudder through the imagination are over-shadowed by the wooded knob east of them. Even The Angle, marked by its historic clump of trees—scene of the climacteric attack and repulse of the third day—must share heart-stirring summons with Little Round Top.

Hills, since man has waged warfare, have constituted natural citadels, centers of swirling conflict, gages of victory or defeat. And Little Round Top on July 2, 1863, became the key bastion of the Union left flank.

It is a small hill, some 200 feet high, but its grades are steep. Motorcars mount the winding, paved road that leads to its summit so easily that it is difficult to picture troops struggling up those slopes in hot haste on that July day when no road existed—through trees and thick underbrush—over ground "up-piled with granite ledges and masses of rocks and strewn with mighty boulders that might be the debris of some antique combat of Titans." [73]

Little Round Top and Big Round Top mark the southern terminus of Cemetery Ridge.[74] It happened that the higher hill was not involved in the main battle, though it was later the scene of a skirmish when it was occupied by several Federal regiments. The Southern assault drove in between the two Round Tops to storm the smaller eminence whose western face had been cleared by woodcutters in 1862.

From the woods along the Emmitsburg Road General E. M. Law, C.S.A., commanding the Alabama Brigade in Hood's Division, Longstreet's I Corps, stared upward to where "Round Top rose like a huge sentinel guarding the Federal left flank." There, he thought, lay the vulnerable point. As near as he could ascertain by observation and scouts, neither of the Round Tops was held by the enemy except for a signal station on the lower hill. If the Confederate right wing circled those heights and swept on to the Taneytown and Baltimore roads, it could smite the left and rear of the Army of the Potomac and crumple it up in rout.

Law's suggestion of a wide flanking movement, forwarded through the chain of command, was rejected in favor of a frontal attack. "Just here," wrote the brigadier, "the battle of Gettysburg was lost to the Confederate arms." [75] That is a concept materially affected by mitigating circumstances: by the continued absence of Stuart's cavalry and neglect to use horsemen at hand for reconnaissance; by "vexatious delays" of which Law himself complained. The morning and most of the afternoon had been frittered away. Longstreet spent precious hours moving his corps into position, attempting to screen his maneuvers, keeping his troops under cover of woods. His men were nevertheless spotted by the Union signalers on Little Round Top. "Old Pete," deliberate, stubborn advocate of defensive rather than offensive action on this field, was a hard hitter when he finally launched an assault, but he did not attack until midafternoon. As culpable was the procrastination of Ewell whose diversionary thrust at the Union right was still later withheld.

Even so victory hovered close. How Longstreet's infantry and artillery smashed Sickles' Union III Corps in the Wheat Field and Peach Orchard and scoured out Devil's Den has been narrated in the previous chapter. Now on the extreme right of the advancing

Gray line a spearhead was leveled and launched at Little Round Top.

If it falls to the lot of a general to be in the right place at the right time, he has a foot in the door of the hall of fame; whether he enters depends, of course, on how he acts upon his advantage. General Gouverneur K. Warren, Chief Signal Officer of the Army of the Potomac, had been ordered by General Meade to check the situation on the Union left flank. His signaler's instinct led him to Little Round Top, empty save for a detail of his own flag men. They had reported glimpses of Rebel troops among the trees off to the west, but those were probably now engaged in the conflict raging along Sickles' front. Approaches to the hill, hidden by masking foliage, showed no signs of life. Yet if regiments were concealed there ready to storm the height, it lay completely at their mercy. Warren recognized at once that Little Round Top was the key to the Union left as Cemetery and Culp's hills were to the right. Preoccupied with the latter, no one else on the staff seems to have realized or at least to have acted to safeguard that vitally important point. That afternoon no cavalry patrolled it. Buford had been stationed there but had been shifted to the rear in the morning, and the remainder of the Blue horse were stationed on the right flank.

Warren sent an orderly to a battery commander whose guns were in position near the foot of Little Round Top, requesting him to drop a round into those masking woods off to the left flank. A piece fired. "As the shot went whistling through the air, the sound of it reached the enemy's troops and caused every one to look in the direction of it," the general recalled. "This motion revealed to me the glistening of gun barrels and bayonets of the enemy's line of battle, already formed and far outflanking the position of any of our troops; so that the line of advance from his right to Little Round Top was unopposed." [76]

Today Warren's statue stands on the summit at the spot where he made that crucial discovery. The life-size bronze figure without a pedestal is affixed to the rocks. Field glasses poised, it seems to come alive and embody the emotions—"intensely thrilling, almost appalling"—that seized its original that July afternoon. Instantly the general dashed off a dispatch to General Meade, urgently asking that a division at least be rushed to the threatened point. His message would bring the V Corps to the rescue. Could it or any part of it arrive in time? Warren wondered tensely. Combat was flaming through the Peach Orchard and Devil's Den. Below he saw the Gray assault waves "in splendid array," rolling up like gale-lashed surf to submerge the hill. Musket balls pinged past him. He ordered the signal detail, about to fold up its flags, to keep them waving. That might give the illusion that there was some force on Little Round Top. Warren mounted and rode his horse down the hill in a reckless scramble to find desperately-needed help.

The fortunes of war were with him. He met a regiment, the 140th New York under Colonel Patrick O'Rorke, of a brigade he had once commanded. Warren shouted and beckoned for them to follow him. O'Rorke protested that his orders directed him to the Peach Orchard.

"Never mind that, Paddy!" Warren called. "Bring them up on the double-quick—don't stop for aligning! I'll take the responsibility."

O'Rorke obeyed, leading his men forward on the run.

BOOTS AND SADDLES

In support of that regiment of a V Corps brigade marched Battery D, 5th U.S. Artillery.

There are moments in the history of wars that conjure up the past. Such a one came now for D Battery, although for its blue-jacketed artillerymen the immediacy of the present sufficed. They were going into action, they knew their duty, and they must play a worthy part. But their guidon flaunted and their guns carried a great heritage. Battery D was the lineal descendant of Alexander Hamilton's famed company of artillery, the oldest unit in the United States Army.

Eighty-seven years before, on a day as cold as this July afternoon was hot, young Captain Hamilton had led the forebear of this battery through the snows to Trenton, patting the barrel of a cannon as he trudged along, for his mount had been harnessed in to help a gun team. His 3-pounders, ancestors of the 10-pounder Parrotts now advancing on Little Round Top, had raked Trenton's Hessian garrison with round shot—boomed at Princeton and Monmouth—fought through to the end of the Revolution. Then in the rapid disbandment of forces only that one company of gunners survived out of the entire United States Army. It served on through the Indian wars. Although the 5th Artillery was a new regiment, organized at the outset of the Civil War, the descent of its Battery D from Hamilton's company was established and is prized to the present time.[77]

One senses a kinship in spirit between the battery's first commander and the officer who led it at Gettysburg, handsome men of high courage both. First Lieutenant Charles E. Hazlett, tall as Hamilton was short of stature, had been color sergeant of the Corps of Cadets at West Point. His immediate predecessor in command of D had been Stephen Weed, who had graduated a few classes earlier. Now Weed, promoted to a brigadier generalcy,[78] headed the brigade Hazlett's guns supported. Upon the younger man and his battery lay an obligation as compelling as the tradition behind them. They fought under the eye of their old leader and they must never fail him.

Little Round Top, its slopes dotted with blue-clad infantrymen toiling upward, loomed above them. They might have unlimbered and hauled their guns up by hand as Smith had at Devil's Den. But time was short, and the need critical. Hazlett thought he could make it horsed. He signaled forward and led the way.

Each gun and each caisson team was pulling approximately 3,800 pounds. Such were the loads with which Battery D, six

10-pounder Parrott rifles, faced that roadless, wooded acclivity. Drivers on the near animals of the six-horse teams bent low over maned necks. The faithful beasts, climbing almost like cats, thrust mightily into their collars, tugging at the traces. Branches buffeted them and the men on their backs. Underbrush clutched at hoofs. Here and there whips rose and fell, lashing discouraged animals that began to lag. More often it was shouts, endearments, or oaths that urged them. For every driver it was as if he were climbing and pulling with his pair. By voice, leg, and hand he strove to make his strength flow into theirs.

Teams and drivers did not struggle upward unaided. Every cannoneer, sweating and gasping, clutched spokes of the slow-turning wheels and heaved, or shoved and pushed with all his might against gun axles, the backs of chests, and any part of the carriages where a man could place a shoulder or hands. Infantrymen converged on the battery and pitched in to help their comrades of the artillery. There was sore need of these guns on the hill, which soldiers of the two arms would defend together.

It was a splendid moment when the guidon of Hazlett's Battery, followed by the guns, surmounted the crest of Little Round Top. "The passage of the guns through the roadless woods and amongst the rocks was marvelous," General Hunt acclaimed. "Under ordinary circumstances it would have been considered an impossible feat, but the eagerness of the men to get into action with their comrades of the infantry, and the skillful driving, brought them without delay to the very summit, where they went immediately into battle. They were barely in time, for the enemy were also climbing the hill." [79]

Unlimber and action front. The Parrotts thundered, skidding back in recoil on the rocky surface of the summit. Bullets from Rebel sharpshooters hummed like a flight of angry bees, dropping a cannoneer here and there. Below resounded the din of volleys of Gray troops advancing to seize the hill. D's cannon could not be depressed sufficiently to take them under fire, but they poured a hail of shells into reinforcements coming up to support the assault.

"Little Round Top, crowned with artillery, resembled a volcano in eruption."

O'Rorke's New York infantry had climbed the hill with Hazlett's Battery and lent a hand pushing the carriages, and the guns had broken through the files of the leading company to go into position. O'Rorke peered down into the maelstrom of combat where a hard-pressed Union brigade, closing in from the left, was striving desperately to stem the Confederate onslaught. He did not give his men time to load or fix bayonets. "Delay was ruin. Hesitation was destruction." The colonel swung out of the saddle and tossed the reins of his mount to his sergeant major. "This way, boys!" he shouted, and led his regiment pell-mell down the slope. They hit the Gray ranks like a battering ram and, body to body, smashed them back. O'Rorke, a bullet through his neck, fell dead, but that heroic counterattack, for the moment at least, had saved Little Round Top.

Presage of another assault, the Rebel yell shrilled high. Hazlett's guns pounded supporting waves but still could not bear on the van. Fortunately for the Union, other cannon commanded that dead space. One section of Captain F. C. Gibbs' Battery L, 1st Ohio Artillery, was posted on the northern slope of Little Round Top, with a second section at its base, and the third in reserve. Those few guns, firing at top speed, flung shell after shell into a ravine where the enemy was concentrating for the final storming of the key hill.

Meanwhile General Weed brought the remainder of his brigade to the defense of the summit. Surely the brigadier, as his riflemen formed to the right and left of Hazlett's guns, gave the commander and men of his old battery the accolade of approval they must have hoped for from him. There could have been time for no more than a few words and a quick smile. Confederate artillery was playing on the summit. Deadlier still was the fire of sharpshooters in Devil's Den, crack shots with good rests for their rifles and fine cover. They took deliberate aim. Little puffs of smoke blossomed in the gaps between the boulders.

Weed turned to give an order to Hazlett. What it was will never be known. It was less likely that it was a command to hold the hill to the last—that went without saying—than that it was some direction of fire, given by an old artilleryman to his one-time lieutenant. Then a Minié ball hit him, and he slumped to the ground, dying. At the instant Hazlett bent anxiously over him a second sharpshooter fired. Mortally wounded, the younger West Pointer fell across the body of his chief.

A stanza of the West Point song, written years later, can serve as hail and farewell to three gallant men of the long gray line of the Corps of Cadets who fell on Little Round Top: Weed, O'Rorke, and Hazlett.

> The Corps! Bareheaded, salute it
> With eyes up, thanking our God
> That we of the Corps are treading
> Where they of the Corps have trod.
> They are here in ghostly assemblage,
> The men of the Corps long dead,
> And our hearts are standing attention
> While we wait for their passing tread.[80]

Battery D, its command taken over by Lieutenant Benjamin F. Rittenhouse, fought on with vengeful intensity. The sound of its guns served as Hazlett's requiem, as he was carried back to a hospital to die that night. Down on the slope Gibbs' Ohio cannoneers still laced the ravine with explosives. Not far away the 3rd Massachusetts Battery had been placed in position on rocky, marshy ground by one of Sickles' staff officers. General Charles Griffin, an old artilleryman, rode by and frowningly noted the poorly-chosen spot. "Get that battery out of there," he ordered. "You can't live in that place five minutes." Before the teams could come up it was too late. A Rebel charge swept forward. Lieutenant Aaron F. Walcott of the 3rd succeeded in spiking one of his pieces before the position was overrun. But the enemy were not destined to keep their trophies long. A Pennsylvania regiment counter-attacked and recaptured the six 12-pounders whose gunners re-turned to drag them off by prolonges.

Along Cemetery Ridge the Union defenses held. In the center Hancock's II Corps stanchly backstopped the shattered III. Meade drew reinforcements from the XII on his right to aid the em-battled V on his left. There, as afternoon dwindled into evening, the Confederate attack, pressed to the limit of endurance, finally spent itself. Though its tide ceased to flow, it did not ebb from the ground it had gained: the Emmitsburg Road, Peach Orchard, Devil's Den, and the fields over which it had fought its way to the bases of the Round Tops, a blood-soaked expanse, strewn with bodies in gray and blue, which would be known as "The Valley of Death." Toward dusk Union officers became concerned that the enemy might succeed in placing artillery on Big Round Top and thus command the smaller hill. They sent two regiments, which secured it after a brief clash resulting in the capture of a Rebel staff officer and 30 men.

The battle of the second day did not end with the failure of the Confederate attempt to turn the Union left. It would carry on through twilight into bitter and spectacular combat at night.

While on the Confederate right the fierce drive of Longstreet's belated attack still maintained its impetus, guns boomed and leaped along the arc of the Gray line. North of I Corps the artillery of Hill's II and that of the reserve joined the bombardment. Poague's, Pegram's, and McIntosh's battalions blazed away from Seminary Ridge, here and there moving batteries forward to cover advancing infantry. Some succeeded in partially enfilading Federal artillery along the Emmitsburg Road, and that flanking fire was of great assistance to Alexander's I Corps gunners when they charged the Peach Orchard and blasted out the infantry and isolated batteries of Sickles' ill-fated Union Corps.

Major Lane's Sumter, Georgia, Battalion was equipped with a number of long-range cannon: two 20-pounder Parrotts, which would carry 1,900 yards at 5 degrees of elevation, and three 3-inch navy rifles. These and other pieces, including some of Garnett's Battalion, engaged the Blue artillery on Cemetery Hill. Fifty-five guns, all told, of Hill's Corps were in action, though mostly at extreme limits of effective fire.

Battalions of the II Corps artillery, for which Ewell had vainly waited on the first day, were now in position. The commander of the group attached to Johnson's Division, Lieutenant Colonel R. Snowden Andrews, had been wounded and was not sufficiently recovered to be present, yet the stamp of that accomplished and resourceful artillerist was on his battalion. When he was captain of the 1st Maryland Artillery at a winter station in Virginia, he decided to demonstrate the effect of different kinds of ammunition to his battery. The target he chose was a flock of canvasback ducks in the Potomac. One of his 12-pounders let fly a charge of canister. It was as deadly to birds as it would be for Yankees. The Marylanders plunged into the icy river and retrieved a fine Christmas dinner.[81] Andrews bagged a greater trophy when he managed to obtain possession of a Federal book on field artillery, showing drawings of the new Napoleon gun, which he republished in a volume of his own.[82] From those plans cannon were cast in the Richmond Tredegar Iron Works and put into service, though Andrews, after the capture of an enemy battery, was forced to admit that Napoleons manufactured in the North were superior.

In Andrews' absence his battalion was led by an able subordinate, Major Joseph W. Latimer, not yet twenty-one. Benner's Hill, providing little shelter and exposed to crossfire, was the only commanding position he could find. He crowded 14 guns into the cramped space and opened at about 4 P.M. At once he became the object of furious cannonading from every Union battery on Cemetery and Culp's hills that would bear. One of them moved pieces forward to enfilade the Alleghany Battery. Captain John C. Carpenter, who had commanded it since the death of his brother, saw his guns silenced one by one. Brown's 4th Maryland was so severely pounded that only two of its pieces could be manned.

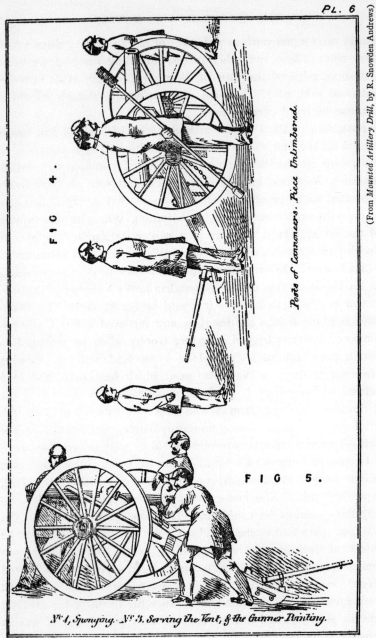

(From *Mounted Artillery Drill*, by R. Snowden Andrews)

FIG 4.

Posts of Cannoneers. Piece Unlimbered.

FIG 5.

Nº 1, Sponging. Nº 3. Serving the Vent, & the Gunner Pointing.

Evans & Cogswell, lith, Columbia, S C.

Finally all but four guns were ordered withdrawn from ground strewn with broken carriages, dead horses, and dead and dying men. Latimer and his mount were hit. Pulled half dazed from beneath his horse, the gallant Virginia Military Institute graduate, who had won even Stonewall Jackson's sparing praise, continued to direct his battalion and would not leave for the rear until night. The "Boy Major" died when gangrene infected his wound.

Adjutant Robert Stiles of the Richmond Howitzers, carrying a message, rode past the smoke-wreathed, littered hill as the deluge of Union shells overwhelmed Latimer and his artillery. Never had he seen "fifteen or twenty guns in such a condition of wreck and destruction as this battalion was. It had been hurled backward, as it were by the very weight and impact of the metal from the position it had occupied on the crest of a little ridge into the saucer-shaped depression behind it; and such a scene as it presented—guns dismounted and disabled, carriages splintered and crushed, ammunition chests exploded, limbers upset, wounded horses plunging and kicking, dashing out the brains of men tangled in the harness; while cannoneers with pistols were crawling around through the wreck shooting the struggling horses to save lives of the wounded men."

The "Boy Major's" cannon had been given neither support nor relief by other units of Ewell's artillery. Inexplicably Carter's and Nelson's battalions had not been brought into action but stood idle in their positions north of Gettysburg. It was one of those failures by the Confederates to exert the full strength of the gunners' arm, failures which characterize the battle and would be repeated on the following day with direr consequences.

It was sunset before the infantry attack, for which Latimer's and later Dance's guns had been striving to pave the way, was tardily launched. Those well-emplaced Blue batteries it faced had already impressively proved their power. Some of the assaulting troops must have been reminded of Malvern Hill where Hunt's massed Union guns had inflicted more than half of that battle's casualties, "an unprecedented thing in warfare." General D. H. Hill in after years declared, "Give me Confederate infantry and Yankee artillery and I'll whip the world!"

Now at the end of Gettysburg's second day took place a trial of strength between Gray foot and Blue cannon. The fate of the fishhook end of the Union line trembled in the balance. Formidable as the position was, it by no means defied conquest, for Meade withdrew a large part of its garrison when he shifted most of XII Corps to the defense of his imperiled left.

The cemetery gate with its flanking houses became at once a cenotaph and *point d'appui* of attack. South of it, to fill a gap between the Union I and II Corps, Hunt placed the batteries of the XII: Rugg's F, 4th U.S. (six 12-pounders); Kinzie's K, 5th U.S. (four 12-pounders); Winegar's M, 1st New York (four 10-pounders); Atwell's E, 1st Pennsylvania (six 10-pounders). These guns were later pulled out to accompany XII Corps infantry. Encircling Cemetery and Culp's hills, north and south of the Baltimore Pike, were the battered I and XI Corps batteries—some refitted, some only partly serviceable, which had retreated to that vicinity at the end of the first day. Hunt reinforced them with five Reserve batteries: Eakin's H, 1st U.S. (six 12-pounders); Taft's 5th New York (six 20-pounders); Hill's C, 1st West Virginia (four 10-pounders); Norton's H, 1st Ohio (six 3-inch); and Edgell's 1st New Hampshire Battery.

The commander of the last mentioned was a veteran of the war with Mexico. Captain Frederick M. Edgell had served with Missouri artillery under Doniphan at the Battle of Sacramento in 1847. The Granite State unit had been his since Second Bull Run where it had been roughly handed, its first leader and 11 men captured. At Antietam it had taken revenge when it silently moved its guns to the rim of a ravine where a Rebel division had bivouacked for the night. The New Hampshire howitzers poured canister down into the sleeping foe with terrible slaughter. "It seemed cruel," wrote the battery historian, "but when is war anything else?" [83]

General Hunt was satisfied with the disposition he had made of his artillery, arranged to meet any attack the enemy could launch.[84]

He suffered only one regret. Two batteries of 4 ½-inch siege guns, 1st Connecticut Heavy Artillery, remained with the supply train at Westminster. Had they been ordered forward, they would have proved highly useful on both the second and the third days. So thought even the horse artilleryman, Captain John C. Tidball. Despite his command of a brigade of light, mobile pieces, supporting the Cavalry Corps, he respected the capabilities of the siege guns and believed they could have been employed to advantage at Gettysburg. He laid the blunder of leaving them in the rear to the fact that "the management of artillery affairs was not yet fully in the hands of those to whom it belonged."

For the batteries of the Union right it had been a long day of growing tension. They could see the enemy massing in the edge of the woods that fringed Seminary Ridge, but no attack came until the solid crash of the gunfire around the Peach Orchard was heard about four o'clock in the afternoon.

Battery B, 4th U.S., after its valiant stand beside the railroad cut on the first day, had four pieces still serviceable. Those were posted in front of the cemetery gate, a point which gave Cannoneer Buell a splendid view of the conflict now raging.

> Looking down the Emmitsburg Road, the fields west of the Round Tops were alive with moving masses of infantry enveloped in flame and smoke; a dozen batteries in different positions were blazing and roaring; shells were bursting in every direction; buildings and haystacks were on fire here and there; pandemonium broke loose generally, and the fight down about the Peach Orchard increased in uproar until its grandeur passed description. All the men strained their eyes in that direction in spite of the frequent commands, "Attention! Eyes front! Stand to posts!" I don't believe there was ever discipline in any army that could make men keep "eyes front" when one of the most desperate struggles in history was going on over their left shoulders a mile and a half away and in plain sight. Moreover, it is terribly de-

moralizing to stand idle when such fighting is being done in another part of the line, and you are waiting momentarily for a strong fire on your own front to begin. The suspense is awful. We knew that if the enemy drove in our troops down there by the Peach Orchard, we would be taken by reverse in left and rear. So we actually longed for Ewell's men in our own front to come on.[85]

Release from gnawing inaction arrived with the bombardment by Latimer's Gray battalion from Benner's Hill. Around the cemetery defenses gun-pointers eagerly sighted their pieces. Rifled guns replied to the Confederate fire with the deadly effect already mentioned, while ammunition passers for the smoothbores looked to the canister supply to meet the infantry attack that was certain to develop. On lower ground in advance of Battery B the 3-inchers of Wiedrich's Battery I, 1st New York, and those of Bruce Ricketts' F and G, 1st Pennsylvania, blazed away. Some 200 yards to B's right crews swarmed around the guns of Stevens' 5th Maine and Reynolds' L, 1st New York. All the perimeter of stout breastworks and emplacements circling the hills was rimmed with flame.

The courage of the attack by Confederate General Ewell's II Corps was unquestionable, its coordination lamentable. Early's infantry made a charge on East Cemetery Hill, "seldom, if ever, surpassed in its dash and desperation," but Rodes' division failed to advance from the town in time to support it. The fire of the Gray cannon, heavily counterbatteried, was not strong enough to crack defenses, constructed from timber and handy cordwood by woodsmen of the Union regiments. Yesterday Ewell had made "a pause at the door of victory." Late today one of his divisions, Johnson's, would repeat that fatal hesitation.

Yet twice that door was forced ajar. A long Rebel line swept toward Cemetery Hill. The setting sun deepened the field of the Stars and Bars, tossing above its ranks, from scarlet to blood-red. Blue guns, shifting to canister, tore great gaps. Rear files filled them, and the attack drove on. Union musketry opened with a solid

crash "like a million trees falling at once." Still the charge surged
forward. It broke on a XI Corps regiment, sent it flying. Now it
flooded over the gun positions of Wiedrich's Battery I, 1st New
York Artillery, and into those of Ricketts' F and G, 1st Pennsylvania.
Cannoneers fought hand to hand with the Louisiana Tigers, tough
men determined to take those batteries.

Close combat among the guns rises to blind fury with few
parallels. Prized trophies, the cannon themselves, are at stake. To
lose them is a disgrace that will long rankle in the gunners'
memories as it will serve as a reproach to the infantrymen who
failed to support them. For attacking infantry here is an opportunity
to take revenge for comrades cut down by blasts from the still-
smoking muzzles they strive to seize and turn against the enemy.

Bayonets stabbed, and clubbed muskets smashed in that fierce
conflict in the gathering darkness. Artillerymen wielded their trail
handspikes like maces, swung rammer staffs, thrust with a guidon
lance, blazed away with the few pistols they had. Others, weapon-
less, flung stones or crushed skulls with them. Men fought with
fists, kicked and gouged. Here and there a gunner struggled to
keep from being dragged off a prisoner.[86]

Cheering Rebels spiked one of Ricketts' guns. In the turmoil
Lieutenant Charles B. Brockway of that battery saw an enemy
infantryman seize the Pennsylvanians' guidon, leap on a horse,
and spur off. With a well-aimed rock Brockway bowled him out
of the saddle. As he fell, the officer wrested the guidon from him
and lifted it high in triumph. At that moment a bullet severed its
staff. A Gray color-bearer planted his flag in an emplacement of
Wiedrich's battery, demanding its surrender. He was knocked
down by an onrush of cannoneers, and his colors captured. But the
guns were all but lost, and the defending line fatally breached
when a brigade from Hancock's II Corps, rushed to the rescue,
came up at a headlong run. "There was a confused sound of
pounding feet and colliding human bodies, grunts and yells and
curses and a crackle of rifle fire—and the last of the Confederates
were driven out." [87]

The final bolt of the attack was not yet shot. Gray columns veered off toward Culp's Hill, bastion of the extreme Union right. Heavily wooded, rocky, precipitous in part, Culp's was a replica of Little Round Top except that it was strongly fortified and held—or had been until General Meade ordered out all but one brigade of its XII Corps garrison to the aid of his hard-pressed left. Though the timbered entrenchments of the hills had looked like log forts to Confederate observers during daylight, their strength did not deter the attempt now made to carry them. Culp's was a prize worth striving for. If it were taken, flanking the Federal right, its captors would stand astride the Baltimore Pike, menace the reserve artillery and wagon trains of the Army of the Potomac, and cut off the retreat of two thirds of Meade's forces.

Captain Stevens' 5th Maine Battery had made one of the stubborn stands in the course of the I Corps retreat on the first day. Through the war it had established a reputation as a crack unit. Its position on the second day was a knoll on the saddle between Cemetery and Culp's hills, with a fine field of fire. One of the 5th's lieutenants, Edward N. Whittier, filled the time before action manipulating a French-made instrument called an "ordnance glass," the nearest approach to a range-finder for light artillery then known.

That instrument, rarely used in the Civil War, was a precursor of modern artillery fire-direction equipment. Whittier, sighting through it that afternoon, measured ranges to all prominent objects on his battery's front. Granted that measurements were correct, the usual guesswork would be eliminated. Elevation of the pieces could be set, and shell fuses cut so as to explode the projectile on target. Here was the technique of the barrages of World War I, fired from predetermined data, and of the pinpoint shooting and concentrations of World War II and Korea. Whittier, given permission to test the accuracy of his estimates, fired a single round. It landed squarely on his target, a clump of trees on the Culp farm.[88]

His "registration," as future artillerymen would term it, paid off handsomely. When Early's Confederate division formed to deliver its assault that evening, the 5th Maine opened with shrapnel. Each shell burst "as if on measured ground at the right time and the right place in front of their formation." Volleys blasting from the six 12-pounders, other batteries chiming in, sounded to supporting infantry "as if a volcano had been let loose."

Early's men maneuvered magnificently despite the devastating fire. Rifles spurting, they swept past the left flank of the Maine guns. Bullets dropped Captain Stevens and a lieutenant, and Whittier, the only surviving officer, assumed command. His left guns poured in canister at short range, but his right half-battery was no longer able to bear. He ordered it limbered to the rear, a feat skillfully performed in deepening dusk. Circling around to the left, it joined the other half. Again six muzzles erupted canister, using double charges. So fast and furious was their rate of fire that cannoneers fell exhausted in the still sultry heat. Volunteers from the infantry took their places. By the time the battery's ammunition had been spent, and it was forced to withdraw to refill its caissons, the attack had been broken.

Although Cemetery Hill was secure for the time being, Culp's was not, and the latter dominated the lower eminence west of it. Simultaneously with Early's assault, Johnson's Division swung east and tackled Culp's. Flashes of artillery lit the night sky like sheet lightning. Rifle fire zigzagged, outlining the entrenchments and the progress of ranks mounting the slopes. Brief crimson flares gleamed among the branches of trees where sharpshooters had taken post. The night conflict, blotting out powder smoke and magnifying din, was gorgeous with pyrotechnics.

Johnson, baffled by the steepness of the northern side of Culp's and the strength of its breastworks, fell back across Rock Creek and tried it again from the southeast. There success was almost his. Confederate infantry flooded into entrenchments vacated by two XII Corps brigades, ordered to the Union left flank. A remaining brigade, warned by pickets, groped through an inky traverse to meet the onslaught. Confused combat raged in the trenches and the darkness of the dense woods. Only by the flash of musketry could men distinguish friend from foe—who wore blue, who gray. The weight of the Southern attack bore back a regiment on the Union right and drove in behind the breastworks.

Daylight would have shown General Johnson the value of the penetration he had made and the threat that could have been exploited against the enemy's rear. Darkness bred irresolution, as reinforcements rushed to the aid of the hard-pressed Blue brigade. The Confederate leader retreated before the counterstroke to maintain a lodgment at the foot of the hill, a point from which he could assault again next morning. It would be too late then. Detached XII Corps divisions were already on their way back and would man Culp's at full strength.

Night brought some measure of relief from the burning heat of that day of battle, heat which veterans long remembered when wounds and the death of comrades half faded in memories. A sudden stillness fell, almost painful to the senses after the roar of conflict. The beams of a full moon, which had failed to filter through leafy branches to light dark combat in the woods of Culp's Hill, shed ghastly illumination on the open fields whose beauty First Lieutenant Frank Aretas Haskell, aide to General Gibbon of the Federal II Corps, had admired that morning.

They are desolate—trampled by the countless feet of the combatants, plowed and scored by the shot and shell, the orchards splintered, the fences prostrate, the harvest trodden in the mud [he wrote].[89] And more dreadful than the sight of all this, thickly strewn over all their length and breadth are the habiliments of the soldiers, the knapsacks cast aside in the stress of the fight, or after the fatal lead had struck; haversacks, yawning with the rations the owner will never call for; canteens of cedar of the Rebel men of Jackson, and of cloth-covered tin of the men of the Union; blankets and trowsers, and coats, and caps, and some are blue and some are gray; muskets and ramrods, and bayonets, and swords, and scabbards and belts, some bent and cut by the shot and shell; broken wheels, exploded caissons, and limber-boxes, and dismantled guns, and all these are sprinkled with blood; horses, some dead, a mangled heap of carnage, some alive, with a leg shot clear off, or other frightful wounds, appealing to you with almost more than brute gaze as you pass; and last, but not least numerous, many thousands of men—and there was no rebellion here now—the men of South Carolina were quiet by the sides of those of Massachusetts, some composed, with upturned faces, sleeping the last sleep, some mutilated and frightful, some wretched, fallen, bathed in blood, survivors still and unwilling witnesses of the rage of Gettysburg.

Artillery Horses

(From *How the Battle Was Fought*, by James F. Long)

That vivid description indicates how great a degree of the devastation the artillery had wrought and suffered. Final decision, as always, was achieved by the might of the infantry, but again and again on that second day the guns had swayed the fortunes of battle.

Indubitably the advantage had lain with the Union, with Meade enabled to shift troops from one threatened flank to the other. "Yet, in the main, the tactical conduct of the defense was as fine as that of the offense was faulty." The Confederate artillery, for all its valor, was outfought, not because it was outgunned but because it failed to make effective use of its available cannon. Its corps commands did not cooperate, and there were repeated instances of batteries that might have been brought into play remaining inactive. Its ablest protagonist, Colonel Jennings C. Wise,[90] declares that neither Brown nor Walker, the II and III Corps chiefs of artillery, nor General Pendleton, the army chief, had any idea of maneuvering to obtain positions from which the II Corps artillery north of the town could concentrate its fire with that of the III upon the Federal defenses of Cemetery and Culp's hills. Thus the Army of the Potomac was able to bring into action 100 guns per mile of front, while the Army of Northern Virginia opposed them proportionately with only 40. The Confederate guns are described by Colonel Wise as positioned along the rim of a wheel, the Union's at its hub. The former, with liberty of maneuver, might have concentrated and crossed fire along lines represented by the wheel's spokes. Blue batteries, immobile in a limited area, necessarily dispersed their fire. Artillery techniques—the application of maximum fire power at the proper point—were potentially in favor of the Confederates.

But the tactical conceptions of the Confederates were still those of Napoleon whose short-range guns required the massing of artillery in order to obtain a concentrated fire. They did not perceive that with increased ranges there existed no relation between massed guns and concentrated fire save insofar as the range of the guns and their target required the proximity of the pieces. The result was that the force of the Confederate Artillery was mechanically misapplied, or applied in a way that could not accomplish the possible result.[91]

In contrast the Union artillery was brilliantly employed. General
Hunt, Meade's chief, again proved to be

> the Nemesis of the Confederates, and time and again his
> artillery was found massed just at the right point to deny
> them success, for it was McGilvery at Plum Run who checked
> Longstreet, and it was Stevens on the right who hurled Early
> from the ridge he had all but won. During Longstreet's
> attack, Hunt had supported Sickles with 11 batteries with
> 60 guns of his general reserve alone. In addition to these
> guns, the 2d, 3d, and 5th Corps had 80 guns in action. Against
> these 140 pieces, Longstreet had but 62 guns on the field, and
> Anderson's Division but 5 in advance of Seminary Ridge.
> ... After the most persistent and heroic efforts on the part
> of Alexander's artillerymen to silence the enemy's batteries,
> at the close of the day they were rewarded by seeing not less
> than 75 Federal guns in position with ever-increasing infantry
> supports nearby.[92]

For that second day of Gettysburg a cynical maxim of Napoleon's
is apt: "God fights on the side with the best artillery."

General J. E. B. Stuart and his cavalry had arrived at last after
a long circuit around the Army of the Potomac during its march
to Gettysburg. His absence, gravely felt, has been spoken of as
depriving the Army of Northern Virginia of its "eyes." And yet a
brigade and part-brigade of Gray horse had accompanied that
army's advance. That they were not used to best advantage in the
first two days of the battle—as effectively, for example, as Buford's
division of Union cavalry on the first day—must be scored against
General Lee. His dependence was great upon Jeb Stuart, with his
flair for reconnaissance and his frequent reports, so competently
performed and rendered as a cavalry function. It may be assumed
that Stuart's personal presence had been more sorely missed by Lee

than that of his command. Now the cavalry leader was on hand
with two fine brigades and a battalion of six crack batteries of
horse artillery. Brief clashes with Blue horse, patrolling the roads,
heralded their coming. Stuart and his men would fight a pitched
battle on the third day. Their attack then, in the phrase that must
so often be used of the Confederate efforts at Gettysburg, came
too late.

At the end of the second day General Meade convened a council
of war at his headquarters. All the Union corps commanders attended, including Sedgwick whose VI Corps had reached the
field after a long march from Manchester. Meade's chief of staff,
General Butterfield, and his engineer and signal chief, General
Warren, were also present. General Hunt, his artillery chief, although summoned, was not there.[93] Evidently he had requested
and received permission to perform duties which would occupy
him through most of the night. His absence would have an unfortunate consequence. Had he been on hand to speak for his arm
and assert his authority over it, he could justly have complained
of that unwarranted interference by Sickles' officers when they
ordered several batteries into ill-chosen positions.

It is [Hunt would later state] an odd notion, which could
not find a lodgment in any army but our own, that an artillery
commander-in-chief, himself a "corps commander," and
provided with a staff of his own, is "one of the staff-officers"
who runs about a battlefield carrying "the actual and
authentic orders" of the general-in-chief to *other* corps
commanders. A "staff-officer" is an officer attached to the
person or headquarters of a general as his aide or assistant
...Frederick the Great...was an "artillery specialist" of
the highest order, yet I have never heard that this unfitted
him for "ordering a line of battle." He was also a discipli-
narian of the sternest school, yet he "almost preached in-
subordination" in order to reduce to a minimum the mischief

that meddling with the artillery by any general, even the general-in-chief, might occasion.[94]

Hunt on the morrow would experience such meddling on a larger scale than today's and with an important bearing on the battle.

Whether to stay and fight was the first question put to the council. That was a gauge of how severely shaken the Army of the Potomac had been by assaults that had come close to shattering first its left then its right flank. By custom the first to answer was the junior officer present, General Gibbon, who had taken over the II Corps from Hancock, now commanding the III vice the wounded Sickles. Gibbon's reply, in which the rest concurred, was: "Remain here, and make such correction in our position as may be deemed necessary, but take no step which even looks like a retreat." The next question was: "Should the army attack or await the attack of the enemy?" Wait was the verdict. For how long then? "Until Lee moves."

At the end of the voting Meade announced quietly and firmly, "Such then is the decision." As the generals left, the Commander-in-Chief made a prophetic remark to Gibbon whose II Corps held the center of the line.

"If Lee attacks tomorrow," he said, "it will be on *your front*. . . . He has made attacks on both our flanks and failed, and if he concludes to try it again it will be on our center." [95]

Hoofbeats through the night, and the moonlit figures of horsemen riding from one battery position to another and through the parks of the reserve guns. Chiefs of artillery, army and corps, made thorough inspections. It is understandable why General Hunt had asked for leave of absence from the council. The night was not long enough for tasks to be done—for repairing damages, replenishing ammunition, and reducing and reorganizing batteries which had lost so many men and horses they could not handle their full quota of cannon. Those duties must be performed before daylight;

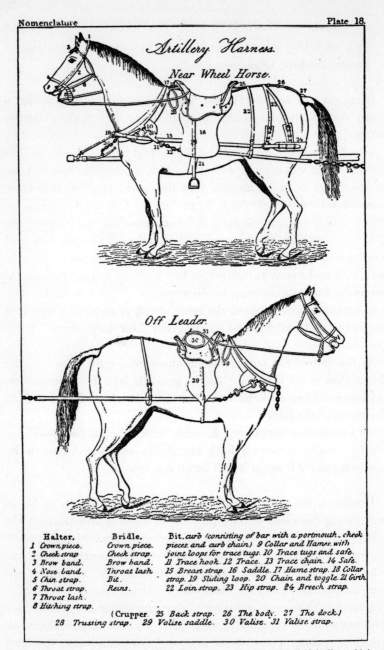

Artillery Harness.

Near Wheel Horse.

Off Leader.

Halter.	**Bridle.**	**Bit.** *curb (consisting of bar with a portmouth., cheek*
1 *Crown piece.*	*Crown piece.*	*pieces. and curb chain)* 9 *Collar and Hames. with*
2 *Cheek strap*	*Cheek strap.*	*joint loops for trace tugs.* 10 *Trace tugs and safe.*
3 *Brow band.*	*Brow band.*	11 *Trace hook.* 12 *Trace.* 13 *Trace chain.* 14 *Safe.*
4 *Nose band.*	*Throat lash*	15 *Breast strap.* 16 *Saddle.* 17 *Hame strap.* 18 *Collar*
5 *Chin strap.*	*Bit.*	*strap.* 19 *Sliding loop.* 20 *Chain and toggle.* 21 *Girth.*
6 *Throat strap.*	*Reins.*	22 *Loin strap.* 23 *Hip strap.* 24 *Breech strap.*
7 *Throat lash.*		
8 *Hitching strap.*		

(*Crupper.* 25 *Back strap.* 26 *The body.* 27 *The dock.*)
28 *Trussing strap.* 29 *Valise saddle.* 30 *Valise.* 31 *Valise. strap.*

(From U.S. War Department: *Instructions for Field Artillery,* 1864)

General Henry Jackson Hunt
(from *Battles and Leaders of the Civil War*)

"Feed it to 'em!" (from *The Cannoneer*, by Augustus Buell)

Hazlett's Battery on Little Round Top (from *The Battle of Gettysburg*, by Jessee B. Young)

The Ninth Massachusetts Battery Galloping into Action
(from *History of the Ninth Massachusetts Battery*, by L. W. Baker)

The Ninth Massachusetts Battery Under Fire
(from *History of the Ninth Massachusetts Battery*, by L. W. Baker)

A 20-pounder Parrott
(*Library of Congress photograph*)

The Artillery Duel (from *In Camp and Battle with the Washington Artillery of New Orleans*, by W. M. Owen)

Cushing's Last Gun and General George Armistead
(from *Leslie's Illustrated History of the Civil War*)

if impossible, the units must be withdrawn and replaced from the Reserve until they were back in condition. Similarly General Pendleton, the energetic Colonel Alexander, and other chiefs were readying the Confederate artillery for action, preparing it to open the concentrated cannonade which General Lee had ordered for as early as possible on the morning of July 3.

Refill your chests with shell and shrapnel and canister before you sleep, you artillerymen of the Blue and the Gray. Swab clean the powder-fouled bores of your guns. Inspect axles, wheels, and poles and replace them if there is need. Run over your implements, spare parts, and all equipment—everything from rammer staffs to vent picks and thumbstalls—and see that you have them at hand, for there will be no other chance to supply them.

Water and feed your horses before you eat your own rations. Refit harness to the new animals you drew to fill gaps in the teams. If your battery has suffered so many casualties that you cannot man all your guns, apply for drafts from the infantry. You'll get them more or less willingly, since they've seen your fire mow down enemy ranks sweeping across the field. Naturally the doughboys won't give you their best men. Make do with what you're granted. They may turn out to be better redlegs than they were riflemen. Appoint them higher-numbered cannoneers and teach them how to pass shells.

You young lieutenants, who have taken over from a captain wounded or killed, still your misgivings. You must handle your battery—must continue to come through tomorrow. It's up to you now. Call over your trusted top sergeant to check over everything with you again. Hide the thrill it gives you when he salutes and snaps out, "Sir, the First Sergeant reports to the Battery Commander." Then take brief hours of the night still left for sleep before the dawn of a third day of battle.

CHAPTER 7

The Third Day of Battle

MUSTERING OF THE CANNON

Battery E, 1st Pennsylvania Artillery
Battery M, 1st New York Artillery
Battery F, 4th U.S. Artillery
Battery K, 5th U.S. Artillery
Battery A, Maryland Artillery
Battery A, 4th U.S. Artillery

Richmond Fayette Artillery
3rd Company, Washington Artillery

All other batteries, U.S.A. and C.S.A.

At dawn on July 3 the guns sounded a reveille for another long day of battle.

REVEILLE

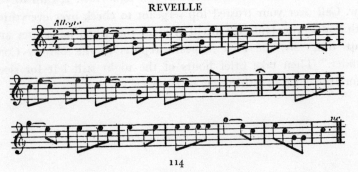

Smoke billowed about Culp's Hill. Shell and Minié balls shattered its trees, withering them into the dead forest they would remain for years after the war. As Gray troops of Ewell's Confederate II Corps advanced to storm the stronghold they had failed to capture the previous evening, men in blue prepared to charge and oust them from their foothold.

The Union XII Corps, returned from the left during the night to reman its entrenchments, was set for defense, assault, or counterattack, and two brigades from the fresh VI were moving up to reinforce it. All four of the XII's batteries opened a rapid bombardment at ranges of no more than 800 yards—Atwell's E, 1st Pennsylvania, and Winegar's M, 1st New York, from south of the Baltimore Turnpike—Rugg's F, 4th U.S., and Kinzie's K, 5th U.S., from west of the road. The six 3-inch rifles of Rigby's Battery A of Maryland from the Reserve added their fire.

No Rebel artillery replied. The hillside was considered too steep and its approaches too difficult to drag guns into position or to bring them to bear from the east side of Rock Creek.[96] No battery attempted to duplicate Hazlett's feat at Little Round Top. The Gray infantry therefore attacked without artillery support, but took full advantage of the cover of the woods.

Shells crashed among their ranks. For the Yankee guns, firing over the heads of their own infantry, it was close shooting. There were several instances of short bursts, due either to defective fuse or misjudgment of range. A Federal colonel, seeing one of his men lose both arms from the explosion of a projectile that came from the rear, sent wrathful word back to the battery commander that if it happened again he would face his regiment about and charge his own guns.[97]

Rifle fire spurted along the line of the Union trenches. The cannon fell silent, as bayonets were fixed, and a blue wave of steel swept downhill to clash with its counterpart in gray. Combat swayed back and forth on the slopes. The Confederates, stubbornly contesting every foot, finally yielded most of the ground gained yesterday. Once more the Union right rested secure, and the threat

to its rear was ended for that morning. Half an hour after the
attack, now repulsed, had been launched, and too late for it to be
stayed, an order to delay it had been received from General Lee.
Longstreet's I Corps was not yet ready to deliver a stroke which
should be made simultaneously with Ewell's. Again the same fatal
lack of coordination, turnabout this time between the Confederate
corps, had been manifested. Thus battles are lost. But General Lee
was not yet ready to concede defeat at Gettysburg.

Some of the Blue artillerymen on Cemetery Hill had thought the
Union Army was about to be surrounded. They heard the din of
conflict on Culp's behind them and in front, and to their left,
through the haze of another hot, murky day, they saw Rebel infantry and guns moving into position along Seminary Ridge. So far
as they knew, the enemy had fought his way well around their left
flank yesterday. Now he appeared to be closing in, tightening the
cordon. To the men in the Union ranks things looked distinctly
alarming—"skittish" they called it.

The visible mustering of those Gray cannon was enough to give
qualms to any spectator anticipating their fire.

All morning there had been a ceaseless, ominous activity,
with more and more Confederate batteries coming up into
one prodigious line that began at the Peach Orchard and
ran north along the Emmitsburg Road and just west of it—
scores and scores of guns, more of them than the Federals
had ever seen in one row, bleak and silent in the bright light,
their muzzles staring blankly toward the center of Cemetery
Ridge. Farther north the Confederates had still more guns
glinting out of the shade on Seminary Ridge, and off to
northwest on Oak Hill a few long-range pieces were placed
in order to bear on Ziegler's Grove and the cemetery.[98]

Seventy-five guns under Alexander were ranked in a curved line
1,300 yards long: his own battalion, Cabell's, Dearing's, Eshleman's,

and Henry's. Nine short-range 12-pound howitzers of Garnett's Battalion prepared to move out as accompanying guns with the infantry advance. Several hundred yards to the left and rear of Alexander's line were posted Walker's 60 pieces. They were stationed along the ridge as far as the Hagerstown Road. A mile to their north Hurt's two Whitworth rifles were emplaced. Filling in the intervals were ten guns of Walker's Battalion and ten more of the command that had been Latimer's, now under Captain Raine. Batteries of Jones' and Nelson's battalions backed them up. Some of Poague's guns had been in action early in the morning, but after an interchange that cost them eight horses and the Federals one exploded caisson, they had ceased fire, saving ammunition.

Here was indeed a formidable array of ordnance. Unfortunately for the cause that was to be lost, all its might would not be exerted today. In the artillery preparation preceding Longstreet's forthcoming assault, 25 rifled cannon and 16 Napoleons of the II Corps and 15 12-pound howitzers of the III would remain unemployed, and if ever there was an occasion when every available piece was needed in the front line, it was then. For that remissness General Pendleton, Lee's Chief of Artillery, must bear the final responsibility.[99]

However, Pendleton, declares Freeman in *Lee's Lieutenants* (III, 179), "had neither the prestige nor authority to assure the employment of all the guns as one weapon under one leader. He appears in the campaign more as a consultant than a commander." Both cooperation and liaison between the artillery of the three Confederate corps were woefully deficient. A similar situation would not infrequently obtain in future wars, with divisions and corps maintaining a jealous control over their own cannon and resisting their diversion to a front other than their own. Colonel Alexander believed that if the III and II Corps artillery had been massed to silence the Union batteries on Cemetery Hill, the attack would have been spared the deadly flanking fire it met from that quarter. Instead, 80 of the 84 guns assigned to fire on that bastion were posted in a line parallel with that of the enemy. The opportunity for an effective enfilade, possible if those batteries had been properly placed, was lost.

On the Union side General Hunt mustered 166 guns before the attack commenced. During the battle he reinforced them with 10 batteries from the reserve.[100] Thus 220 guns of the Blue finally faced 172 of the Gray. When the last great Confederate charge swept across the fields against the center of Meade's line, artillery odds tilted in favor of the Federals still more markedly because of the placement of the guns.

Guns and men to work them—horses to pull them into action—ammunition to feed them. In that last essential the odds—more shells and better fuses—also lay with the Union on that third day of July. Some Southern batteries, because of defective fuses, were reduced to using round shot only. Moreover, many Gray artillerymen, Alexander and Poague excepted, were not conscious of the vital necessity of conserving their limited ammunition. Ominous in extreme was the shortage that threatened in view of the great cannonade about to be fired. Each Gray battery had carried from 130 to 150 rounds into Pennsylvania. In the ammunition train were no more than 100 rounds per gun—even less in the opinion of Alexander, who estimated the amount at 60. Short of the capture of shells from the enemy's train or from one of his arsenals, no more would be forthcoming.

In contrast General Hunt not only had seen to the provision of an ample supply but sternly preached and strictly enforced its sparing use. In that respect alone he ranks as a great artillerist.[101] In the Army of the Potomac the transport of ammunition had proved so great a burden that the allowance of 400 rounds per gun had been reduced to 250. If a battery by reckless expenditure exceeded that quota, it was in Hunt's opinion suspect of having fired off all its shells in order to find an excuse for quitting the field to replenish its chests; by his orders it must remain on the ground until more ammunition was furnished it. During campaigns in 1862 as many as 300 to 400 rounds had been squandered in small skirmishes, a rate of fire exceeding one round per gun per minute. That was too much, Hunt stated, except for canister at short ranges; the rate should not be faster than one round per gun in two minutes and that only at critical moments. He stressed the accuracy of rifled cannon when carefully sighted and how far better results could be obtained from 12 well-aimed shots than from 50 delivered in haphazard haste.[102]

"Artillery," its chief for the Army of the Potomac declared, "should be used only against large bodies of men, rarely against small groups, never in cannonading individuals, which is too often done, especially if they ride white horses." [103]

There are two curious and contrasting commentaries on Hunt's precepts in regard to economy of ammunition. "When that gallant boy Cushing [C.O., Battery A, 4th U.S. Artillery], during the great cannonade in which he was killed [at Gettysburg], applied for more ammunition, the [corps] chief of artillery [Captain John G. Hazard] replied, 'Young man! are you aware that every round you fire costs $2.67?' " [104] A hang-the-expense attitude, on the contrary, would prevail in the campaign of 1864 when an artillery chief warned his corps commander that the supply of shells was being dangerously reduced by an unnecessary bombardment and was curtly informed that the cannonade would be continued if it cost $100,000! [105]

A special ammunition column had been formed by General Hunt and attached to the Artillery Reserve, as already stated.[106] It carried 20 rounds per gun, over and above the authorized amount, for every gun in the army, in order to meet unexpected shortages. Such deficits already had arisen and been promptly remedied. The III Corps in its haste to reach the battlefield had left all its artillery ammunition behind, and the II Corps half its train, while other commands for various reasons of improvidence had run short.[107] Because of Hunt's foresight shells had not been lacking for the Union guns in the first two days of battle nor would they fail them in their imperative need on the third. Yet tremendous as the volume of fire was for that period,[108] and adequate and effective in the crises, the official report on expenditure demonstrates how faithfully Hunt's orders were followed. His 310 cannon, exclusive of those of the horse artillery, fired 32,781 rounds—an average of 106 per gun and well below the supply of 270 rounds for each piece. And of the shells listed as used a considerable number were lost when limbers and caissons were exploded by the enemy's fire.

Cannoneer Buell from the position of his battery, B, of the 4th U.S., near the cemetery, had watched that massing of enemy artillery along Seminary Ridge. He

> could see over across the valley a line of Rebel guns reaching from near the Seminary on the north clear down to a point nearly opposite the Peach Orchard on the south, lining that ridge for over a mile in length with what was almost one unbroken battery, over 100 guns strong! I venture to say that no man now living in this country will ever see another artillery line like it, at least not on our own soil. Looking southward along Cemetery Ridge on our own side, so far as we could see, what appeared to be the whole artillery of the Army of the Potomac was in similar formation, though we could not see it all from our position.

The hours ticked past noon. It had fallen so quiet along the front that the young artilleryman could hear the humming of honeybees. He was reminded of his home farm, and a wave of homesickness swept over him. A veteran on the verge of battle, he chided himself, should not give way to such sentiment. He "braced up" and dismissed it, scowling toward the enemy and fingering his thumbstall. Better put his mind on the duty he would soon be performing: stoppering the vent of his gun with that piece of padded leather when a powder charge was rammed down to the breech.

Buell looked up at the approach of a mounted officer. It was General Hunt on a tour of inspection. The cannoneer saw him frown as he checked the battery's depleted resources. After the punishment it had taken during its gallant fight on the first day, B possessed four of its quota of six Napoleons, only two caissons, scarcely enough horses to pull its carriages, and 50 men all told. Its one remaining officer, Captain Stewart, had gone to the surgeon to have his wounds dressed.

Hunt spoke to Orderly Sergeant John Mitchell, temporarily in command. "If I had known that you were in this condition, I would have relieved you this morning with a battery from the Reserve. I had no idea you were so much cut up."

"We have suffered some, sir," the sergeant replied, "but we do not want to be put out of action!" At that the men set up a cheer. The general smiled, nodded, and rode on. Battery B stayed in the line.[109]

Like young Cannoneer Buell, General Hunt from Cemetery Ridge surveyed the marshaling of the might of the enemy's artillery. To his practiced eye it presented an even more magnificent and significant display. "Our whole front for two miles was covered by batteries already in line or going into position—apparently in one unbroken mass—from opposite the town to the Peach Orchard, which bounded the view to the left, the ridges of which were planted thick with cannon. Never before had such a sight been witnessed on this continent, and rarely, if ever, abroad." [110]

It was Hunt's task to fathom the purpose of that threatening gun power. Would it support another attempt by Ewell on the Union right or guard the Confederate line against a counterstroke from that quarter? No, it was probably designed to cover an attack on the center, as General Meade had forecast—to cause the Blue batteries to exhaust their ammunition in reply—to crush them—to shake defending infantry—to pave the way for their own assault troops advancing over open ground. In that event the cannonade must be a long and heavy one. While the defenders still quivered under its impact, charging brigades would hit them and roll over their remnants.

All the artillery on his own front, General Hunt resolved, whether of the army corps or of the Reserve, must act as a unit to repel the redoubtable blow he anticipated.[111] For fifteen or twenty minutes after the enemy's bombardment commenced his gunners must stand and take it. Most of his batteries could survive it, protected as they were by earthworks or stone walls. Then let them open, concentrat-

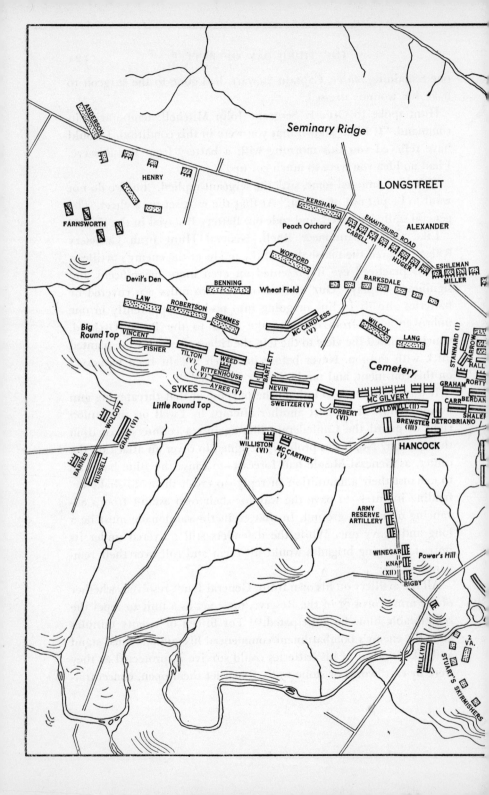

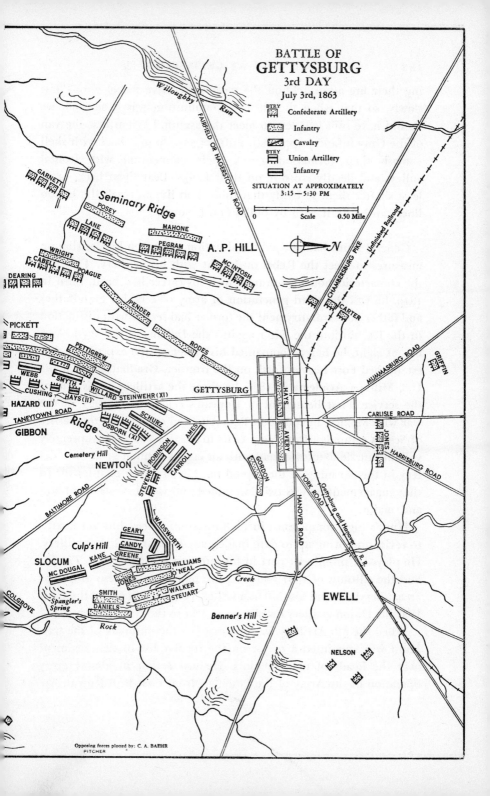

BATTLE OF
GETTYSBURG
3rd DAY
July 3rd, 1863

BTRY		Confederate Artillery
		Infantry
		Cavalry
BTRY		Union Artillery
		Infantry

SITUATION AT APPROXIMATELY
3:15 — 5:30 PM

0   Scale   0.50 Mile

N

Willoughby Run

FAIRFIELD OR HAGERSTOWN ROAD

GARNETT

Seminary Ridge

POSEY

LANE

MAHONE

WRIGHT

PEGRAM

A. .P. HILL

CABELL

POAGUE

MC INTOSH

DEARING

PENDER

PICKETT

RODES

CARTER

PETTIGREW

Unfinished Railroad

CHAMBERSBURG PIKE

WEBB

SMYTH

WILLARD STEINWEHR (XI)

CUSHING

HAYS (II)

HAZARD (II)

GETTYSBURG

HAYS

MUMMASBURG ROAD

GRIFFIN

TANEYTOWN ROAD

OSBORN (XI)

SCHURZ

AVERY

GIBBON

Ridge

AMES

CARLISLE ROAD

JONES

Cemetery Hill

ROBINSON

CARROLL

GORDON

NEWTON

STEVENS

HARRISBURG ROAD

YORK ROAD

WADSWORTH

Gettysburg and Hanover R. R.

HANOVER ROAD

GEARY

Culp's Hill

CANDY

GREENE

KANE

WILLIAMS

O'NEAL

Creek

SLOCUM

MC DOUGAL

JONES

COLGROVE

SMITH

WALKER

STEUART

EWELL

Spangler's Spring

DANIELS

Benner's Hill

Rock

NELSON

Opposing forces plotted by: C. A. BAEHR
PITCHER

ing their fire accurately on the most destructive Rebel guns—"but slowly, so that when the enemy's ammunition was exhausted, we should have sufficient left to meet the assault." When first the van of the Gray infantry appeared, shift targets. Pound them with shell —smash their formations—check their momentum with frontal volleys and deadly crossfire on their flanks. Beat them back, or at least shatter them so badly that those who live to reach the Union lines can be dealt with by bullet and bayonet.

General Hunt had assayed the situation and taken his decision on measures to meet the Rebel onslaught with his artillery. This was the climacteric moment toward which his career had built. Born in 1819, he was the third generation of army officers, his grandfather and father both infantrymen; the former had served with distinction in the Revolution, the latter against the Indians in the West. As a boy of eight, he had accompanied his father on the expedition that established Fort Leavenworth on the frontier. Graduating from the U.S. Military Academy in 1839, he chose the artillery as his arm of the service. First lieutenant of Duncan's celebrated battery in the war with Mexico, he fought at Palo Alto and through all the battles of Scott's campaign from Vera Cruz to Mexico City. His supremely valiant muzzle-to-muzzle duel with an enemy cannon at Molino del Rey in the storming of the capital has already been mentioned. In that engagement he was twice wounded and won brevets as captain and major.

Hunt's high competence in his profession placed him on boards to revise and bring up to date inadequate systems for light artillery. He played a prominent part in formulating *Field Artillery Tactics,* and the editions of 1861 and 1864 are monuments to his ability as an artilleryman and his skill as a writer. For its efficiency in the Civil War the Union artillery owed a great debt to those regulations.

When the 5th Artillery was organized at the outbreak of the war, Hunt was appointed a major on the regular list in that regiment over the heads of many seniors. He saw action in almost every operation of the Army of the Potomac, from First Bull Run to Appomattox, as a battery commander, leader of the Reserve, and then Chief of Artillery. It was at Malvern Hill that "in a masterpiece of fire direction he controlled a group of sixty cannon as if they were one huge battery—as if he were an organist pulling the stops for the instrument's mightiest diapason." [112] At Fredericksburg his massed guns covered the crossing of the Rappahannock.

In attempting to do justice to the great value of his leadership of the artillery at Gettysburg, this book echoes the praise of contemporary and other works. Every general in chief under whom he served, from McClellan to Grant, acclaimed him with the exception of Hooker, who paid for his disregard of his gunner chief. At Chancellorsville "Fighting Joe," having relegated Hunt to administrative duties in the rear soon after the opening of the battle, grossly mismanaged his artillery. His crushing defeat when Stonewall Jackson turned his right might well have become disaster had not Hunt, freed at last to reach the field, shielded the retreat with his guns.

Successive awards for gallant and meritorious conduct in action promoted Henry Hunt to a brevet major generalcy. Although his command was equivalent to that of a corps, he never received the consonant rank, as was his due. After his retirement for age, Congress tardily sought to honor him by conferring upon him the rank of major general on the retired list. The bill, unfortunately, was killed by President Arthur's pocket veto and was never revived. However, on Hunt's death in 1889 a fitting valedictory was pronounced in Secretary of War Redfield Proctor's obituary order: "It is needless to recite his deeds; the army today knows them; the army of the future will find them in history." [113]

On that third crucial day of Gettysburg Hunt lacked time to report the steps he intended taking to counter the Confederate attack to General Meade, nor did he deem it necessary to notify the Commander-in-Chief whose full confidence he held. Rapidly he rode along the full line of his guns, from right to left, issuing his orders to corps artillery and battery commanders. In his thoroughgoing way he covered them all—the Regular batteries of the 1st through

5th regiments—Volunteers from twelve states—the Reserve he had called upon in emergencies and would summon up again today. While he issued orders to the Regulars, he must have recalled his own service as an officer with batteries of the 2nd and 3rd U.S. What a galaxy of noted names the roster of the latter regiment held! Meade himself, Commander-in-Chief of the Army of the Potomac. Sherman, Grant's right hand in the West, and Thomas W. Sherman. Stanch George H. Thomas, who would soon win the title of "The Rock of Chickamauga." John F. Reynolds, killed in action on Gettysburg's first day. High-ranking Confederates, Braxton Bragg and Jubal A. Early. A. E. Burnside, whose doubts of his ability to command the Union Army had proved too well justified. Robert P. Parrott, the cannon founder, many of whose pieces would thunder in today's cannonades.

Surely Hunt paused a little longer to talk with battery commanders he knew. One likes to think he had a special word for First Lieutenant Alonzo H. Cushing, brevetted a major for gallantry in action at Chancellorsville. Cushing was twenty-one but seemed younger. To one of his corporals he "looked more like a schoolgirl than a warrior, but he was the best fighting man I ever saw." His Battery A, 4th U.S., was posted with the II Corps in the center of the Union line which, Meade had predicted, would bear the brunt of Lee's main assault on this third day. If that happened, there could be no doubt that Cushing and his cannoneers would stand to their guns.

At length the general reached the left flank, the crest of Little Round Top, where along with Gibbs' Battery, Battery D, 5th U.S. Artillery, was still posted, ably carrying on under Lieutenant Rittenhouse since the mortal wounding of Hazlett. On that vantage point Hunt remained to await the opening of the attack.

The main body of the Confederate offensive, to be supported by that great array of cannon which had so deeply impressed those who beheld it from the other side, slowly flexed its muscles. Longstreet, whose I Corps was to serve as the spearhead of the assault, was ob-

stinately reluctant to deliver it. To General Lee he voiced his fore-
bodings of failure and urged alternatives: another attempt on the
Union left, or reversion to the defensive forcing Meade to take the
offensive. Indeed he had already drafted preparatory orders for the
former.

Lee shook his head. He was convinced that the only practicable
course left the Confederates was to break the Union center, launch-
ing the attack from the strong positions already gained in the Peach
Orchard and its vicinity. He firmly believed that his men were un-
defeated, invincible—that earlier failures had been due to lack of
coordination. Once the enemy's center was shattered, the road to
Philadelphia and Baltimore would be opened.

One concession the Commanding General did make to Longstreet's persistent opposition and an added objection that if he
assaulted with his whole corps, its left flank would be dangerously
exposed. Let Longstreet anchor it with two divisions then. In their
place Lee would turn over to him troops from Hill's III Corps. That
expedient was a grievous mistake on two counts. Numbers of Hill's
men were weary and depleted by losses in the first day's fighting.
And the plan shifted the direction of attack farther toward the
Federal right, bringing it within range of the massed batteries on
Cemetery Hill.

Prolonged discussion of command decisions at the Battle of Gettysburg is not the province of this record of its artillery actions. Suffice
it to state that General Lee, his belief in the invincibility of Southern arms unshaken, overruled his stubborn subordinate and ordered
the assault.[114]

It was to be made by Pickett's fresh division, with Pettigrew's on
his left. Reinforcements raised the total to 10 brigades—15,000 men.
That was not enough, Longstreet strongly objected to Lee, for a
charge over 1,400 yards of open ground, a charge he considered to be
"desperate and hopeless." Not only must it face frontal fire throughout its advance but enfilading shelling from Federal artillery on
Little Round Top would rake its ranks.

Colonel Armistead L. Long, of Lee's staff and the general's link with his artillery, spoke up for his chief. Long had been the original commander of a famous battery, the 1st Company, Richmond Howitzers, in which Robert E. Lee, Jr., had once served as a private. The words of such a veteran artillerist, unwarranted as was the assumption they voiced, carried weight when he declared that the guns on Little Round Top could be silenced.[115] Neither Lee nor Longstreet questioned his statement. The latter turned away to order reluctantly his dispositions for the attack.

After the repulse of Ewell's early-morning attempt to seize Culp's Hill, the front had fallen quiet, "as silent as a churchyard," except for sporadic bursts of gunfire. Poague had broken off one such duel to conserve ammunition. Another followed an hour before noon when a Blue regiment tried to take a barn which was a nest of sharpshooters. Some 60 cannon of Hill's III Corps, C.S.A., replied to by the Federals, engaged in that minor clash, the opposing batteries banging away at each other for half an hour. Confederate Colonel Alexander withheld all his 75 pieces from the action. To support the forthcoming charge he knew he would need every round of ammunition in his chests, and that supply, he gravely feared, would prove insufficient.

A reliable and self-reliant officer, that crack artilleryman. His broad brow must have been wrinkled with anxiety that third day of July, and his firm lips, half hidden by a drooping mustache but partly revealed by low-shaven chin whiskers, surely were tightly compressed. A dreadful responsibility had been laid on his shoulders. General Longstreet had ordered him to take position where he could observe the effect of the bombardment by his guns and then to give the word that would launch Pickett's charge.

Hands of watches moved inexorably on toward one o'clock. Again the battlefield was wrapped in ominous silence, its every detail brightly etched by the rays of a burning sun. All was in readiness for the supreme effort. Gray brigades, mustered for the charge, rested on their arms in the grateful shade of the woods. In the long line of artillery, cannoneers took posts, lanyards stretched. Ears tensely strained for the sound of signal guns.

Firing those two signal shots was an honor that could well be coveted. It might have been allotted to one of the I Corps batteries from South Carolina, which had organized one of the oldest gunner units in the country: the Charleston Artillery Company, founded in 1757 and preceded only by the Ancient and Honorable Artillery Company of Boston (1638) and the Philadelphia Company (1755). The Richmond Fayette Artillery, though it did not originate until 1824, could fairly make a claim. The crossed cannon of its insignia could be considered to represent the two 6-pounders Lafayette gave it when he visited the city, pieces he brought from France during the Revolution and through whose gift the battery had been named for him. However, the signal guns chosen, more on the spur of the moment than through premeditation, belonged to the Washington Artillery of New Orleans, founded in 1838, a dashing, hard-fighting battalion.

A few minutes before 1 P.M. a courier galloped up to that battalion with an order forwarded through the corps artillery chief. It read:

Colonel: Let the batteries open. Order great care and precision in firing. If the batteries at the Peach Orchard cannot be used against the point we intend attacking, let them open on the enemy on the rocky hill. Most respectfully, J. Longstreet, Lieutenant-General commanding.

Major Eshleman of the Washingtons spoke rapidly to one of his battery commanders, Captain M. B. Miller of the 3rd Company. Miller raised an arm and swept it downward. One hundred thousand men tensed as the sharp report of Number 1 gun shattered the stillness. Again Miller's arm gave the signal to fire. A gunner jerked the lanyard of the second piece, but its friction primer failed to explode. That moment's delay [116] before the second shot was fired was only a short interval, "but during it the heart of two great armies could almost be heard to throb." [117]

Hard on the echo of the boom of the second gun came the thunderous crash of a cannonade that would reverberate through American history.

CHAPTER 8

The Third Day of Battle

CANNONADE

‹‹‹›

Georgia Regular Battery

Battery B, 1st New York Artillery
Battery A, 1st Rhode Island Artillery
Battery B, 1st Rhode Island Artillery
Battery I, 1st U.S. Artillery
1st Massachusetts Battery
1st New York Battery
3rd New York Battery
Battery C, 1st Rhode Island Artillery
Battery G, 1st Rhode Island Artillery
Battery D, 2nd U.S. Artillery
Battery F, 5th U.S. Artillery
Battery A, 1st New Jersey Artillery

‹‹‹›

It was as if the signal had set off a chain of huge firecrackers. Detonations crashed along the line of the Gray batteries. Some fired salvos, reports rippling from piece to piece. In others the cannon blazed away simultaneously in volleys. Soon the explosion of powder charges and the clamor of bursting shells merged in one continuous, thunderous roar. The earth trembled. A pall of smoke and dust darkened the sunlit sky.

For a few minutes guns of the Union strained at their leashes, lanyards taut in the hands of cannoneers. No longer could they withhold their reply. As the flashes of hostile batteries were spotted, commanders estimated ranges. Gun pointers sighted along barrels and spun the wheels of elevating screws. Fuses were cut carefully. Projectiles sped in screeching flight. Eighty Blue cannon, all that would bear at the moment, blasted away at the 138 Confederate guns in furious action.

"Let the batteries open," General Longstreet had ordered. To him the obedient fulmination along Seminary Ridge and its echo from the Federal side sounded "like mighty wild beasts growling at each other and preparing for a death struggle." One of his brigade commanders, General Law, was placed where he could look up the valley toward the town of Gettysburg. He saw the hills capped with crowns of flame and fumes while the guns vomited their iron hail upon one another. "Dense clouds of smoke settled over the valley, through which the shells went hissing and screaming on their errand of death. Numbers of these exploded midway over the valley, apparently with venomous impatience, as they met each other in mid-air, lighting up the clouds with their snake-like flashes." [118]

This rumbling, roaring tempest of sound and fury was more terrifying than a sudden thunderstorm, which catches a man in the open or cowering under riven trees, for the vivid lightning streaks and crashing bolts it reproduced were not impersonal but direct menaces. Veterans felt again the half-forgotten tightening in the pits of their stomachs of their first time under fire. They prided themselves on having withstood the heavy bombardments of Second Bull Run, of Antietam and Fredericksburg, but those were dwarfed by this tremendous cannonade, incessant, ceaseless. For Union artillerymen it muffled the reports of their own pieces to the proportions of toy pistols.

Over on the Union right cannoneers not yet engaged watched the
fiery drama unfold with admiration. In B of the 4th U.S. they exchanged critical comments on the performance of various Confederate batteries, meanwhile regretting that the range was still too
great for their own brass smoothbores to be brought into play.
"Oh, well, boys, be patient," Sergeant Mitchell told them. "All this
is to hammer our folks down to the left and pave the way for their
infantry. There's going to be a —— of a charge pretty soon, along
the whole line, and then we'll come in for our share. Keep your
shirts on, boys!" [119]

One group of Gray guns whose practice could be singled out for
special praise was Captain John Milledge's Georgia Regular Battery.
With enterprise and efficiency it had found a position under good
cover on the flank of Cemetery Hill. From that vantage point it
suddenly and swiftly flung 48 telling rounds on batteries of the XI
Corps.

> The gunners got our range at almost the first shot [Colonel
> Osborn, the corps artillery chief acknowledged]. Passing low
> over Wainwright's guns, they caught us square in flank and
> with the elevation perfect. It was admirable shooting. They
> raked the whole line of batteries, killed and wounded the
> men and horses, and blew up the caissons rapidly. I saw one
> shell go through 6 horses standing broadside.
>
> To meet this new fire I drew from the batteries facing
> west the 20-pounder Parrott battery of Capt. Taft, and wheel-
> ing it half around to the right brought it to bear on them.
> I also drew from the reserve one battery and placed it in
> position on Taft's right.
>
> Fortunately for us these batteries, placed in the new line,
> at once secured the exact range of their immediate adver-
> saries. In a few minutes the enemy's fire almost ceased, and
> when it opened again, and while the fire was progressing, it
> was irregular and wild. They did not again get our range as
> they had it before we replied.[120]

Prompt counterbattery, particularly the weight of metal of the big 20-pounders, had ended the threat of the Georgia guns. It was not pleasant for Northern artillerymen to contemplate what might have happened if the rest of Nelson's Confederate battalion, or Jones', had also been put in position where they could have joined in enfilading the line of massed Union cannon. Milledge, like Latimer on the second day, received neither support nor relief.[121]

Elsewhere in the Blue defenses gun crews were taking a share of punishment. Enduring it stoically, they worked their pieces with precision, firing deliberately and accurately. Automatically cannoneers followed the familiar routine so long drilled into them—the training which turns frightened, bewildered recruits into veterans steady under the ordeal of battle. Each calm command was smoothly executed. "Sponge—thumb the vent—ram—correct the aim—trail right—trail left." A lieutenant watched one of his gunners lying

> stretched along the trail, setting off his elevations by 1, 2, and 3 finger breadths, just as he measured his whiskey in happier days, and checking every move of his cannoneers. Suddenly a round shot carried away the head of No. 1, and his body fell across the gun breech—blood and brains spattering and splashing the gunner from head to waist. Deliberately, the gunner wiped the ugly mess from his face, cleared his eyes, lifted the corpse from the gun, laid it on the sod, resumed his post and continued operations with scarcely the loss of a count.

The lieutenant, in after years when he commanded a regiment, would relate that incident to his young officers and tell them: "That was discipline—the discipline that every man must acquire before he can call himself a field artilleryman." [122]

But the worst fury of the Confederate cannonade did not fall upon opposing artillery and infantry in the front lines. Shells, soaring in long trajectories, swooped over Cemetery Ridge and burst well down on its reverse slopes, wreaking havoc in rear areas. Meade

was all but blasted out of his farmhouse headquarters. Shot riddled
it, one smashing the jamb of a door in which he was standing. Cool
under fire as always, the general suggested to his staff that a shift to
another command post would be sensible and leisurely led the way,
narrating a humorous story from his Mexican War days—how General Zach Taylor had found a wagoner crouching behind a small
cart as flimsy shelter from an enemy bombardment and called out:
"You damned fool, don't you know you are no safer there than
anywhere else?" And the man had shouted back, "Don't suppose I
am, General, but it kinda feels so."

Another old artilleryman, who abruptly found himself on the
receiving end, was General Gibbon. The first avalanche of Rebel
shelling caught him at headquarters of his 2nd Division of the
II Corps, with his aide-de-camp, Lieutenant Frank A. Haskell.
Gibbon buckled on his sword and looked for his horse. His mounted
orderly, leading up the animal, was killed and toppled from the
saddle, and the two horses ran away. As the general started for the
front on foot, he noted the behavior of the gun and ambulance
teams. Even when a bursting missile slaughtered one or a pair, the
rest stood stolidly as though saying to themselves, "It is fate. It is
useless to try to avoid it." Men, he reflected, outwardly take it a good
deal the same way, hiding their fear. It was absurd to say you were
not scared. "None but fools, I think, can deny that they are afraid
in battle." [123] Haskell, too, confessed he was steadied by the com-
posure of his mount, which insisted on finishing its feed of oats
while its owner was trying to bridle it. While the aide forced bit
between munching teeth, he saw the headquarters mess wagon
struck by a shell. Its pair plunged, reins were dragged from the
driver's slack hands, and all smashed into wreckage against a tree.
A second shell demolished two pack mules, loaded with boxes of
ammunition. Haskell rode forward, overtaking the general, who
had been provided with a mount by another orderly. Dismounting
just behind the rise, they strode on into the front line where the
Union guns, "the guardian lions of the crest, quick to awake when

the danger comes, have opened their fiery jaws and begun to roar—
the great hoarse roar of battle."

Death and destruction reigned on the ground they quitted. There
behind the crest, which falsely promised protection, torrents of
Rebel shells swooped down in hissing arcs on the eastern slopes.
They spread carnage among the clerks, cooks, musicians, and medi-
cal personel—men whom front-line troops scornfully called non-
combatants. Give them rifles and put them in battle and they
would, as many had on other fields, acquit themselves gallantly. Now
in terror of the deadly rain of metal from the skies hundreds broke
and fled in wild panic. Ambulances could not run the gantlet of
that shellfire to bring back wounded from the front, nor could
stretcher-bearers thread it with their burdens and live. For a time
only caisson drivers, "fantastically brave or reckless," risked it,
galloping their teams across that perilous space to fetch ammunition
to the insatiable guns. Some of them made it; others, as a bursting
round exploded on their loaded chests, were smashed to bits.
Blindly the shells searched out the spot where the reserve artillery
was parked, presumably under cover of a hill, awaiting a call into
action. A dozen caissons blew up with a roar. In hot haste the batteries limbered and retreated beyond the enemy's range.

The fire of the Confederate guns, lethal as it proved to be on the
Union rear area, was in great measure wasted. Its bursts in artillery
parlance were "lost"—that is, they were unobserved and therefore
went uncorrected. Ranges were not shortened so as to achieve the
primary objective of the cannonade: knocking out the bulk of the
Blue batteries along the ridges and softening the defending infantry.

Yet the front line of the Army of the Potomac, safe though it was
in comparison with the rear, did not escape unscathed, and the
II Corps, to be the *point d'appui* of attack, bore the brunt. Haskell
saw cannoneers reel and drop, as solid shot crushed the cannon they
were serving into heaps of twisted metal and splintered wood.

The great oaks there by Woodruff's guns heave down their
massy branches with a crash. The shells swoop down among

the battery horses standing there apart. A half a dozen horses start, they stumble, their legs stiffen, their vitals and blood smear the ground.... Only a few yards off a shell exploded over an open limber box in Cushing's battery, and at the same instant, another shell over a neighboring box. In both boxes the ammunition blew up with an explosion that shook the ground, throwing fire and splinters and shells far into the air and all around, and destroying several men.[124]

So wrote Gibbon's aide, Lieutenant Haskell. No one has described artillery in the heat of battle more vividly than that young infantry officer, who possessed the gift of words, of poetic prose; he would not survive the war to develop that gift further. As he stood among the batteries on the crest he saw the guns as

great infuriate demons, not of the earth, whose mouths blaze with smoky tongues of living fire, and whose murky breath, sulphur-laden, rolls around them and along the ground, the smoke of Hades. These grimy men, rushing, shouting, their souls in frenzy, plying the dusky globes and the igniting spark, are in their league, and but their willing ministers.... Besides the great ceaseless roar of the guns, which was but the background of the others, a million various minor sounds engaged the ear. The projectiles shriek long and sharp. They hiss, they growl, they sputter; all sounds of life and rage; and each has its different note, and all are discordant. Was ever such a chorus heard before?...

We watched the shells bursting in the air, as they came hissing in all directions. Their flash was a bright gleam of lightning radiating from a point, giving place in the thousandth part of a second to a small, white puffy cloud, like a fleece of the lightest, whitest wool. These clouds were very numerous. We could not often see the shell before it burst; but sometimes, as we faced toward the enemy, and looked above our heads, the approach would be heralded by a prolonged hiss, which always seemed to me to be a line of something tangible, terminating in a black globe, distinct to the eye, as the sound had been to the ear. The shell would seem to stop, and hang suspended in the air an instant, and then vanish in fire and smoke and noise. We saw the missiles tear and plow the ground. All in rear of the crest for a thousand yards, as well as among the batteries, was the field of their blind fury. . . .

The percussion shells would strike, and thunder, and scatter the earth and their whistling fragments; the Whitworth bolts would pound and ricochet,[125] and bowl far away sputtering, with the sound of a mass of hot iron plunged into water; and the great solid shot would smite the unresisting ground with a sounding "thud," as the strong boxer crashes his iron fists into the jaws of his unguarded adversary. . . .

Our artillerymen upon the crest budged not an inch, nor intermitted, but, though caisson and limber were smashed, and the guns dismantled, and men and horses killed, there amidst smoke and sweat, they gave back, without grudge, or loss of time in the sending, in kind whatever the enemy sent, globe, and cone, and bolt, hollow or solid, an iron greeting to the rebellion, the compliments of the wrathful Republic.

From Little Round Top General Hunt had witnessed the cannonade open and swell toward a crescendo. Batteries near him, Rittenhouse's and Gibbs', far from being silenced as Confederate Colonel Long had predicted, boomed in reply. To Hunt the scene was indescribably grand. Yet the enemy's fire in this thunderous prologue to assault appeared to his practiced eye to be scattered, overshooting, and relatively ineffective. Someone over there was missing opportunities. If it became massed and concentrated, he must be ready to deal with it. He rode rapidly toward the station of the reserve artillery. Its batteries must be alerted to bolster threatened points in the line.

The dozen exploded caissons in the abandoned park told the story.

The reserve guns and the ammunition train had decamped from that unhealthy spot, but messengers had been left to receive and convey his orders. He hurried them off to bring up fresh units and returned to the ridge.

His batteries there were firing with the steady deliberation he had enjoined. However, a glance at their chests showed him that ammunition was running low. A cessation of fire must be ordered to save shells to meet the forthcoming attack. The artillery commander went in search of Meade to confirm his judgment. Not being able to find the new headquarters, Hunt ordered a cease fire on his own authority, a decision which, as he shortly learned, anticipated the wishes of the General-in-Chief.

CEASE FIRING

On the II Corps front cease-fire orders, given by General Hunt to its artillery chief, Captain Hazard, were countermanded by the corps commander, General Hancock. It was an action soon to be fraught with such important consequences that a reconstruction of the scene from available facts may be allowable.

Winfield Scott Hancock, intrepid and efficient, was undeniably one of the top Union generals at Gettysburg, a peer of Meade and of Reynolds, who fell on the first day. One can picture him frowning when he noticed the slackening of the fire of his II Corps batteries and demanding the reason for it from Hazard.

Why are the guns ceasing fire, Captain?

On orders from General Hunt, sir. We were told to save ammunition to meet the attack.

General Hunt is the army's Chief of Artillery. I'm in command of this Corps, and that includes its guns. My infantry is taking a pounding from the Rebels. Hunt's a gunner officer—always has been. He doesn't realize what it means to infantry's morale to have to take a cannonade like this without their own artillery paying any of it back. Resume firing.

Very good, sir.

So the interchange probably ran, and as a result the II Corps batteries again opened with shell. It is unlikely that Hazard ventured to point out to Hancock that the guns emplaced on the crest were enduring greater punishment than the infantry, under cover behind it and comparatively unexposed, a condition that Hunt had taken into account. "I knew the severity of the trial to which I was subjecting all the troops," the artillery chief later stated. "I knew, also, that while the batteries would be the direct object of the enemy's fire, their men must stand idle at the guns and bear its full fury, while the infantry lying on the reverse slope of the ridge and out of the enemy's sight would be partly sheltered from it. Yet I felt no misgivings as to the fortitude of my cannoneers, and no doubt as to that of the infantry." [126]

Hunt did not question Hancock's authority over his corps guns but maintained his right as the head of a special arm and speaking for the Commander-in-Chief to give orders affecting the part to be played in battle by the artillery as a whole.[127] That he had anticipated Meade's wishes and had carried them out by the cease-fire direction has already been noted. Hancock evidently was not so informed. The upshot was that Hazard's batteries continued to expend their shells, and the supply in the chests dwindled toward the point when only short-range canister would remain.

GALLOP

Rumble of wheels, beat of hoofs, jangle of harness, a blare of bugles. Forward galloped fresh batteries from the reserve. Fitzhugh's K of the 1st New York with guns of the 11th New York Battery attached; Weir's C, 5th U.S.; Wheeler's 13th New York; Parsons' A of New Jersey; Cowan's 1st New York Battery. The last relieved Brown's Battery B, 1st Rhode Island, which along with Battery A from the same state had been too badly crippled to continue in action. One of B's guns, while being loaded, had been struck squarely on the muzzle. The round killed the cannoneer holding the rammer staff and wedged itself in the bore. New arrivals were put in position on the II Corps front near a clump of trees, soon to become a historic landmark.

Colonel Alexander, C.S.A., scanned smoke-wreathed Cemetery Ridge from the observation station, just on the left of the line of guns, where General Longstreet had ordered him to estimate the effect of the fire. Even the straight shoulders of an old West Pointer must have bowed under the weight of his responsibility. A courier from Pickett's Division, holding his horse, stood by his side. Alexander, when he judged the moment propitious, was to send that orderly galloping off to launch the charge.

When would that moment strike? Porter Alexander, a top artillerist, was competent to determine it if anyone was. Still, how could anyone yet give an answer, with the target obscured by billowing clouds of smoke and dust? Here and there a geyser of flame, an exploding caisson, flared in the field of his sweeping glasses, but the roar of the Blue batteries continued undiminished. He could see their shells bursting over the positions of his own pieces. The Gray guns must be enduring another "artillery hell," as their ordeal at Sharpsburg had been branded. Indeed the losses in his own battalion, now under Major Huger, were rising toward their total of 114 men, including infantry volunteers, and 116 horses. Confederate infantry, although it kept sheltered, was suffering also. Such Federal cannon as were not engaged in counterbattery combed likely cover for concentrations. Shells crashed down on the apple orchards where men in gray congregated to seek shade from the burning sun. As explosions of jagged steel ripped through the branches, the agonized shrieks of the wounded rose. Rifles, swords, haversacks, and fragments of human flesh and bones flew through the air. The ground trembled as if shaken by an earthquake.

What toll were the Confederate batteries exacting in turn? A heavy one beyond the crest, but that holocaust was hidden, and their primary mission was to batter the Union front-line defenses. Alexander could only hope that advantage was being taken of the single benefit of the extended exterior line of the artillery of the Army of Northern Virginia. A deadly enfilade and crossfire might be delivered, especially by the guns of Ewell's II Corps on the extreme left. Only Milledge's Battery seized that opportunity and it was soon neutralized.

Small wonder that Alexander, while Pickett's courier waited, let the cannonade boom on past the fifteen minutes he had originally intended. As he hesitated, a dispatch from Longstreet arrived, heaping his dilemma higher. It was the first in an extraordinary interchange of messages between the I Corps commander and his acting artillery chief.

> Colonel: If the artillery fire does not have the effect to drive off the enemy or greatly demoralize him, so as to make our efforts pretty certain, I would prefer that you should not advise General Pickett to make the charge. I shall rely a great deal on your good judgment to determine the matter, and shall expect you to let General Pickett know when the opportunity offers.

Alexander ran a startled glance over the paper. If the assault was to be made on General Lee's judgment, he told himself, that was all right, but he did not want it made on his. He was too experienced a soldier to allow such a command decision, no matter for a subordinate, to be foisted on him. He took time to draft an astute and carefully-worded reply.

> General: I will only be able to judge of the effect of our fire on the enemy by his return fire, for his infantry is but little exposed to view and the smoke will obscure the whole field. If, as I infer from your note, there is any alternative

to this attack, it should be carefully considered before opening our fire, for it will take all the ammunition we have left
to test this one thoroughly, and, if the result is unfavorable,
we will have none left for another effort. And even if this is
entirely successful, it can only be so at a very bloody cost.

There was another "if" in Longstreet's answer, leaving his
artillery chief still in a quandary.

Colonel: The intention is to advance the infantry if the
artillery has the desired effect of driving the enemy off, or
having such other effect as to warrant us in making the
attack. When the moment arrives, advise Gen. Pickett, and of
course advance such artillery as you can use in aiding
the attack.

Only General Lee could countermand the charge. Would he do
so if the remonstrances Longstreet already had made were but-
tressed by an opinion from Alexander that the artillery preparation
was insufficient? Such a possibility remained, but it was not yet to
be considered. Moreover, much of Alexander's uncertainty had been
dispelled by a visit to Pickett, whom he found ready and eager to
go forward, and he had "returned to his post stimulated by the
contagious spirit of the gallant infantry leader."

Cast down the gauntlet then. Let the moment be chosen. Alexander, shouldering his burden, wrote a brief reply to Longstreet.

General: When our artillery fire is at its best, I shall order
Pickett to charge.

"Advance such artillery as you can use in aiding the attack,"
Longstreet had ordered. Alexander already had sent a courier to
alert a group of howitzers of Garnett's Battalion to be prepared to
move forward with Pickett. They could not be found. Without
notification General Pendleton had shifted them back under better

cover.[128] Also the Chief of Artillery had removed the ordnance train to a more distant point to escape fire. Caissons dispatched to the new location to be refilled had not yet returned, and ammunition was running low.[129] In default of the howitzers Alexander drew accompanying guns from other battalions: five from Garden's and Reilly's batteries of Henry's Battalion and four from the Washington Artillery.

Still the Gray storm troops waited poised in the woods. Choice of the moment for the charge, implacable, inexorable, inescapable—an agonizing "when"—increased its dead-weight pressure upon Colonel Alexander. Minutes, each one lessening the ammunition supply by 100 shells, ticked past in almost unendurable suspense. The artilleryman could not help but yield to it as the cannonade thundered in crescendo. He rushed off a message to Pickett:

"If you are coming at all, you must come at once, or I cannot give you proper support; but the enemy's fire has not slackened at all; at least 18 guns are still firing from the cemetery itself."

Then, mercifully, a little later, he thought his sweeping field glasses had given him an answer. Rolling smoke clouds from the Union batteries along Cemetery Ridge were breaking up into isolated puffs. Hunt's orders to cease firing and save ammunition to meet the assault were beginning to take effect in most sectors of the Blue line. An observer on the other side could interpret that diminished reply as the conservation measure it actually was, or he could lay it to the silencing of the hostile guns by his own artillery fire. The former seemed less likely. Federal guns, more plentifully supplied with shells, usually were not compelled to resort to frugality forced upon the Confederates, a practice which had been both economy and high strategy when Lee held his masked guns on Marye's Hill out of action until the time arrived to smash Burnside's charges at Fredericksburg.

Besides, Alexander's glasses offered additional evidence. They showed him remnants of enemy batteries withdrawing from positions littered with the bodies of cannoneers and horses and wrecked carriages. Never before had he seen the Federals pull out guns simply to save them up for an infantry attack. He told himself: "If they do not run fresh batteries in there in five minutes, this is our fight." [130]

Five minutes passed without a sign of life in the deserted positions. Now, at last, was the moment. A courier galloped with Alexander's second message to Pickett:

"For God's sake, come quick. The 18 guns are gone; come quick, or my ammunition won't let me support you properly."

For good or ill the word had been given.

Meanwhile Pickett had taken the artilleryman's first note to Longstreet. "Old Pete" read it—made no comment. Pickett pressed him. "General, shall I advance?" Still Longstreet uttered not a word.

Another general in a war to come would write of the awful responsibility of command.

> . . . It is true that the responsibility for orders that send men into battle, when it may mean death to men that you know personally, when it may maim and destroy men with whom you have spoken within the hour, is not lightly to be borne by any man. It leaves invisible scars, and the very recollection of it brings a spiritual humility of soul. . . .[131]

Such was now the unavoidable duty of James Longstreet. He would later declare that he foresaw what his men would meet and would gladly have given up his position rather than share in the responsibilities of that day.[132] He had already shifted some of the onus on to Colonel Alexander. In totality its weight would fall upon General Lee in obedience to whose orders the charge was to be executed. And yet Longstreet could not or would not open his lips. Some say he simply turned his face away; others that he let his chin drop upon the collar of his tunic. He himself stated that he bowed.

For the eager Pickett a gesture sufficed. He saluted and said, "I am going to move forward, sir," and galloped back to his division.

Even then the actual onset hung once more in abeyance. As

Longstreet joined Alexander, the latter expressed his apprehension that his ammunition on hand might be exhausted before the crisis of the attack. The corps commander snapped: "Stop Pickett immediately and replenish your ammunition." At once the artilleryman protested. The reserve also was scant, and resupply would take too long. In the interim all the effect of the preparatory fire would be lost.

Deed silenced words. Under the gaze of the watching officers Gray battle ranks emerged from the woods and marched steadily into the open fields toward the center of the Union line.

CHAPTER 9

The Third Day of Battle

CHARGE

‒‒‒

There was a death-torn mile of broken ground to cross,
And a low stone wall at the end, and behind it the Second Corps,
And behind that force another, fresh men who had not yet fought.
They started to cross that ground. The guns began to tear at them.

Stephen Vincent Benét: *John Brown's Body*

‒‒‒

Three Gray lines came out of the woods, with skirmishers fanned out ahead. Pickett's Division on the right and to its left Pettigrew's, not abreast but somewhat behind. Fifteen thousand men. Ranks dressed and intervals so beautifully kept that the assault waves seemed to merge into an unbroken sea flooding the valley. Sun glinted on the slanted rifle barrels and on the drawn swords of a few mounted officers, looming above its broad expanse. Red battle flags, slashed by starred, blue Greek crosses of St. Andrew, clothed it with grandeur, calling Solomon's phrase down through the centuries to acclaim it that afternoon at Gettysburg: "terrible as an army with banners."

It was three o'clock. The mighty cannonade was momentarily hushed. No paean of Rebel yells rose from the serried ranks—it

144

was not time for that yet. By sudden stillness the drama of the onset was intensified a hundredfold.

Along the Union defenses ran exclamations: "Here they come! Here comes the infantry!" They had met charges before, these men in blue, and delivered them—fourteen desperate, sacrificial ones, for instance, at Fredericksburg, shattered by Lee's massed cannon. As brave men they paid this onslaught due tribute, though they did not yet know the height of its valor even at the outset. Three of the Gray brigadiers, Armistead, Garnett, and Kemper, and two colonels, Hunton and Williams, were riding because they were too sick to march on foot. They had quitted ambulances and field hospitals to take part in this charge.[133] Not a few men in Pettigrew's Division wore "the red badge of courage" before they emerged from the woods: bandaged wounds suffered on the first day. They had been called back to fill the ranks along with orderlies and others.

Supporting brigades formed to follow the attacking divisions. Once the Union center had been broken by the main assault, these troops would rush in to widen the gap and roll back its edges, right and left, in rout. But by failures and confusion in command from corps downward the reserves were improperly placed and not the best that could have been selected as to leadership and quality. Left-flank units were weak and less battle-wise.

The first unfolding of the spectacle had no witness more eloquent than Lieutenant Haskell, watching from the lines of the II Union Corps.

None on that crest now need be told *that the enemy is advancing.* Every eye could see his legions, an overwhelming resistless tide of an ocean of armed men sweeping upon us! Regiment after regiment, and brigade after brigade, move from the woods and rapidly take their places in the lines forming the assault. Pickett's proud division, with some additional troops, hold their right; Pettigrew's (Worth's) their left. The first line at short interval is followed by a second, and that a third succeeds; and columns between support the lines. More than half a mile their front extends; more than a thousand yards the dull gray masses deploy, man touching man, rank pressing rank, and line supporting line. The red flags wave, their horsemen gallop up and down; the arms of eighteen thousand men, barrel and bayonet, gleam in the sun, a sloping forest of flashing steel. Right on they move, as with one soul, in perfect order, without impediment of ditch, or wall or stream, over ridge and slope, through orchard and meadow, and cornfield, magnificent, grim, irresistible. . . . Should these advancing men pierce our line and become the entering wedge, driven home, that would sever our army asunder, what hope would there be afterwards, and where the blood-earned fruits of yesterday?

On they came and on. Their firm tread covered 200 yards, and still scarcely a shot had been fired at them. Vulnerable to rifled cannon from first appearance, they were now within the range even of smoothbores. It was as if the Union gunners were caught in a trance, fascinated by that splendid display of martial pageantry—the last great charge in the old tradition. Men would not look upon its like again.

Shoulder to shoulder marched the ordered ranks. So had men charged since organized warfare began. Here once more was the onsweep of the infantry mass, flung full in the face of the enemy, to be halted only to fire a volley or by its own destruction. The increased range of muskets had not altered or abated its grim finale. It must still be driven home with the bayonet. Not for this charge and on this field were the wide deployment, the advances by rushes, and the prone firing, with groups covering each other's forward movement—tactics the past had occasionally witnessed and future combat would demand. Upright, aligned, close-ranked, they marched on.

And then—"The guns began to tear at them."

Parrott and 3-inch ordnance rifle. Rodman and James and Napoleon. They flamed and thundered—leaped back in recoil—were rolled back into battery—loaded, sighted, and fired again and again. Artillerymen, pounding the enemy masses, knew the fierce joy of battle. Here was retaliation for the punishment they had suffered from the enemy's cannonade. They saw their shells rip rents in the oncoming ranks and the flags reeling and going down. Green fields in the wake of the charge were tinged with the gray uniforms of still or writhing bodies. In future wars it would seldom be given gunners, placing indirect fire on unseen targets, to witness the dreadful destruction they wrought. They saw it plain at Gettysburg.

Despite that iron scourging the gallant charge drove forward, its center guiding on the clump of trees and toward the low stone wall of The Angle. It did not halt or hesitate except to dress ranks or to break openings in fences that barred the way. When the line thickened into columns to pass through the channels, Federal artillery concentrated on them and shredded them. They poured through regardless, formed up again, and marched on. Blue troops on the ridge could not withhold admiration for the steadiness of that beautifully marshaled array, which cannon rent but could not demolish.

Even from far away on the Confederate right rear the spectacle was immensely impressive. Sergeant Neese of Chew's Battery, en route with his unit and a cavalry detachment to guard that flank, caught a distant glimpse from a hilltop. He saw

a vast bank of thick battle smoke, with thousands of shells exploding above the surface of a white, smoking sea. The sight was grand beyond description and awe-inspiring in extreme. Our line looked to me from our point of observation to be about three miles long and enveloped in thick smoke, from which came a fearful roar and clash of musketry accompanied with a deep, continuous roll of booming artillery, such as an American soldier never heard before on this continent. The artillery fire at one time was so heavy that the hills shook and the air trembled, and the deep thunder

rolled through the sky in one incessant roar like as if the
giants of war were hurling thunderbolts at each other in the
clouds and rushing their war chariots across the trembling,
sounding welkin.

Second Lieutenant John H. Lewis, marching at his post with the
file closers of one of Pickett's companies, would always remember
its superb steadfastness.

The crash of shell and solid shot, as they came howling and
whistling through the lines, seemed to make no impression
on the men [he recalled]. There was not a waver; but all was
as steady as if on parade.... "Steady, boys," came from the
officers, as we advanced. Crash after crash came the shot and
shell. Great gaps were being made in the lines, only to be
closed up, and the same steady, move-forward; the division
was being decimated. Its line was shortening, but as steady as
ever, the gallant Armistead still in the lead, his hat working
down to the hilt of his sword, the point having gone through
it. He seemed to be as cool as if on drill, with not a sound of
cannon near.[134]

Musketry punctuated the din of artillery as Pickett's skirmishers
brushed aside those of the Union, who fell back toward their lines
on the crest. Confederate guns, firing over the heads of their advancing infantry, beat a tattoo of drumfire. At points columns of
flame and smoke, exploding caissons, testified to their aim, but there
was still no diminuendo in the defense's answering roar. Neither
the preliminary cannonade nor the present bombardment had
succeeded in crushing those Blue guns. The 18 seen leaving the
vicinity of the cemetery had quickly been replaced by reserve
batteries. Yankee infantry behind earthworks and stone walls was
waiting up there on the ridge, little scathed by long-range and
wide-scattered fire, to meet the charge.[135]

Move up the Gray guns, then, to close the range and support the assault. In the center only one in four could comply. Batteries pooled their dwindling supply of ammunition and turned most of it over to the one piece they advanced. On the right Alexander led forward a group of guns from Henry's Battalion, the Washington Artillery, and the Troup Battery to a swell of the ground just west of the Emmitsburg Road. They unlimbered well ahead of the route Pickett's column was following and opened a sudden and lethal fire that enfiladed Union infantry massed to repel the attack. Before 'the advantage gained could be exploited 20 Union cannon smothered them with a blanket of shells. With a number of pieces wrecked, and many men and horses down in a bloody welter, these accompanying guns were virtually silenced.[136] Their oncoming infantry must press the charge home without their aid.

Like pointing fingers the muzzles of guns on the Federal right and left commenced to follow the Rebel brigades, as their swinging tread carried them over the level ground, and they began to ascend the lower slopes. On Little Round Top Rittenhouse's and Gibbs' batteries, gunners peering along barrels, sighted eagerly. To their north that fine artilleryman from Maine, Lieutenant Colonel Freeman McGilvery, commanding the 1st Volunteer Brigade of the Reserve, alerted his 39 pieces. While he had caused earthworks to be thrown up in front of each to protect crews, every battery was well aware that he would not hesitate, if the need arose, to sacrifice it as he had Bigelow's 9th Massachusetts in the Peach Orchard on the second day. He would as readily, as he then had, offer his own life, but the time for that had not yet come. In the next year of the war, then in command of 100 guns, he would be wounded in the hand and die under anesthetic during the amputation of a finger.

Three of McGilvery's batteries began to volley on the orders of a general to reply to the enemy cannonade. The colonel sternly countermanded that fire after a few rounds and reduced the rate to a slow, well-directed counterbattery. He had strict instructions from General Hunt to conserve ammunition for the infantry charge and he faithfully followed them.

Now the moment was at hand. On came the long, sweeping assault, its right driving straight for his position. Every gun broke into full fury. Shells smashed into the Gray waves and spattered them into crimson spume. Under that blast of metal remnants drifted to the left. McGilvery shouted orders. Cannoneers sprang to wheels and trails. That whole line of artillery swung obliquely to the right. The guns, firing at top speed, took the enemy in the flank and raked all three of his lines. Little Round Top batteries joined the deadly enfilade.

Yonder on Cemetery Hill the guns were flaming, too. The charging brigades had entered the concave arc formed by the Union defenses and they were caught by a frightful crossfire from right and left. A little farther, and Blue riflemen also would pour a hail of bullets into both those exposed flanks. Death folded its wings around them.

Like the Light Brigade at Balaklava they had cannon to right of them, cannon to left of them, cannon in front of them. So thought a watching lieutenant of Union artillery.[137] But that famous charge, he remembered, was the rash act of an angry commander and, delivered by cavalry at full gallop, it was all over briefly. These men in gray, crossing nearly a mile of open ground at a measured tread, were infantry. Even without fences to break through they could not cover that distance at the quickstep in much less than fifteen minutes. Still they came on indomitably, traversing a fiery gantlet with a nerve the young officer on the ridge had never seen equaled. Cannon, as in the Crimea, must shatter this charge.

The range was scarcely half a mile now. Even tyro gunners could not have missed, and the Blue artillerymen were veterans, cool in action and firing with precision in spite of the rapidity with which they worked their guns. Jagged holes opened wider in the oncoming ranks. The lines stretched thinner to fill them. Colors swayed and fell. It was longer before they were caught up and carried on, and there were fewer of them. Segments of that inflexible advance wavered and dragged. Corpses more thickly strewed the ground behind, and among them lay living men who could no longer force themselves to face that merciless blast. Volley on volley of the murderous crossfire crashed out. Sometimes a single shell scythed a swath of ten men before it burst.

On the left glimpses of retreat—scores of men running to the rear —showed through the smoke and dust. But the center and the right, veering toward it, marched indomitably on, though the flanks withered. As smartly as if on a drillground, Pickett swung his brigades half-left, a battering ram concentrating its impact to smash through the middle of the Union line.

There where the II Corps manned the stone walls of The Angle, and the little clump of trees beckoned the final assault, the guns had fallen tragically silent. They had no ammunition left but short-range canister, having exhausted their supply of shells when General Hancock countermanded Hunt's cease-fire orders and directed the batteries to continue replying to the Confederate cannonade. To the end of his life the Chief of Artillery believed that the fire those batteries would have added, had his orders not been superseded, would have broken the charge before it reached the Union position, as half of it had been beaten back—that the crushing of the onslaught in mid-career would have given the Army of the Potomac its only opportunity for a successful counterattack.[138]

But the charge, though its flanks were shriveling, had not been broken. It was a bludgeoned antagonist, arms hanging limp, who would not give up but lowered his head and plunged at his foe. And Pickett's brigades, strength and sinews for the final thrust, drifting farther to the left under the pounding by McGilvery's guns, would squarely strike this II Corps front.

Blue-clad infantry and artillery made ready, the former little hurt as yet, the latter badly battered while they kept their guns in action and bore the brunt of the Rebel cannonade. Battery B of Rhode Island had been knocked out, and A from that state was nearly disabled. Rorty's B, 1st New York, and I of the 1st U.S., commanded by chunky little "Dad" Woodruff, who had been one of the shortest men in the Corps of Cadets, U.S. Military Academy, and was all fighter, were in better shape. The battery which had suffered most severely was Cushing's A, 4th U.S. Graduated in 1861 from West

Point as a second lieutenant, he had been promoted to a first before leaving the hall. That was still his rank on the Regular list, although he had been a brevet major since Chancellorsville for gallantry in action there. His good-natured, youthful face was grim now. He had seen his men and horses mowed down and three of his limber chests blown up—had watched one of his cannoneers, caught in the roaring blast of exploding ammunition, go hopping a few steps toward the rear on one leg, shreds of the other dangling. Wheels of several of his guns had been shattered but replaced. Cushing ordered them rolled down to the stone wall where enemy shells still burst. He and the other battery commanders loaded with canister and waited for the upsweeping Gray tide to come within range.

Down through the bores of their rifles infantrymen had rammed the heavy, round Minié balls, bullets that inflicted more dreadful wounds than their conical, steel-jacketed successors. At Spotsylvania they would hew down oaks twenty-two inches thick. Some men with smoothbores loaded with improvised buckshot cartridges. Now the Blue and Gray ranks blazed away at each other with deafening volleys, small arms taking over from artillery except for the canister-shotted guns.

Confederate Colonel Alexander and his batteries, which had fallen silent as the adversaries closed, watched the conflict "as men with a life-and-death interest in the result. If it should be favorable to us, the war was nearly over; if against us, we each had the risks of many battles yet to go through. And the event culminated with fearful rapidity. Listening to the rolling crashes of musketry, it was hard to realize that they were made up of single reports, and that each musket-shot represented nearly a minute of a man's life in that storm of lead and iron. It seemed as if 100,000 men were engaged, and that human life was being poured out like water."[139]

Infantry and artillery crossfire continued to converge from the arc of the Union line upon the assault. Its flanks melted and swayed backward. Not so its hard-cored center. Seemingly immortal, irresistible, the charge drove on. Now they who watched from Seminary

Ridge and the death-littered valley could follow it no longer. Billowing powder smoke and clouds of dust curtained its fiery denouement.

Before that shrouding pall closed down the watchers caught one last glimpse. Yonder on the ridge the rays of the sun gleamed on the folds of the Stars and Stripes. "The flag was still there."

At a gasping, stumbling run Pickett's waves mounted the last yards of the rising slope and dashed toward the stone wall. Rifles flaming, bayonets charged, drawn swords flashing. A Confederate captain paused for a last look at his dying son, then rejoined the rush. They charged straight into the bullet storm and into the mouths of cannon belching double and triple charges of canister. Blue regiments to right and left poured fire into their flanks. The spearhead drove on. Nothing, apparently, could blunt it. High above the clamor quavered the shrill Rebel yell.

Rolling, rattling rifle volleys—"as thick the sound as when a summer hailstorm pelts the city roofs; as thick the fire as when the incessant lightning fringes a summer cloud"—swept the Union batteries. Officers and cannoneers toppled around their guns. Woodruff was down, mortally wounded. Rorty and one of his lieutenants were killed. Remnants of the New Yorkers fought desperately to save their guns from the enemy storming in among them. A gray-clad officer planted colors beside one piece with a triumphant cry, "This is ours!" Sergeant Emil Darveau shouted defiantly back, "You lie!" He threw away his empty revolver, snatched up a trail handspike, and brained the gun's captor. Scarcely had he struck before he fell riddled with bullets.

Down at the stone wall Cushing's last two guns blazed away with canister. The rest of his battery had been knocked out, and Lieutenant J. S. Milne, his second in command, killed. Cushing himself had been hit in both thighs when a shell blew up one of his limbers and was hobbling about on bloodily bandaged legs. He pitched in to help a depleted crew serve one of his pieces. Stoppering the vent with a hand unprotected by a thumbstall, the searing hot barrel burned him to the bone. He sucked the agonizing thumb and called for faster fire. The Rebel waves surged on over the last lap— 400, 300, 200 yards. Cushing poured double canister into them, ripping open huge gaps. But one of his guns was wrecked now, and he could not halt the onrush.

Two bullets struck him, one piercing his right shoulder, the other inflicting a dreadful stomach wound. Sergeant Frederick Fuger caught his reeling commander in his arms and begged him to go to the rear.

"There's no time, Fuger," Cushing refused. "I stay right here and fight it out, or die in the attempt."

The sergeant held him up while he called for triple canister. "I'll give them one more shot," Cushing said.

As Fuger jerked the lanyard, a third bullet drilled his chief through the head, killing him instantly.

Cushing ran the last of his guns to the battle line.
The rest had been smashed to scrap by Lee's artillery fire.
He held his guts in his hand as the charge came to the wall.
And his gun spoke out for him once before he fell to the ground.* [140]

Men in blue and gray mingled in a wild melee of hand-to-hand combat. Sergeant Fuger, who would win a commission for gallantry this day, rallied his surviving cannoneers. They closed with the enemy and fought them with sabers, trail spikes, rammer staffs, and the bayoneted rifles of the fallen. Among them was the Chief of Artillery. As General Hunt galloped to the threatened point, his horse had been shot under him. He dragged himself clear, drew his revolver, and strode toward the clump of trees, joining his gunners in their last stand.

All The Angle and abutting battle lines ran red with carnage. Whistling ball, stabbing bayonet, clubbed musket, and butts jabbed

* From *Selected Works of Stephen Vincent Benet,* Rinehart & Company, Inc. Copyright © 1927, 1928 by Stephen Vincent Benet. Copyright renewed 1955, 1956 by Rosemary Carr Benet.

into contorted faces. General Hancock, a bullet through a thigh, slid from the saddle of his tottering horse. Gibbon, faint from the shock of a slug through one shoulder, was carried to the rear. But the Confederate leaders had fallen also. Garnett was dead and Kemper dangerously wounded. Armistead laid one hand on the breech of Cushing's last, silent gun; the other held aloft his saber waving his men on, the hat that had been on its tip now become its sheath. At that moment a bullet cut off his life. He lay close to the dead battery commander, their arms stretched toward each other. Still the Gray tide, not yet dammed, foamed forward.

"The fate of Gettysburg hung upon a spider's single thread!" So believed Lieutenant Haskell, galloping through the press of combat to rally regiments to the threatened point. Was he right, or had the charge been foredoomed? One faces again the teeming "ifs" of the battle.[141] Suffice the facts that the charge now had spent itself—that supports had not been able to reach it—that it had cracked the Union center but not crushed it.

Borne back by the final, furious impetus of the attack, the stubbornly gallant defense gave but would not break. File closers of the 19th Massachusetts joined hands and held the regiment's battered, bending line in place. From right and left reinforcements dashed in at the double. Minnesota and Maine, Pennsylvania and Michigan, Vermont volleying from a flank—the loyal states rallied and rushed into the fray. Pickett's men, their backs to the stone wall they had crossed, fought and died or surrendered to odds they could no longer withstand. Remnants reeled back. The Gray tide, risen to high-water mark, sank and ebbed.

Recoil and recessional. Blue cannon pounding the mangled brigades in retreat, exacting an even bloodier toll than they had of the advance. Survivors, dazed but still defiant, limping past sad-faced General Lee, astride "Traveller." The Gray leader's atonement and accolade to the grief-stricken Pickett. "This has been my fight and upon my shoulders rests the blame. The men and officers of your command have written the name of Virginia as high today as it has ever been written before."

They mustered to meet the expected counterattack. Even men of the ranks, shattered in the assault, shook their fists and dared the enemy to charge *their* heights.[142] Lee and Longstreet little doubted that it would be delivered. Federal skirmishers flowed down from Cemetery Ridge as if to herald it. Alexander's forward guns beat them back with canister. Other batteries, having partially refilled their ammunition chests at the train, came back into line.

Meanwhile on the northern and southern flanks of the battle lines more artillery had been in action, the sound of its guns faint echoes of the thunders of the crucial conflict in the center. These were cannon of the cavalry corps, the élite, fast-moving, hard-hitting horse batteries.

CHAPTER 10

The Third Day of Battle

THE HORSE BATTERIES

Breathed's (Va.) Battery
2nd Baltimore Light Artillery
Hart's (S.C.) Battery
McGregor's (Va.) Battery
Charlottesville (Va.) Horse Battery
Louisiana Guard Battery
German (S.C.) Artillery
Rowan (N.C.) Light Artillery

9th Michigan Battery
6th New York Battery
Batteries B and L, 2nd U.S. Artillery
Battery M, 2nd U.S. Artillery
Battery E, 4th U.S. Artillery
Batteries E and G, 1st U.S. Artillery
Battery K, 1st U.S. Artillery

Horsemen, guardians of the flanks through the history of warfare, hovered on the right and left of the opposing armies that third day of Gettysburg—the cavalry corps and their horse artillery—Jeb Stuart's gray-clad riders and Alfred Pleasonton's who wore the blue.

The proud mounted arm had long since yielded pre-eminence, first to the English longbow, then to modern fire power. To charge entrenched infantry and massed cannon meant destruction. Yet it could serve invaluably in support and fight its own battles at it had less than a month previously in the hard-clashing, almost purely cavalry combat at Brandy Station where the Union horse had for the first time held their own against the long-superior Southerners.

The fortunes of war at Gettysburg had been swayed during the first two days by failure to use cavalry in missions where it excelled: in reconnaissance and as protection for flanks. Lee and his corps commanders did not call upon their horsemen for information which might have led to the success of assaults on the Federal right and left. It was Confederate infantry scouts who discovered that Little Round Top had been left unguarded when Buford's cavalry division was ordered from its post there to the rear, a gross error on the part of the Union staff. Earlier knowledge and a prompt attack might well have stormed the key hill before Warren could rush troops to its summit.

But on the afternoon of the third day Gray and Blue cavalry and their batteries stood to horse in readiness on the wings, as Pickett's and Pettigrew's divisions began their epic charge on the Union center.

TO HORSE

Rifled or smoothbored guns of the horse artillery waited limbered. Cannoneers, each one individually mounted, clasped their horses' bridle reins near the bit. Their comrades in the light artillery rode on limber chests and caissons, which would never do for a horse battery. It took fast going to keep up with the cavalry. Try to sit a seat on a carriage at a headlong gallop into action over rough ground, and the air would be full of hurtling cannoneers, jolted loose from the most frenzied grip on chest handles. A man needed saddle leather under him in the horse artillery, and its quota of 12 more mounts and two more men per piece than the light gunners were allotted was essential for its duty. Numbers 9 and 10 of the gun squad were horse holders. When cannoneers dismounted to unlimber, they turned their reins over to the horse holders, two mounts to either side, to be led back with the limbers. Good horsemen, the holders must be prepared to gallop back to the guns and return the led animals to their riders when the battery made one of the frequent changes of position demanded.

A member of Stuart's horse artillery, which was about to fight at Gettysburg, wrote a stirring description of mounted gunners in action on another field.[143]

Down the crowded highway galloped a battery, withdrawn from some other position to save ours. The field fence is scattered while you could count thirty and the guns rush for the hills behind us. Six horses to a piece, three riders [drivers] to each gun, over a dry ditch where a farmer would not have driven a wagon, through clumps of bushes, over logs a foot thick, every horse on the gallop, every rider lashing his team and yelling. The sight behind us makes us forget the foe in front. The guns jump two feet high as the heavy wheels strike rock or log, but not a horse slackens his pace, the cannoneer leaning forward in his saddle. Six guns, six caissons, seventy-two horses, eighty men race for the brow of the hill, as if he who reached it first was to be knighted. A moment ago the battery was a confused mob. We look again and the six guns are in position, the detached horses hurrying away, the ammunition chests open, and along our line runs the command, "Give them one more volley and fall back in support of the guns."

We have scarcely obeyed, when boom! boom! boom! opens the battery, and jets of fire jump down and scorch the green trees under which we fought and despaired. What grim, cool fellows those cannoneers are! Every man is a perfect machine.

Bullets splash dust in their faces, but they do not wince. Bullets sing over and around them, but they do not dodge. There goes one to the earth, shot through the head as he sponged the gun. The machinery loses just one beat, misses just one cog in the wheel and then works away again as before. Every gun is using short fuse shell. The ground shakes and trembles. The roar shuts out all sounds from a battle line three miles long, and the shells go shrieking into the swamp to cut trees short off, to mow great gaps in the bushes, to hunt out and shatter and mangle men until their corpses cannot be recognized as human.

You would think a tornado was howling through the forest, followed by billows of fire, and yet men live through it, aye, press forward to capture the battery. We can hear their shouts as they form for the charge.

Now the shells are changed to canister, and the guns are served so fast that all reports blend into one mighty roar. The shriek of a shell is the wickedest sound in war, but nothing makes the flesh crawl like the demoniac, singing, purring, whistling grape shot and the serpent-like hiss of canister. Men's legs and arms are not shot through but torn off. Heads are torn from bodies and bodies cut in two. Grape and canister mow a swath and pile the dead on top of each other.

Swift movement, rapid, accurate fire, and often dashing, independent actions—such were the tenets these mounted gunners lived by. They prided themselves on being able to go anywhere they were needed. "Never say a cliff's inaccessible; just say difficult for horse artillery."[144] Gallantly they upheld the splendid traditions of the flying batteries in the war with Mexico and established their own. Pelham, Chew, and other Confederate commanders led their guns in charges with the cavalry. At Fredericksburg the former, constantly shifting position and finally with only one gun undisabled, beat back the advance of 10,000 Yankee troops for almost an hour. Union horse gunners, long a *corps d'élite,* displayed the élan and efficiency of their Rebel counterparts and they would demonstrate it again this last afternoon at Gettysburg.[145]

It had been Union General Buford's dismounted troopers, stemming for a time the enemy's advance on July 1, that opened the battle, and Calef's horse battery, A of the 2nd U.S., that fired the first artillery shots. Now carbine and saber and accompanying cannon were about to conclude the conflict.

The two sharp clashes of cavalry that took place on the afternoon of July 3 are confused by some historians. Both hinged on Pickett's charge. Confederate General Stuart rode to circle the Federal right flank and strike the enemy's rear. On the left wing of the Army of the Potomac Union General Kilpatrick sent his horsemen galloping down on Rebel infantry and artillery in the woods to support the counterattack he believed Meade would make after he had repulsed Lee's thrust at the center.

Plumed Jeb Stuart led his four brigades toward the Baltimore Pike, sabers and accouterments jangling, horses seeming to step to the rhythm of his battle song:

> If you want to smell hell—
> If you want to have fun—
> If you want to catch the devil—
> Jine the cavalry!

Wheels of horse artillery, cavalry with cannon, rumbled a bass accompaniment. Griffin's 2nd Baltimore Battery. Thomas E. Jackson's from Charlottesville, Virginia. A section of Green's Louisiana Guard guns. Breathed's and McGregor's Virginia batteries. Those last two were short of ammunition and were ordered to save it until critical moments. Unfortunately, also, three crack units had been detached. A Virginia battery under the able Robert Preston Chew had been left in the rear between Hagerstown and the river. So had Moorman's from the same state, each of whose gunners fought by the code of the Vikings: "Attack two men, stand before three, give

ground a little to four, and run from five." Hart's South Carolina
Battery had been attached to Longstreet's Corps. Those artillerymen
had been armed with four British Blakely guns, imported on blockade runners by Wade Hampton, one of Stuart's brigade commanders,
at his own expense. The scarred veterans from South Carolina,
steadily in action since 1861, could be depended upon to live up to
the song sung to them by women dressing their wounds in hospitals:

> Stand firmly by your cannon,
> Let your balls and grapeshot fly.
> Trust in God and Davis,
> But keep your powder dry.[146]

Jeb Stuart, moving on to terrain which afforded a splendid field
of fire for artillery, would regret the absence of those batteries—
would even more keenly miss the gallant Pelham, the greatest horse
artilleryman of all, killed in a cavalry charge the previous year.

The Gray horsemen mounted Cress's Ridge, two and a half miles
east of the town of Gettysburg. Thence a tempting prospect of the
roads in rear of the Federal lines spread out before them. They saw
no sign of the enemy; the ground looked empty and the way clear.
Perhaps because Stuart suspected an ambush he ordered one of
Griffin's guns to advance to the edge of the woods and fire a number
of random shots in several directions, shots that might be expected
to develop the presence of hostile forces. On the other hand, they
may have been a signal to General Lee that the cavalry was in position and ready to attack. In any event those ringing reports disclosed
Stuart's own whereabouts.

For a time there was no reply. Stuart, keeping his horsemen
under leafy cover, moved his guns forward. He stationed Jackson's
Battery on the northern wooded slope of the ridge and occupied
the buildings of Rummel's farm with sharpshooters. Two cavalry
brigades were posted on the right and the other two, under towering
Wade Hampton and Fitzhugh Lee, Robert E. Lee's nephew, were
placed on the left. They waited, poised for a sudden onset which,

once Pickett's charge was driven home, might roll up the right of the Army of the Potomac in disorganized rout.

From opposite woods the watchful Union cavalry division of General David Gregg heard the opening rounds and caught the glint of sabers among the trees on the ridge. John B. McIntosh mustered his brigade for action. That of George A. Custer, which had been ordered to shift to the left flank, was recalled to meet the forthcoming attack.

Now one of the best Union horse artillery batteries in the service, M of the 2nd U.S., commanded by Lieutenant A. C. M. Pennington, Jr., took Griffin's guns under fire. M's six 3-inch rifles laid down such a rapid and accurate hail of shells that the Gray pieces were disabled and what was left of the unit compelled to limber and find shelter in a hurry.

As dismounted Yankee skirmishers advanced, a second Rebel battery, Jackson's, opened on them. Pennington, shifting aim to this new adversary, was joined in his bombardment by Captain Alanson M. Randol's combined E and G of the 1st U.S. Heirs to the traditions of two fine old Regular regiments, they rained iron on Jackson's unit. Pennington stood beside his second piece and directed the sergeant, acting as pointer, to knock out a certain gun of the enemy's. The sergeant sighted carefully, stepped clear, and gave the order to fire. The round struck the target gun squarely on the muzzle, ruptured the barrel, and dismounted it. It was good shooting at three quarters of a mile.

Pennington said: "Well done. Now try that left gun." The sergeant came through with a shot that hit a wheel hub, smashed the piece, and killed the crew. Remnants of Jackson's Battery hastily quit the ridge, and the Union artillery shifted its fire to Rummel's barn. Shells crashed through its walls, burst within, and scoured out the sharpshooters. In the fields dismounted troopers, reinforcements for both sides crowding up, locked in combat, and the battle swayed back and forth.

Then Hampton's horsemen, followed by Lee's, rode out of the woods on the left of Stuart's line. They formed in close column of squadrons, "advancing as if in review, with sabers drawn and glistening like silver in the bright sunlight." Union batteries swung their guns on them. Cavalrymen fighting on foot fell back, clearing the field of fire, and the Blue cannon opened with shrapnel. Ammunition passers ran up with armloads of canister rounds, for those oncoming gallopers would close the range in a matter of seconds.

As fast as the guns could fire, the widespread sections of M of the 2nd U.S. and E and G of the 1st poured shell, then canister, into the broad column swooping down on them. They pounded its center and both flanks. Great gaps appeared in the ranks of the hurtling horsemen and were as quickly filled. Massed cannon could have crushed them in mid-career, but these guns were too few. Some of the Federal horse artillery, including the 9th Michigan Battery, had been detached to meet Pickett's charge, and other batteries were with the cavalry on the left wing.

As the Gray riders thundered on, General Gregg ordered a countercharge. Custer, yellow hair streaming, led his Michiganders in one of the whooping, hell-for-leather onslaughts he loved. Pennsylvania cavalry dashed in from another quarter. Horse crashed against horse, sabers rising and falling, revolvers flaming. Hampton, cut to the skull, was carried from the field. The Confederate column, its edges fraying away, gave ground and recoiled. When the horsemen drew apart, Breathed's and McGreggor's Gray guns engaged in a spirited duel with the Union batteries, staving off pursuit. The Confederate artillerymen were handicapped by defective ammunition; not a few shells burst short, endangering skirmishers of their supporting troops. Stuart's lines held until nightfall, then retreated. His attempt to strike the rear of the Army of the Potomac had failed like the assault on its center.

On the Union left the tide of battle was reversed in a conflict in which Blue cavalry engaged Gray foot and guns.

It was five o'clock, and Pickett's charge had ebbed, when small arms and cannon fire broke out in the direction of Devil's Den and the Round Tops. There Confederate troops held ground gained on the second day, the right of their line angling sharply and facing south. Confronting them was Union General Kilpatrick's cavalry division, guarding the flank, and with orders that directed the commander "to press the enemy, to threaten him at every point and to strike at the first opportunity." [147]

Kilpatrick believed his moment now had come. He tried, with far less prospect of success, to accomplish the same sort of turning maneuver Jeb Stuart had attempted at the other end of the line. If he brought it off and rolled up the Southern right in conjunction with the counterattack he assumed Meade would deliver on Lee's center, he felt assured that the entire Rebel army would collapse in rout.[148]

"Kill-cavalry" they called Kilpatrick because he wore out troopers and horses by hard marches. He was about to live up to the nickname further by the charges he recklessly ordered his horsemen to make —attacks over broken ground, obstructed by fences and stone walls, against steady infantry and artillery.

Two batteries of Union horse artillery unlimbered and went into action: Captain Samuel S. Elder's E of the 4th U.S. and Captain William M. Graham's K, 1st U.S. They were not used in the close support of the cavalry they were designed to give. The 1st West Virginia Cavalry launched a charge on a Texas regiment behind a rail fence, staked and bound with withes. Vainly the front rank tried to hack a way through with their sabers. Shells should have leveled that barrier. The troopers fell back, re-formed, and charged again, only to be beaten back with heavy losses from deadly volleys.

Kilpatrick rode up to one of his brigade commanders, General Elon J. Farnsworth, recently brevetted to that rank for gallantry in action, and ordered a third charge. The brigadier protested, "General, do you mean it? Shall I throw my handful of men over rough ground, through timber, against a brigade of infantry? The 1st Vermont has already been fought half to pieces; these are too good men to kill."

"Kill-cavalry" barked at him. "Do you refuse to obey my orders? If you are afraid to lead this charge, I will lead it." Farnsworth, at that questioning of his courage, rose in his stirrups and hotly demanded, "Take that back!" For seconds his superior officer glared at him, then apologized, "I did not mean it; forget it."

A captain who had overheard the interchange caught Farnsworth's last remark that he would make the charge but it must be on Kilpatrick's responsibility.[149] The brigadier placed himself at the head of his men.

As the cavalrymen, sabers drawn, rode forward in column of fours, through the woods, their supporting artillery shifted fire to cover the assault. Shells shrieked close overhead through the trees, showering the troopers with leaves. No order to charge with the cavalry, as the Confederate horse artillerymen, Pelham and Chew, had done so dashingly and effectively, was given the commanders of the Blue batteries.

Rippling rifle volleys met Farnsworth's 300. From higher ground they were shelled frontally and raked with enfilading fire by the guns of Bachman's German Battery of South Carolina and those of James Reilly's Rowan, North Carolina, Light Artillery. Saddles emptied, and horses toppled. The charge was the forlorn hope Farnsworth was certain it would be, but he and his troopers pressed it valiantly two miles deep into the enemy lines. Had it coincided with a counterattack on the center of the Army of Northern Virginia, it might have served a purpose. As it was, it became a futile sacrifice. Farnsworth, leading back survivors, fell with five mortal wounds.

The smoke of battle cleared away, its last thin, white wisps dissolving in the deepening blue sky of the waning afternoon. Sounds of combat on the flanks, counterpoint and postlude to the thunderous symphony of the center, dwindled into stillness. In that ominous quiet the Army of Northern Virginia girded itself on Seminary Ridge and its slopes for anticipated counterattack. Only let the enemy exchange roles—defense for assault. Let some Yankee general charge with 15,000 men, or twice as many, over that bloody mile of open ground. Then the South's bitter pangs of defeat would be assuaged.

Gray batteries and the ammunition train made anxious counts of their remaining rounds. There were enough left for one day's fight. Forward guns, which had beaten back a Union reconnaissance with canister, made ready for its seemingly inevitable sequel, a full-scale onset. As dusk began to fall, and there was still no enemy cannonade or any signs of an advance, the waiting artillery was gradually withdrawn to the ridge in preparation for a general retreat.

It was dark when General Longstreet rode out to inspect the skirmish line. Down in the hard-won Peach Orchard he found a battery in a perilously advanced position far ahead of the infantry. Whose are these guns? he demanded. A tall man stepped up and identified himself as the captain. Longstreet recognized his friend, "Buck" Miller, commanding the 3rd Company, Washington Artillery. "Why," the general asked, "was the battery so far out in front?" Miller answered cheerfully, "I am out here to have a little skirmishing on my own account, if the Yanks come out of their holes." [150] Longstreet, even after that disastrous day, could still laugh at the idea of using 12-pound howitzers for a skirmish.

But the Yankees would not attack, neither that night nor the next day, in spite of the hope, voiced by Rebel gunners, that the enemy artillery would celebrate it at noon with a salute to the "Glorious Fourth." The Blue batteries, ran the surmise, were too badly crippled to fire it.

General Meade, criticized for inaction, was to be defended by his Chief of Artillery.

Our own line [General Hunt declared] was in more or less disorder, as the result of the conflict, and in no condition to advance a sufficient force for a counter-assault ... [which] would have brought them directly in front of the numerous batteries which crowned the Emmitsburg Ridge, commanding that line and all the intervening ground; a farther advance, to the attack, would have brought them under additional heavy flank fires. [That is, they would have been exposed to the same deadly enfilade that shattered Pickett's wings.]

It needs but a moment's examination of the official map [Hunt continued] to see that our troops on the left were locked up. As to the center, Pickett's and Pettigrew's assaulting divisions had formed no part of A. P. Hill's line, which was virtually intact. The idea that there must have been "a gap of at least a mile" on that line, made by throwing forward these divisions, and that a prompt advance from Cemetery Ridge would have given us the line, or the artillery in front of it, was a delusion. *This* was not a "Waterloo defeat" with a fresh army to follow it up, and to have made no provision against a reverse would have been rash in extreme. An advance of 20,000 men from Cemetery Ridge in the face of the 140 guns then in position would have been stark madness; an immediate advance from any point, in force, was simply impracticable, and before due preparation could have been made for a change to the offensive, the favorable moment— had any resulted from the repulse—would have passed away.[151]

Under a drenching downpour of rain on the afternoon of July 4 the Army of Northern Virginia commenced its retreat. First the long wagon train, laden with wounded, jolted southward over the rough roads—stretching out to "seventeen miles of agony." Then marched the worn infantry and light artillery. Backward glances alert for pursuit, weary cavalry and horse batteries guarded the rear. So they quitted that lost field of battle where they had acted their part with gallantry, their military honor untarnished.

Perforce they left behind them their 2,592 dead and some of their 12,709 wounded. Men missing, 5,150, raised the total Confederate casualty list to 20,541. The artillery's share of those losses was: killed, 94; wounded, 437; missing, 77. That arm lost 627 horses.

Three thousand and seventy-two soldiers of the Union had given "the last full measure of devotion." Wounded were 14,497 and missing 5,434—total casualties of 23,003. In the artillery 105 were killed, 565 wounded, and 67 missing, with 881 horses killed or disabled.[152]

General Lee conducted the retreat with his old-time skill. The Army of the Potomac slowly followed, its V and VI Corps in the van. In sharp fights Union cavalry harassed the long column but were fended off by Gray horse and artillery. At Williamsport the Potomac River, too high to be forded and bridges out, barred the way. Giving his wagon train a twelve-hour start, Lee shifted his troops to Fairfield and Hagerstown. As Meade poised for attack, the river receded, and the Confederates crossed by-now practicable fords and a new-built bridge. The Army of Northern Virginia was safely back on its home soil, and there were twenty-two more grim months of war to be faced.

As in the case of the withheld counterattack, General Meade was castigated for failure to seize the opportunity to crush the enemy in retreat—for allowing "a defeated army, short of ammunition, encumbered with its wounded and prisoners and its wagons, thirty to forty miles from the Potomac, with a mountain defile to pass and a wide river to cross, to march off 'unmolested' and remain eleven days between Gettysburg and the Potomac without once being seriously attacked." [153]

Yet the glory of the Union victory at Gettysburg shone bright. Invasion had been halted and beaten back. A potent legend, the invincibility of Southern arms, had been destroyed. The manpower of the Confederacy could not replace the losses of those three July days. While the great battle around the little town of the crossroads was not the end, it was the turning point and the beginning of the end.

The part played by artillery in the Battle of Gettysburg was one of the most notable ones in the annals of the arm.

Gallant in extreme had been the conduct of Union batteries on the first day. When the tide turned against the I and XI Corps, they fought near-sacrifice, rearguard actions which covered the retreat to Cemetery Hill. Their fire and stanch infantry regiments prevented that retreat from degenerating into a disorganized rout. There was plenty of fight left in them when they reached the hill, threw up breastworks in front of the guns, and prepared to defend that bastion to the last. They lost eight cannon of which six were later recovered. Considering the odds against them, the record of the 11 Federal batteries (66 guns of which 60 were in action) was especially admirable. They were opposed by 90 enemy pieces, and by nightfall as many more were in position.

That day the Confederate artillery was well served and swiftly maneuvered. Its weight of metal, along with converging infantry assaults, half crippled the Blue batteries and forced them to pull out, as well as helping materially to break the rallies of the Blue foot. Guns sited on Oak Ridge delivered telling crossfires. It was not the fault of the Gray gunners that their preponderant might was not exerted in an attack on Cemetery and Culp's hills that evening—the attack Lee planned and Ewell failed to make—the attack that would have won the battle.

The second day also saw supremely valiant stands by Union artillerymen in the Peach Orchard, Devil's Den, and the Wheat Field after the III Corps' unauthorized advance created a dangerous salient and risked its destruction. One battery's losses ran to 50 per cent and others' were inordinately high. The handling of the Reserve artillery, with units rushed into action to meet recurrent emergencies, was superb. At one time a line of 24 guns, unsupported, filled a wide gap in the Blue line, checked the enemy's advance for precious minutes, and then covered the III Corps withdrawal and aided counterattacks. Batteries on and beside Little Round Top helped the infantry save that crucial eminence. Meeting the Confederate assault on Cemetery Hill, Union artillerymen suffered severely but stood to their guns, fought for them hand to hand when two batteries were overrun, and contributed greatly to the repulse of that determined attempt to roll up the Federal right. Through the long hours of battle the weight of the guns tipped the scales from imminent defeat toward victory. Of the 218 engaged, with 80 supporting III Corps, 18 were captured but all but four retaken, in most instances by spirited infantry charges.

The Army of Northern Virginia had 181 guns available on the second day. Seventy-eight were employed with efficiency and élan against the Union left, as witness the splendid charge of a battalion into the Peach Orchard. These guns gave increasingly strong support to the attack in that quarter; although their fire was finally unable to pave the way for the attempt to turn the enemy's flank, they aided in holding the advantageous ground gained and occupied strong positions for the delivery of the next day's cannonade. Delays and failures in coordination by the corps commands are not chargeable against the Gray gunners. However, on the Confederate left artillery chiefs, within the limitations of their authority, can be accused of lack of drive and enterprise and must bear a measure of responsibility for repulse of the second attack on Cemetery Hill. To allow their cannon on Benner's Hill to be blasted off it, while two battalions which might have supported and relieved them stood idle, seems inexcusable. On both flanks it was a near thing the second day, with victory for Southern arms hovering close. Certainly on their left the full power of their artillery was not used to achieve success.

On the third day the artillery of the three Confederate corps, jealously maintaining control of their guns, displayed little cooperation and liaison. No authoritative, over-all command forced the united action that was essential to success. While cannon of I Corps were ably handled in comparison with those of the other two corps, the Gray artillery as a whole stands guilty of heinous sins of omission and commission: placement of 80 out of the 84 guns, assigned to bombard Cemetery Hill, in a parallel line instead of in positions that would have permitted an effective enfilade; some 56 II and III Corps guns never brought into action at all in those critical hours when every piece was imperatively needed; that unjustified estimate that Federal batteries on Little Round Top would be neutralized; a shift without due notification of a battalion of howitzers to a new location where it could not be found when required and of the ammunition train to a more sheltered point with a resultant loss of precious time in replenishing caissons.

The tremendous cannonade by 138 guns, preceding the charge, was preparatory fire that did not prepare. True, observation was highly difficult because of smoke and dust, but that is by no means complete extenuation for the overshooting that largely missed primary targets. The bulk of the havoc it wreaked was in rear areas, leaving defending infantry little harmed and knocking out only a few front-line batteries. Guns moved forward to support the charge were either counterbatteried or became otherwise ineffective. Sorely hampered by shortage of ammunition, defective fuses, and other factors already mentioned, the Confederate artillery failed to fulfill its mission. Yet, its fighting spirit undampened, it stood ready to crush a Federal counterattack, and the Gray cannon bore a gallant part in protecting the retreat.

Two hundred and twenty Union guns replied to the enemy cannonade and thundered against the historic charge. Heavy casualties suffered by rear elements and center batteries did not affect the final result. Frontally, by those lethal crossfires from both flanks of the fishhook line, and at last with double and triple canister at close range, they shattered all but the spearhead of the assault, its wings withered, its support battered back. Premature exhaustion of the II Corps' long-range ammunition on its commander's orders, superseding General Hunt's cease fire, may well have been the factor that saved the charge from repulse before it reached The Angle. It was the high toll exacted by the Union cannon that enabled the infantry to blunt and beat back Pickett's final thrust into the lines. And the Blue guns took an even heavier toll of the Gray waves in retreat than in advance.

At Gettysburg both sides served their guns with equal bravery. On all other counts the artillery of the Army of the Potomac was superior—in number of pieces, weight of metal, equipment in general, supply and quality of ammunition, in organization and command. Yet most of those odds had favored the Union on other fields and had not prevailed. It was the last two counts that made the difference, along with the marked advantage conferred by defensive action. The record of the Blue guns at Gettysburg stands as an enduring tribute to the organizing and commanding genius of General Henry Jackson Hunt. By his provision of ammunition and by his brilliant tactics, particularly in the use of guns from the Reserve, he proved himself a great Chief of Artillery, unsurpassed in American history.

On the battlefield they gathered the wounded and buried the dead. The orderly sergeant of a crippled battery [154] called the roll in a faltering voice, pausing for answers that never came. Its wounded captain, waiting to take the report, turned and walked away to hide his emotion.

Lieutenant Haskell, stiff in the saddle from a bullet bruise on his right leg, rode over the battlefield before rejoining his command. Never elsewhere had he seen "such abundant evidences of a terrific fire of cannon and musketry. . . . Along the enemy's position, where our shells and shot had struck during the cannonade of the third, the trees had cast their trunks and branches as if they had been icicles shaken by a blast. And graves of the Rebels' making, and dead horses and scattered accouterments, showed that other things beside trees had been struck by our projectiles."

He rode on through the town, miraculously only one of its folk killed by a bullet of the conflict that had raged through and around it. Then he let his horse pace slowly through the burying ground on Cemetery Hill. "How," he reflected, "these quiet sleepers must have been astounded in their graves when the 20-pound Parrott guns thundered above them and the solid shot crushed their gravestones! . . . A dead horse lay by the marble shaft, and over it the marble finger pointed to the sky. The marble lamb that had slept its white sleep on the grave of a child now lies blackened upon a broken gun-carriage. . . .

"I looked away to *the group of trees*—the Rebel gunners know what ones I mean, and so do the survivors of Pickett's division—and a strange fascination led me thither. How thick are the marks of the battle as I approach—the graves of the men of the 3d Division of the 2d Corps; the splintered oaks, the scattered horses—seventy-one dead horses were on a spot some fifty yards square near the position of Woodruff's battery, and where he fell." [155]

Marshaled headstones would multiply in the citadel cemetery on the hill, dedicated in November, 1863, by President Lincoln's immortal address. In after years another President and General of the Army would build his home nearby.

Monuments and statues and the towering shaft of the Peace Light, surmounted by its eternal flame, rose on the hallowed ground of that shrine of valor and remembrance. And among them the guns still stand at Gettysburg.

TAPS

Appendix A

List of guns on the battlefield, Gettysburg National Military Park. Capabilities of various pieces of ordnance used in the battle, and details of ammunition and equipment.

This tabulation is a recent revision by Dr. James C. Hazlett of the official 1932 list in *The Location of the Monuments, Markers, and Tablets on the Battlefield of Gettysburg*. After repeated visits to the Park and considerable research, Dr. Hazlett, an assiduous student of Civil War ordnance, made a number of corrections in identities and calibers. Particularly interesting is his conclusion that some of the guns designated as Napoleons are actually altered 6-pounders.

"The 6-pounders," at Gettysburg (on the Federal side) he states [letters to the author, October 3, and November of 1957], "were deliberately altered after the war to resemble Napoleons, because they didn't have enough of the latter to go around. There are several points that favor this view. They are the only guns there with what I call a muzzle enlargement, where the bore of the gun has been increased in diameter to a *variable* distance down the barrel. This enlargement gives them a false muzzle diameter of 4½ inches, while the true Napoleon is 4⅝ inches. Most, if not all of them, show signs of having been turned in a lathe *after* the inscriptions were placed on the muzzle. On several of the guns the inscriptions on the muzzles are nearer the bore edge of the gun than usual, and in two cases part of the initial has actually been machined away, because the muzzle enlargement impinges upon them. The guns are placed

175

in pairs except in one spot (East Cavalry Field) where they are not too close to Napoleons for direct comparison. The 6-pounder on the Confederate side (where there is supposed to be one) is not altered in this manner.

"The Brooke rifles were simply mistaken for 20-pounder Parrotts, and it is natural that two of them were placed on the Federal side in Taft's New York Battery. With this exception, and the one Confederate Napoleon on the Federal side (F-166)—also two of the spurious Napoleons (6-pounders in disguise), the guns have been placed on the field with great care and accuracy.

"As I have commented in the notebook,* the presence of the 3-inch Ordnance rifles and Parrotts on the Confederate side is perfectly natural." [Captures from the Union Army in previous battles.]

UNION

Culp's Hill—two 12-pounders, two 10-pounder Parrotts	4
Stevens Knoll—one 12-pounder, five 6-pounders	6
Baltimore Pike—one 12-pounder, two 20-pounder Parrotts, two 20-pounder Brooke rifles	5
East Cemetery Hill—two 12-pounders, eighteen 3-inch rifles	20
Evergreen Cemetery—two 20-pound Parrotts	2
National Cemetery—six 12-pounders, two 10-pounder Parrotts, eight 3-inch rifles	16
Hancock Avenue—twelve 12-pounders, eight 6-pounders, two James, twenty-two 3-inch rifles, ten 10-pounder Parrotts	54
Trostle Field—two 3-inch rifles	2
Meade Avenue—two 12-pounders	
Pleasanton Avenue—two 3-inch rifles, one 12-pounder	3
United States Avenue—two 12-pounders	2
Peach Orchard—two 12-pounders, four 3-inch rifles	6
Excelsior Field—two 12-pounders, two 10-pound Parrotts	4
Wheat Field Road—two 12-pounders, four 3-inch rifles	6
Emmitsburg Road—ten 12-pounders	10
Hunt Avenue—three 6-pounders. (The other gun, which may or may not have been another 6-pounder, was struck by an automobile several years ago, and as the carriage was demolished, the gun was "retired.")	3
Taneytown Road—two 12-pounders, four 3-inch rifles, two 10-pound Parrotts	8
Seminary Avenue—two 6-pounders	2
East Cavalry Battlefield—four 12-pounders, two 6-pounders, two 3-inch rifles	8
Carlisle Street—two 12-pounders	2

* "Field Artillery on the Gettysburg Battlefield."

Howard Avenue—eight 12-pounders, four 3-inch rifles — 12
Field Northwest of Lee's Headquarters Field—two 12-pounders — 2
Chambersburg Pike—four 3-inch rifles mounted, four unmounted — 8
Reynolds' Avenue—six 3-inch rifles — 6
Sedgwick Avenue—two 3-inch rifles — 2
Sykes Avenue, Little Round Top—four 10-pound Parrotts, two 12-pounders — 6
Wright Avenue—two 12-pounders — 2
Howe Avenue—two 3-inch rifles — 2
Bushman's Woods—two 3-inch rifles — 2
South Cavalry Field—two 3-inch rifles — 2
Sickles Avenue—Devil's Den—four 10-pound Parrotts — 4
Wheat Field—two 12-pounders — 2
Althoff Field—two 12-pounders — 2
Crawford Avenue—two 10-pound Parrotts — 2
Granite Lane—two 3-inch rifles — 2
Powers Hill—two 3-inch rifles, four 10-pound Parrotts — 6

Total — 227

Four limbers, three caissons, Cushing's Battery A, 4th U.S. Artillery.

CONFEDERATE

Seminary Avenue—two 3-inch rifles — 2
West Confederate Avenue—twenty-one 3-inch rifles, thirty-eight 12-pounders, eighteen 10-pound Parrotts, two 20-pound Parrotts, two 20-pounder Brooke rifles, fourteen 12-pounder howitzers, two Whitworth guns, two 24-pounder howitzers — 99
Section 6—two 3-inch rifles — 2
Section 5—six 12-pounders, one 6-pounder, one 12-pounder howitzer — 8
Section 4—six 3-inch rifles, six 12-pounders, two 10-pounder Parrotts, two 12-pounder howitzers, one 20-pounder Parrott, one 20-pounder Brooke rifle — 18
East Cavalry Battlefield—two 12-pound howitzers, ten 3-inch rifles, two 12-pounders, two 10-pound Parrotts — 16
Benner's Hill—three 3-inch rifles, eight 12-pounders, three 10-pound Parrotts, two 20-pound Parrotts — 16
Jones' Battalion—four 3-inch rifles, two 12-pounders, two 10-pound Parrotts — 8
North Confederate Avenue—four 12-pounders, two 3-inch rifles, two 10-pound Parrotts, two Whitworths — 10
Western Maryland Railroad Cut—two 12-pounders — 2

Total — 181

GETTYSBURG ORDNANCE

Based on notes by General C. A. Baehr

Guns

At Gettysburg the proportion of guns in both armies was 50 per cent smoothbores, mostly Napoleons, and 50 per cent rifles, mostly 3-inch.

Napoleon: bronze smoothbore; weight 1,200 pounds; caliber 4.62 inches; charge 2½ pounds; projectile 12 pounds; range 1,566 yards.

3-inch Ordnance Rifle: wrought-iron sheets rolled on mandrel, welded and turned to shape; 850 pounds; charge 1½ pounds; projectile 10 pounds; range approximately 2,800 yards.

3-inch Parrott Rifle: cast-iron tube, interior cooled, reinforced by iron breech hoop shrunk on; 900 pounds; 1½ pounds; projectile 9¾ pounds; range approximately 3,000 yards.

HOWITZERS

	32 Pounder	24 Pounder	12 Pounder
Diameter of Bore (Caliber)	6.4 in.	5.82 in.	4.62 in.
Length	82 in.	71.2 in.	58.6 in.
Weight of Howitzer	1890 lbs.	1318 lbs.	788 lbs.
Weight of How. and Carriage	4575 lbs.	4036 lbs.	3214 lbs.
Propelling Charge	3.25 lbs.	2.5 lbs.	1.25 lbs.
Shell-Bursting Charge Weight Complete Round	1 lb. 24.6 lbs.	12 oz. 18.8 lbs.	7 oz. 9.35 lbs.
Spherical Case Shot Number of Musket Balls Bursting Charge Weight Complete Round	245 1.4 lbs. 32.72 lbs.	175 1.2 lbs. 24.64 lbs.	76 1 lb. 12.2 lbs.
Maximum Range with Shell	1,500 yds.	1,325 yds.	1,070 yds.

20-pounder Parrott Rifle: same construction as 3-inch; caliber 3.67 inches; charge 2 pounds; projectile 19½ pounds; range approximately 3,000 yards.

Whitworth Rifle (English): breechloader; hexagonal bore; caliber 2.75 inches; weight 1,100 pounds; projectile 10 pounds; range 5,000 yards plus (estimated as high as 5 miles).

Brooke Rifle: a development by the Confederate Ordnance Department; similar to the Parrott in construction and characteristics; cast iron.

James Rifle: cast bronze; caliber 3.67; 875 pounds; charge .75 pounds; projectile 12 pounds; range 1,700 yards.

Rodman Rifle: cast iron, interior-cooled in forging; caliber 3 inches; 850 pounds; charge 1.50 pounds; projectile 10 pounds; range approximately 2,800 yards.

Powder

Large grains, "tailored" to suit the gun; graphited; charges in woolen bags.

Primers

Friction; some obturating types designed to eliminate erosion of vent; gunners still kept old-style portfires and slow matches on hand for use in case of primer failure.

Projectiles

Solid shot: demolition and ricochet fire; regulations recommended it for ranges over 350 yards, particularly when fired over troops supported.

Shell: hollow cast iron with a bursting charge of 7 to 8 pounds; granulated powder of consistency something like blasting powder; fuse of same type as that for shrapnel but percussion and combination fuses also used.

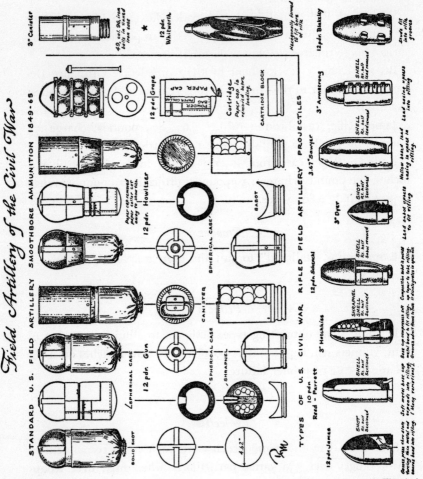

Field Artillery of the Civil War

(From *Military Collector & Historian*)

Shrapnel or Spherical Case; hollow cast-iron container filled with musket balls, sealed in with melted resin; hole in matrix held sufficient powder to rupture case and scatter balls; fuse, usually Bormann type, capable of burning up to 5½ seconds, screwed in before loading; safety limit—ranges over 500 yards.

Canister: tin cylinder filled with cast-iron shot packed in tiers with sawdust filter; 27 to 48 shot in the various types used in field guns; recommended for use up to 400 yards; below 150 yards, double canister.

Grape: large balls fastened around a core of wood or metal, resembling a grape cluster; estimated effective at ranges up to 800 yards.

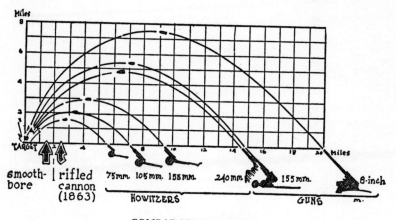

COMPARATIVE RANGES

(From *Artillery through the Ages*, by Albert Manucy)

Fuses

Bormann: punch-type powder train, punched for timing desired.

Hotchkiss: percussion mixture, set off by plunger held by soft metal pin.

Shenkel: wooden, papier-mâché combination.

Also simple wooden or paper tubes cut to desired length on a fuse board.

Fire-Direction Equipment

Tangent sight: shank and bar adjustable for range.

Pendulum hausse: bracket swung to allow for difference in level of wheels.

Quadrant with plumb bob or level bubble.

Tripods and plummets for indirect fire.

Settings of elevations and fuses for various ranges were listed in tables but were usually made by estimation and observation. Deflection, pointing muzzle to right or left, was accomplished by shifting the trail by means of a trail spike.

Appendix B

Organization of the artillery, Union and Confederate armies, at the Battle of Gettysburg, and location of memorials on the field.

(Based on *The War of the Rebellion: Official Records,* Volume XVII, Parts I and II; Wise, *The Long Arm of Lee; The Location of the Monuments, Markers, and Tablets on the Battlefield of Gettysburg.*)

ARMY OF THE POTOMAC

Chief of Artillery. Brig. Gen. Henry J. Hunt.

I Corps. Col. Charles S. Wainwright. East Cemetery Hill.

2nd Battery, 1st Maine Light Artillery. Capt. James M. Hall. Chambersburg Pike, McPherson Ridge; marker, National Cemetery.

5th Battery, 1st Maine Light Artillery. Capt. Greenleaf T. Stevens, Lt. Edward N. Whittier. Slocum Avenue, Stevens Knoll; marker, Seminary Avenue, south of Chambersburg Pike.

Battery L (E attached), 1st New York Light Artillery. Capt. Gilbert H. Reynolds, Lt. George Breck. South Reynolds Avenue and East Cemetery Hill.

Battery B, 1st Pennsylvania Light Artillery. Capt. James H. Cooper. South Reynolds Avenue; marker, East Cemetery Hill; Hancock Avenue (second position).

Battery B, 4th U.S. Artillery. Capt. James Stewart. East Cemetery Hill, Baltimore Pike.

II Corps. Capt. John G. Hazard. Hancock Avenue, near The Angle.

Battery B, 1st New York Light Artillery (14th New York Battery attached). Capt. James McK. Rorty, Lts. Albert S. Sheldon and Robert E. Rogers. Hancock Avenue.

Battery A, 1st Rhode Island Light Artillery. Capt. William A. Arnold. North Hancock Avenue.

Battery B, 1st Rhode Island Light Artillery. Lts. T. Fred Brown and Walter S. Perrin. Central Hancock Avenue; marker, field west of copse of trees.

Battery I, 1st U.S. Artillery. Lts. George A. Woodruff and Tully McCrea. North Hancock Avenue, Ziegler Grove.

Battery A, 4th U.S. Artillery. Lt. Alonzo H. Cushing, Sgt. Frederick Fuger. Hancock Avenue at The Angle.

III Corps. Capts. George E. Randolph and A. Judson Clark. Sickles Avenue, Excelsior Field, and Peach Orchard.

2nd Battery, 1st New Jersey Light Artillery. Capt. A. Judson Clark, Lt. Robert Sims. Sickles Avenue, Excelsior Field, and Hancock Avenue.

Battery D, 1st New York Light Artillery. Capt. George B. Winslow. Sickles Avenue, Wheat Field.

4th New York Battery. Capt. James E. Smith. Sickles Avenue, Devil's Den Hill, and Crawford Avenue (section).

Battery E, 1st Rhode Island Light Artillery. Lts. John K. Bucklyn and Benjamin Freeborn. Emmitsburg Road, north of Peach Orchard.

Battery K, 4th U.S Artillery. Lts. Francis W. Seeley and Robert James. Emmitsburg Road near Smith House.

V Corps. Capt. Augustus P. Morton. Sykes Avenue, north slope
Little Round Top.

3rd Massachusetts Battery. Lt. Aaron F. Walcott. Field north of
Valley of Death.

Battery C, 1st New York Light Artillery. Capt. Almont Barnes. South
Sedgwick Avenue.

Battery L, 1st Ohio Light Artillery. Capt. Frank C. Gibbs. Sykes
Avenue, Little Round Top.

Battery D, 5th U.S. Artillery. Lts. Charles E. Hazlett and Benjamin
F. Rittenhouse. Same location.

Battery I, 5th U.S. Artillery. Lts. Malbone F. Watson and Charles C.
McConnell. Swisher Field.

VI Corps. Col. Charles H. Tompkins. Sedgwick Avenue.

1st Massachusetts Battery. Capt. William F. McCartney. National
Cemetery.

1st New York Battery. Capt. Andrew Cowan. Hancock Avenue, High
Water Mark.

3rd New York Battery. Capt. William A. Harn. Taneytown Road,
southwest corner National Cemetery.

Battery C, 1st Rhode Island Light Artillery. Capt. Richard Water-
man.

Battery G, 1st Rhode Island Light Artillery. Capt. George W.
Adams.

Battery D, 2nd U.S. Artillery. Lt. Edward B. Williston. Taneytown
Road, south of S. Patterson buildings.

Battery G, 2nd U.S. Artillery. Lt. John H. Butler. North Hancock
Avenue, Ziegler Grove.

Battery F, 5th U.S. Artillery. Lt. Leonard Martin. North Hancock
Avenue, Ziegler Grove.

XI Corps. Maj. Thomas W. Osborn. Howard Avenue, west section.

Battery I, 1st New York Light Artillery. Capt. Michael Wiedrich.
East Cemetery Hill.

13th New York Battery. Lt. William Wheeler. West Howard Avenue.

Battery I, 1st Ohio Light Artillery. Capt. Hubert Dilger. West Howard Avenue; marker, Howard Avenue and Carlisle Road; tablet, National Cemetery.

Battery K, 1st Ohio Light Artillery. Capt. Lewis Heckman. Carlisle and Lincoln streets, Gettysburg.

Battery G, 4th U.S. Artillery. Lts. Bayard Wilkeson and Eugene A. Bancroft. East Howard Avenue, Barlow Knoll.

XII Corps. Lt. Edward D. Muhlenberg. Baltimore Pike, one mile southeast of Gettysburg.

Battery M, 1st New York Light Artillery. Lt. Charles E. Winegar. Powers Hill.

Battery E, 1st Pennsylvania Light Artillery. Lt. Charles A. Atwell. Slocum Avenue, north Culp's Hill (section); Powers Hill.

Battery F, 4th U.S. Artillery. Lt. Sylvanus T. Rugg. Baltimore Pike, H. Spangler Field.

Battery K, 5th U.S. Artillery. Lt. David H. Kinzie. Same location.

Cavalry Corps

1st Brigade, Horse Artillery. Capt. James M. Robertson. Pleasonton Avenue, south end.

9th Michigan Battery. Capt. Jabez J. Daniels. South Hancock Avenue.

6th New York Battery. Capt. Joseph W. Martin. Taneytown Road, north of Meade's headquarters.

Batteries B and L, 2nd U.S. Artillery. Lt. Edward Heaton. Field in front of schoolhouse, Granite Schoolhouse Road; east end, Pleasonton Avenue (second position).

Battery M, 2nd U.S. Artillery. Lt. A. C. M. Pennington, Jr. East Cavalry battlefield, north of Hanover Road.

Battery H (section), 3rd Pennsylvania Heavy Artillery (serving as light). Capt. W. D. Rank. Hanover Road, on right flank; Hancock Avenue (second position).

2nd Brigade, Horse Artillery. Capt. John C. Tidball.
Cavalry Avenue, East Cavalry Battlefield.

Batteries E and G, 1st U.S. Artillery. Capt. Alanson M. Randol. East Cavalry Battlefield.

Battery K, 1st U.S. Artillery. Capt. William M. Graham. Emmitsburg Road, near Keckler Lane.

Battery A, 2nd U.S. Artillery. Lt. John F. Calef. Chambersburg Pike; Reynolds Avenue, south of Springs Road (section).

Battery C, 1st U.S. Artillery. Lt. William D. Fuller. Taneytown Road and Granite Schoolhouse Lane.

Artillery Reserve

Brig. Gen. Robert O. Tyler, Capt. James M. Robertson.
1st Regular Brigade. Capt. Dunbar R. Ranson.
Hancock Avenue near Pleasonton Avenue.

Battery H, 1st U.S. Artillery. Lts. Chandler P. Eakin and Philip D. Mason. National Cemetery.

Batteries F and K, 3rd U.S. Artillery. Lt. John G. Turnbull. Sickles Avenue, Emmitsburg Road.

Battery C, 4th U.S. Artillery. Lt. Evan Thomas. South Hancock Avenue.

1st Volunteer Brigade. Lt. Col. Freeman McGilvery.
Hancock Avenue near railroad crossing;
Excelsior Field.

5th Massachusetts Battery. Capt. Charles A. Phillips. Wheat Field Road, Sickles Avenue.

9th Massachusetts Battery. Capt. John Bigelow, Lt. Richard S. Milton. Same location; also near Trostle House (section and limber chest); North Hancock Avenue, Ziegler Grove (haversack).

15th New York Battery. Capt. Patrick Hart. Sickles Avenue, Wheat Field Road.

Batteries C and F, 1st Pennsylvania Light Artillery. Capt. James Thompson. Peach Orchard (two positions); South Hancock Avenue.

2nd Volunteer Brigade. Capt. Elijah D. Taft.
Baltimore Pike.

Battery B, 1st Connecticut Heavy Artillery. Capt. Albert F. Brooker.
Battery M, 1st Connecticut Heavy Artilley. Capt. Franklin A. Pratt.
2nd Battery, Connecticut Light Artillery. Capt. John W. Sterling. South Hancock Avenue.
5th New York Battery. Capt. Elijah D. Taft. National Cemetery; Baltimore Pike; Evergreen Cemetery (section).

3rd Volunteer Brigade. Capt. James F. Huntington.
National Cemetery.

1st New Hampshire Battery. Capt. Frederick M. Edgell. National Cemetery.
Battery H, 1st Ohio Light Artillery. Lt. George W. Norton. Same location.
Batteries F and G, 1st Pennsylvania Light Artillery. Capt. R. Bruce Ricketts. East Cemetery Hill.
Battery C, West Virginia Artillery. Capt. Wallace Hill. National Cemetery.

4th Volunteer Brigade. Capt. Robert H. Fitzhugh.
Hancock Avenue near The Angle.

6th Maine Battery. Lt. Edward B. Dow. South Hancock Avenue.
Battery A, Maryland Artillery. Capt. James H. Rigby. Powers Hill.
1st Battery, New Jersey Light Artillery. Lt. Augustin N. Parsons. South Hancock Avenue.
Battery G, 1st New York Light Artillery. Capt. Nelson Ames. Peach Orchard, Emmitsburg Road; marker, south Hancock Avenue.

Battery K, 1st New York Light Artillery (11th New York Battery attached). Capt. Robert H. Fitzhugh. Hancock Avenue, Meade Statue field.

ARMY OF NORTHERN VIRGINIA

Chief of Artillery. Brig. Gen. William N. Pendleton.

I Corps. McLaws' Division. Col. Henry C. Cabell's Battalion. Battery A, 1st North Carolina Artillery. Capt. Basil C. Manly. Confederate Avenue, south of Wheat Field Road.

Pulaski (Ga.) Artillery. Capt. John C. Fraser and Lt. W. J. Furlong. Same location.

1st Company, Richmond Howitzers. Capt. Edward C. McCarthy. Same location.

Troup (Ga.) Battery. Capt. Henry H. Carlton and Lt. C. W. Motes. Same location.

Pickett's Division. Maj. James Dearing's Battalion.

Fauquier (Va.) Artillery. Capt. Robert M. Stribling. West Confederate Avenue, Pitzer Woods.

Hampden (Va.) Artillery. Capt. William H. Caskie. Same location.

Richmond Fayette Artillery. Capt. Miles C. Macon. Same location.

Lynchburg (Va.) Battery. Capt. Joseph G. Blount. Same location.

Hood's Division. Maj. M. W. Henry's Battalion.

Branch (N.C.) Artillery. Capt. Alexander C. Latham. Confederate Avenue, south of Emmitsburg Road.

Charleston German Artillery. Capt. William K. Bachman. Same location.

Palmetto (S.C.) Light Artillery. Capt. Hugh R. Garden. Same location.

Rowan (N.C.) Artillery. Capt. James Reilly. Same location except for a section at Confederate Avenue, Bushman Field.

Artillery Reserve. Col. J. B. Walton.
Col. E. Porter Alexander's Battalion.

Ashland (Va.) Artillery. Capt. Pichegru Woolfolk, Jr., and Lt. James Woolfolk. Confederate Avenue, south of Wheat Field Road.

Bedford (Va.) Artillery. Capt. Tyler C. Jordan. Same location.

Brooks (S.C.) Artillery. Lt. S. C. Gilbert. West Confederate Avenue, north of Wheat Field.

Madison (La.) Light Artillery. Capt. George V. Moody. Same location.

Richmond Battery. Capt. William W. Parker. Confederate Avenue, south of Wheat Field.

Bath (Va.) Battery. Capt. Esmond B. Taylor. Same location.

Washington (La.) Artillery. Maj. Benjamin F. Eshleman.

1st Company. Capt. C. W. Squires. West Confederate Avenue, north of Wheat Field Road.

2nd Company. Capt. J. B. Richardson. Same location.

3rd Company. Capt. M. B. Miller. Same location.

4th Company. Capt. Joe Norcom and Lt. H. A. Battles. Same location.

II Corps. Rodes' Division. Lt. Thomas H. Carter's Battalion.

Jeff Davis (Ala.) Artillery. Capt. William J. Reese. East slope, Oak Hill; also East Cavalry Battlefield, east of Rummel Woods.

King William (Va.) Artillery. Capt. William P. Carter. North Confederate Avenue.

Morris (Va.) Artillery. Capt. R. C. M. Page. Same location.

Orange (Va.) Artillery. Capt. Charles W. Fry. Same location.

Early's Division. Lt. Col. Hilary P. Jones' Battalion.

Charlottesvile (Va.) Artillery. Capt. James McD. Carrington. East of Harrisburg Road, Frommeyer farm, half mile north of Rock Creek.

Courtney (Va.) Artillery. Capt. W. A. Tanner. Same location.

Staunton (Va.) Artillery. Capt. Asher W. Garber. Same location.

Louisiana Guard Artillery. Capt. C. A. Green. Same location; also East Cavalry Battlefield, east of Rummel Woods.

Johnson's Division. Maj. James W. Latimore's Battalion; Capt. C. J. Raine.

1st Maryland Battery. Capt. William F. Dement. Benner's Hill, south of Hanover Road.

Alleghany (Va.) Artillery. Capt. John C. Carpenter. Same location.

4th Maryland or Chesapeake Artillery. Capt. William D. Brown. Same location.

Lee (Va.) Battery. Capt. Charles J. Raine. Same location.

Artillery Reserve. Col. J. Thompson Brown. Capt. Willis J. Dance's Battalion, 1st Virginia Artillery.

2nd Company, Richmond Howitzers. Capt. David Watson. West Confederate Avenue, Schultz Grove; also at north end of avenue.

3rd Company, Richmond Howitzers. Capt. Benjamin H. Smith, Jr. Seminary Avenue, north of Spring Road.

Powhatan (Va.) Artillery. Lt. John M. Cunningham. Same location.

1st Rockbridge Artillery. Capt. Archibald Graham. Benner's Hill, south of Hanover Road.

Salem (Va.) Artillery. Lt. C. B. Griffin. West Confederate Avenue, south of Hagerstown Road; also east of Reynolds Avenue and north of W. M. Railroad cut.

Lt. Col. William Nelson's Battalion.

Amherst (Va.) Artillery. Capt. Thomas J. Kilpatrick. Benner's Hill, north of Hanover Road.

Fluvanna (Va.) Artillery. Capt. John L. Massie. Same location.

Georgia Regular Artillery. Capt. John Milledge. Same location.

III Corps. Heth's Division. Lt. Col. John J. Garnett's Battalion.

Donaldsonville (La.) Artillery. Capt. Victor Maurin. West Confederate Avenue, south of Hagerstown Road.

Huger (Va.) Artillery. Capt. Joseph D. Moore. West Confederate Avenue, north of McMillan Woods.

Pittsylvania (Va.) Artillery. Capt. John W. Lewis. Same location.

Norfolk Light Artillery Blues. Capt. Charles R. Grandy. Same location.

Pender's Division. Maj. William T. Poague's Battalion.

Albemarle (Va.) Artillery. Capt. James W. Wyatt. West Confederate Avenue, north of Spangler Woods.

Charlotte (N.C.) Artillery. Capt. Joseph Graham. Same location.

Madison (Miss.) Artillery. Capt. George Ward. Same location.

Warrenton (Va.) Battery. Capt. J. V. Brooke. Same location.

Anderson's Division. Maj. John Lane's Sumter (Ga.) Battalion.

Company A. Capt. Hugh M. Ross. West Confederate Avenue, south of McMillan Woods.

Company B. Capt. George M. Patterson. Same location.

Company C. Capt. John T. Wingfield. West Confederate Avenue, Pitzer Woods.

Artillery Reserve, Col. R. Lindsay Walker.
Maj. David D. McIntosh's Battalion.

Danville (Va.) Artillery. Capt. R. S. Rice. West Confederate Avenue, Schultz Grove.

Hardaway (Ala.) Artillery. Capt. W. B. Hurt. Same location; also section, Whitworth guns, North Confederate Avenue.

2nd Rockbridge Artillery. Lt. Samuel Wallace. West Confederate Avenue, Schultz Grove.

Virginia Battery. Capt. Marmaduke Johnson. Same location; also at north end of avenue.

Maj. William J. Pegram's Battalion; Capt. E. B. Brunson.

Richmond Battery (Crenshaw's). Lt. A. B. Johnston. West Confederate Avenue, McMillan Woods.

Fredericksburg (Va.) Artillery. Capt. E. A. Marye. Same location.

Letcher (Va.) Artillery. Capt. Thomas A. Brander. Same location.

Pee Dee (S.C.) Artillery. Lt. William E. Zimmerman. Same location.

Purcell (Va.) Artillery. Capt. Joseph McGraw. Same location.

Stuart Horse Artillery. Maj. R. F. Beckham's Battalion.

Breathed's (Va.) Battery. Capt. James Breathed. East of Rummel Woods; iron tablets on East Cavalry Battlefield.

McGregor's (Va.) Battery. Capt. W. M. McGregor. Same locations.

Chew's (Va.) Battery. Capt. R. P. Chew.

Griffin's (Md.) Battery. Capt. W. H. Griffin.

Hart's (S.C.) Battery. Capt. James F. Hart.

Moorman's (Va.) Battery. Capt. M. N. Moorman.

Jackson's (Va.) Battery. East of Rummel Woods.

Imboden's Horse Artillery.

Virginia Battery. Capt. J. H. McClanahan. On brigade marker, Reynolds Avenue.

NOTE: Absence of markers indicates unit was not engaged.

Appendix C

Reports of Brig. Gen. Henry J. Hunt, U.S. Army, Chief of Artillery,
Army of the Potomac.

ARTILLERY HEADQUARTERS, ARMY OF THE POTOMAC,
September 27, 1863.

GENERAL: I have the honor to submit the following report of the operations of the artillery of this army in the battle of Gettysburg, July 1, 2, and 3:

On July 1, Reynolds' (First) and Howard's (Eleventh) corps and Buford's division of cavalry, the whole under the command of Maj. Gen. J. F. Reynolds, engaged the enemy on the west and northwest of the town of Gettysburg. On the west of Gettysburg, about a third of a mile distant, there is a ridge running nearly north and south, parallel to the Emmitsburg pike. This ridge, on which the seminary is situated, is crossed by the Cashtown pike about 100 or 150 yards north of the seminary, and some 50 yards farther on it is cut by a railroad. On the west of the seminary is a grove of large trees, and the summit of the ridge and the upper part of both its slopes are more or less covered with open woods through its entire length. The ground slopes gradually to the west, and again rising, forms a second ridge, parallel to and about 500 yards distant from the Seminary Ridge. This second ridge is wider and smoother than that upon which the seminary stands, and terminates about 200 yards north of the point at which the Cashtown road crosses it. Near this point, and to the south of it, are a house and barn, with some five or six acres of orchard and wooded grounds, the rest of the ridge being cleared. It was in the skirmish near this house that General Reynolds fell, and over the country covered by the ridge that the First Corps fought. To the north and east, beyond where the Seminary Ridge terminates, the country is more flat, and this ground was occupied by the Eleventh Corps, the front of which was in a nearly perpendicular position to that of the First Corps, and faced the north.

About 10.15 A.M. Hall's battery (Second Maine, six 3-inch) was ordered into action by General Reynolds on the right of the Cashtown road, on the second ridge, and some 500 yards beyond the seminary. The enemy had previously opened fire from a battery of six guns at a distance of about 1,300 yards, and directly in front of this position, on Reynolds' troops, and Hall, on coming into action, replied with effect. In the course of half an hour, a body of the enemy's infantry approached the right of Hall's battery under cover of a ravine, and opened upon him at a distance of 60 or 80 yards, killing and wounding a number of his men and horses. The right and center sections replied with canister, while the left section continued its fire on the enemy's battery. The supports now falling back, Captain Hall found it necessary to retire, which he did by sections.

Soon after, the Third Division (Rowley's), First Corps, occupied the open ground on this ridge with Cooper's battery (B, First Pennsylvania, four 3-inch), which took post in an oat-field, about 380 yards south of the Cashtown road.

The Second Division (Robinson's) occupied a road on the west slope of the Seminary Ridge, north of the railroad, and the Eleventh Corps came into position on the flat ground farther north, and in a position nearly perpendicular to that of the First Corps. Colonel Wainwright, commanding the artillery of the First Corps, sent Stewart's battery (B, Fourth United States, six 12-pounders) to report to General Robinson, and ordered Reynolds to move with his battery to the support of Calef's horse battery (A, Second United States, six 3-inch), which had been placed in position by General Wadsworth

on the spot just occupied by Hall's (Second Maine, six 3-inch), and
was sharply engaged with the enemy's battery in its front. Reynolds
had hardly taken position when the enemy opened a severe fire from
a second battery immediately on his right. The cross-fire of the
enemy's two batteries caused both Calef's and Reynolds' to retire,
Reynolds taking up a new position at right angles to the ridge, with
his left covered by the woods, near the house and barn referred to.
While executing this movement, Captain Reynolds was severely
wounded in the right eye, but refused to quit the field. The enemy's
battery soon after ceased its fire. At the request of General Wadsworth, Colonel Wainwright posted Wilber's section of Reynolds'
battery in the orchard on the south side of the Cashtown road, where
he was sheltered from the fire of the enemy's battery on his right
flank by the intervening house and barn, and moved the other two
sections to the south side of the wood, on the open crest.

In the meantime the Eleventh Corps had taken position, and Dilger's battery (I, First Ohio, six 12-pounders), attached to Schurz's
division, soon became engaged with one of the enemy's batteries at
1,000 yards distance, which was soon re-enforced by another. Dilger maintained his position until re-enforced by Wheeler (Thirteenth New York Independent, four 3-inch), sent to his assistance
by Major Osborn, commanding the artillery of the corps, when a
sharp contest ensued, the result of which was one piece of Wheeler's
dismounted and five of the enemy's, which Major Osborn states they
left on the ground. The enemy suffered the most loss. During this
action, Captain Dilger several times changed the positions of his batteries with excellent effect, selecting his ground with judgment.

About 11 A.M. Wilkeson's battery (G, Fourth United States, four
12-pounders) came up, and reported to General Barlow, who posted
it close to the enemy's line of infantry, with which it immediately
became engaged, sustaining at the same time the fire of two of his
batteries.

In the commencement of this unequal contest, Lieut. Bayard
Wilkeson (Fourth U.S. Artillery), commanding the battery, a young
officer of great gallantry, fell, mortally wounded, and was carried

from the field. Lieutenant Bancroft succeeded to the command, and by changing position and distributing his sections, in order to meet the different movements of the enemy, succeeded in maintaining himself handsomely until the division fell back to the town, when he withdrew to Cemetery Hill.

About 4 P.M. the troops were withdrawn to Cemetery Hill, and Schurz's division, with Heckman's (K, First Ohio, four 12-pounders) and Wiedrich's (I, First New York, six 3-inch) batteries, were posted so as to cover the movement of the corps, Wiedrich's being placed on the hill in front of the cemetery entrance. Heckman worked his guns well, and held his ground until the enemy entered his battery. He then retired with the loss of one gun, the battery being so much crippled that it was sent to the rear, and was not again called into action.

Wiedrich's battery was actively engaged, and about 4.30 P.M. the enemy made an attempt to turn our right, but his line was very soon broken by the fire of this battery, and the attempt failed.

The First Corps was withdrawn about the same time as the Eleventh. Colonel Wainwright, commanding the artillery of this corps, understanding the order to hold Cemetery Hill to apply to Seminary Hill, posted Cooper's battery (B, First Pennsylvania, four 3-inch) in front of the professor's house. Captain Stevens (Fifth Maine, six 12-pounders) was soon after posted by General Doubleday on Cooper's right. Soon after, the enemy emerged in two strong columns from the woods in front, about 500 yards distant, outflanked our line nearly a third of a mile, then formed in two lines of battle, and advanced directly up the crest. During this movement, Reynolds battery (L, First New York, six 3-inch) opened on the columns, but the fire of his sections was much interfered with by the movements of our own infantry in their front. Colonel Wainwright therefore moved these two sections, under Lieutenant Breck, to a strong stone wall on the seminary crest, near Stevens' position. The movement was not ordered until the enemy, outnumbering our troops 5 to 1, were within 200 yards of the battery. Lieutenant Wilber's section of the same battery soon after fell back with his supports (L, First

New York, six 3-inch; Fifth Maine, six 12-pounders, and Cooper's, B, First Pennsylvania, four 3-inch) to the same position, thus concentrating sixteen guns. Stewart's battery (B, Fourth United States, six 12-pounders) was also on the same line, half of the battery between the Cashtown pike and the railroad, the other half across the railroad, in the corner of a wood. The enemy's lines continued to advance across the space between the two crests, but when the first line was within about 100 yards of the seminary, Lieutenant Davison, Fourth U.S. Artillery, commanding the left half of Stewart's battery, placed his guns on the Cashtown pike, so as to enfilade the whole line. This movement, well sustained by the other batteries, brought the first line to a halt, but the second, supported by a column deployed from the Cashtown road, pushed on. An order was now received by Captain Stevens from General Wadsworth, directing his battery to withdraw, but Colonel Wainwright, not knowing this, and still under the mistaken impression as to the importance of holding Seminary Hill, directed all the batteries to maintain their positions.

In a few minutes, however, all our infantry were seen rapidly retreating toward the town, and the batteries were all limbered to the rear, and moved off down the Cashtown pike, maintaining a walk until the infantry had left it. By this time our retreating columns were lapped by the enemy's skirmishers, who opened a severe fire from behind a fence within 50 yards of the road. As soon as the road was clear, the batteries moved at a trot, but it was too late to save all the material. Lieutenant Wilber's last piece (L, First New York, six 3-inch) had 1 of its wheel-horses shot, and, by the time this could be disengaged, 3 others were shot and Lieutenant Wilber's own horse killed. It was impossible to move the piece off, and it was lost. No blame apparently can be attached to the officers of this or of Heckman's battery (K, First Ohio, four 12-pounders) for the loss of the two guns in the retiring of the two corps. It was the necessary result of the obstinate resistance made to the enemy, so as to cover the withdrawal of their respective corps. Three of the caisson bodies of Stewart's battery were broken down, 1 of his caissons exploded, 2 of his guns had been disabled by the breaking of their pointing rings, and 3 of Hall's guns dismounted.

The losses of the batteries of the First Corps in these operations were heavy; 83 officers and men killed and wounded, including 6 officers wounded (Capt. G. T. Stevens and Lieut. C. O. Hunt, Fifth Maine, severely; Capt. G. H. Reynolds, L, First New York, severely; Lieut. J. Stewart, Fourth Artillery, slightly; Lieut. J. Davison, Fourth Artillery, severely; Lieut. W. C. Miller, B, First Pennsylvania, slightly), and about 80 horses, a large proportion of the latter between the Seminary Ridge and the town, the enemy having at that time a fire upon them from both flanks and the rear, and no infantry replying. The batteries passed immediately through the town, and were placed with those of the Eleventh Corps in position on Cemetery Hill, so as to command the town and the approaches from the northwest. The batteries north of the Baltimore pike in front of the cemetery gate, under the command of Colonel Wainwright, chief of artillery, First Corps, were posted as follows: Stewart's battery (B, Fourth United States, four light 12-pounders) across the road, so as to command the approaches from town; then Wiedrich's (I, First New York Artillery, four 3-inch), Cooper's (B, First Pennsylvania Artillery, four 3-inch), and Reynolds' (L, First New York Artillery, five 3-inch), in all thirteen 3-inch guns, along the north front, some of them in such a position that they could be turned to bear upon the town and the field of battle of the 1st. Stevens' battery (Fifth Maine, six 12-pounders) was posted to the right and some 50 yards in front of this line, on a knoll, from whence they could obtain an oblique fire upon the hills in front of our line, and a flanking fire at close quarters upon any attacking columns. Each of the guns in these batteries had a small earthwork thrown up in its front, to afford a partial shelter from the fire of the enemy's sharpshooters. Osborn's batteries (Bancroft's, G, Fourth U.S. Artillery, six 12-pounders; Dilger's, I, First Ohio, six 12-pounders; Wheeler's, Thirteenth New York, three 3-inch), of the Eleventh Corps, with the exception of Wiedrich's, transferred to Colonel Wainwright, Heckman's, crippled and sent to the rear, and one gun of

Wheeler's dismounted, were placed in the cemetery grounds, to the north of the Baltimore road.

On the night of July 1, the commanding general left Taneytown, and reached Gettysburg about 2 A.M. of the 2d. Soon after his arrival, he directed me to see to the position of the artillery, and make such arrangements respecting it as were necessary. I examined the positions at Cemetery Hill, so far as the darkness would permit, and then accompanied the general and Major-General Howard in an inspection of the west front of the field, occupied by the Second and Third Corps. Cemetery Hill commanded the positions which could be occupied by the enemy to the north and northwest. Toward the south the line occupied the crest of a gentle elevation, which, concealing everything immediately behind it from the observation of the enemy, commanded the ground to the west, which sloped down gradually for a few hundred yards, and then rising, formed another crest, varying from half to three-quarters of a mile distant. The summit of this crest was wooded, and toward the south bent eastwardly and crossed the Emmitsburg road, forming a very favorable position for the enemy's artillery, and affording concealment to his movements in that direction. About half or three-quarters of a mile south of the cemetery our own crest and the ground in front of it were broken by groves of trees, and still farther on by rough and rocky ground. At a distance of about 2 miles from Cemetery Hill, a high, rocky, and broken peak formed the natural termination of our lines. The broken character of the ground in front of the southern half of our line was unfavorable to the use of artillery. From the cemetery, as a center, the right of our line extended toward the east, and lay on the north of the Baltimore pike. The ground is hilly, heavily wooded, and intersected with ravines and small water-courses, very unfavorable to the use of artillery. The First and Eleventh Corps were stationed on and near Cemetery Hill. The Second Corps (Hancock's) stretched along the crest on the left of the Cemetery Hill, with the Third Corps (Sickles') on its left. To the right of the cemetery lay a portion of the First Corps (Newton's), and beyond it the Twelfth (Slocum's).

At or near daylight, Major-General Slocum reported to the commanding general that there was a gap between the left of his line and the right of the First Corps, which he feared would be taken advantage of by the enemy, as he apprehended an immediate attack. The general commanding then gave me directions to make the necessary arrangements to meet the emergency. I considered this, in connection with the order previously given me, as a recognition, for the present, at least, of the position I had held at Antietam and Fredericksburg, as commander of the artillery of the army, and proceeded to make the necessary dispositions and to give all directions I considered necessary during the rest of the battle. In order to cover the gap between the First and Second Corps, the batteries of the Twelfth Corps (Muhlenberg's, F, Fourth United States, six 12-pounders; Kinzie's K, Fifth United States, four 12-pounders; Winegar's, M, First New York, four 10-pounders, and Knap's, E, Pennsylvania, six 10-pounders) were placed so as to command the outlet from that interval toward the Baltimore pike, and such of the batteries on Cemetery Hill as commanded the ground and its approaches from the side of the enemy were also placed in position. The interval between the lines was too broken and too heavily wooded to permit the artillery to be placed on the immediate line of battle. These positions were held by the batteries until the infantry line was completed and well strengthened, when the artillery was arranged for any attack the enemy could make.

The batteries at the cemetery, under command of Colonel Wainwright, remained as already described, and Major Osborn, chief of artillery of the Eleventh Corps, was directed to take command on the south of the road. I re-enforced him with half of Hall's battery (Second Maine, three 3-inch) from the First Corps, the other half being disabled, and five batteries (Eakin's, H, First United States, six 12-pounders; Taft's, Fifth New York, six 20-pounders; Hill's, C, First West Virginia, four 10-pounders; Huntington's, H, First Ohio, six 3-inch, and Edgell's, First New Hampshire, six 3-inch) from the Artillery Reserve, thus placing at his disposal, including the three batteries (Bancroft's, G, Fourth United States, six 12-pounders;

Dilger's, I, First Ohio, six 12-pounders, and Wheeler's, Thirteenth New York, three 3-inch) of his own corps remaining to him, six 20-pounder Parrotts, twenty-two light rifles, and eighteen light 12-pounders. These were stationed as follows: On the right, resting next the Baltimore road and facing the Emmitsburg, Dilger; on his left, Bancroft; then, in the order named, Eakin, Wheeler, Hill, and Hall. These eighteen light 12-pounders and ten light rifles commanded the enemy's positions to the right of the town. In rear of Bancroft and perpendicular to him were Taft's six 20-pounder Parrotts; on Taft's right and rear were Huntington's 3-inch guns; these batteries facing the north. This arrangement, in connection with that of Wainwright, brought all the positions within range of the cemetery that the enemy could occupy with artillery under a commanding fire. The batteries were all brought into requisition at different periods of the battle.

July 2, during the morning, several moving columns of the enemy, passing toward our right, were shelled, and compelled to make detours, or seek the cover of ravines to make their movements.

At about 3.30 P.M. the enemy established a battery of ten guns (four 20-pounders and six 10-pounder Parrotts) in a wheat-field to the north and a little to the east of the Cemetery Hill, and distant some 1,200 or 1,300 yards, and opened a remarkably accurate fire upon our batteries. We soon gained a decided advantage over them, and at the end of an hour or more compelled them to withdraw, drawing off two of their pieces by hand. Twenty-eight horses were afterward found on the knoll. The enemy suffered severely, and, although we were successful, we had cause to regret that our 4½-inch guns had been left at Westminster, as the position offered great advantages for them.

The enemy endeavored to re-establish his battery farther to his right, but as we could in this position bring a larger number of guns to bear than before, he was soon driven off. Cooper's battery (B, First Pennsylvania, four 3-inch), which had suffered severely in this affair, was now relieved by Ricketts', from the Artillery Reserve.

In this cannonade, Lieut. C. P. Eakin, First U.S. Artillery, was badly wounded and carried off the field, and Lieut. P. D. Mason, First U.S. Artillery, assumed command of the battery.

About the same hour, 3.30 P.M., as the enemy was seriously annoying the left of the Twelfth Corps, three guns of Knap's battery, under command of Lieutenant Geary, and Van Reed's section of K, Fifth U.S. Artillery, were placed in an eligible position, about 200 yards from the right of the First Corps. As soon as their presence (Knap's Pennsylvania Battery, 10-pounders, and Kinzie's, K, Fifth U.S. Artillery, light 12-pounders) was noticed, the enemy turned his battery (eight guns) upon them, but after a spirited contest of thirty minutes, in which he had a caisson blown up, his guns were silenced. The conduct of both Lieutenants Geary and Van Reed is highly spoken of by their chiefs of artillery.

When the infantry of the Twelfth Corps crossed over to the support of the Third Corps, on the left of our line, these guns were withdrawn and rejoined their batteries.

About sunset the enemy again opened from a knoll in front of the cemetery, distant about 1,800 yards, and this was soon followed by a powerful infantry attack on the position by General Rodes' Louisiana [?] brigade.* As their columns moved out of the town, they came under the fire of Stevens' battery (Fifth Maine), at 800 yards' distance. Wheeling into line, they pushed up the hill. As their line became unmasked, all the guns that could be brought to bear upon them, some twenty, were opened, first with shrapnel and then with canister, with excellent effect. The center and left were beaten back, but their right worked their way up under cover of the houses, and pushed completely through Wiedrich's battery (I, First New York, six 3-inch) into Ricketts' (F and G, First Pennsylvania, six 3-inch). The cannoneers of both batteries stood well to their guns, and when no longer able to hold them, fought with handspikes, rammers, and even stones, joining the infantry in driving them out, and capturing several prisoners. This attack of Rodes was mainly repelled by the

---

* Rodes' division comprised only North Carolina, Georgia, and Alabama troops. Reference is probably to Hays' Louisiana brigade.—COMPILER.

artillery alone. The loss of the enemy was reported to be large by their wounded in the affair, who afterward fell under the care of our surgeons in Gettysburg.

About 12 M. a detachment of Berdan's Sharpshooters was sent into the woods near the point where the enemy's crest opposite the left of our army cuts the Emmitsburg road, and reported the enemy as moving in force toward our left flank.

About 2 P.M. General Sickles formed his corps in line to meet an attack from this direction, his right resting on the Emmitsburg road, in a peach orchard, in advance of the center of our left, and his line extending in a general direction toward Sugar Loaf or Round Top, a peak which terminated our line on the left. At this time I reached the ground, and found Captain Randolph, chief of artillery Third Corps, making arrangements to station his battery on the right, those on the left having already been posted as follows: Smith's battery (Fourth New York, six 10-pounders) on the extreme left and on a steep and rocky eminence in advance of Sugar Loaf, and on his right Winslow's (D, First New York, six 12-pounders), in a wheat-field, separated from Smith by a belt of woods. I accompanied Captain Randolph, first sending to General Tyler, commanding the Artillery Reserve, for two batteries, one of light 12-pounders and one of rifles, and assisted him in posting the other batteries as follows: Clark's battery (B, First New Jersey, six 10-pounders) on the line to the left of the peach orchard; Ames' (G, First New York, six 12-pounders), from the Artillery Reserve, in the orchard, both facing the south, and perpendicular to the Emmitsburg road; then along the Emmitsburg road and facing the west, Randolph's (E, First Rhode Island, six 12-pounders), and Seeley's (K, Fourth United States, six 12-pounders) batteries, Seeley's well to the right of Randolph's. While Ames and Clark were moving up, the enemy opened a brisk fire upon them from a position near the Emmitsburg road and on the opposite side of it.

By this time, about 3.30 P.M., Major McGilvery came up from the Artillery Reserve with three batteries—Bigelow's (Ninth Massachusetts, four 12-pounders); Phillips' (Fifth Massachusetts, six 3-inch), and Hart's (Fifteenth New York, four 12-pounders)—which I ordered into position on the left of Clark's. As I saw that more batteries of the enemy were getting into position on the south of the Emmitsburg road and forming opposite to this line, I sent to the reserve for more rifled guns, and then, as Smith (Fourth New York, six 10-pounders) had not opened, I went to his battery to ascertain the cause. When I arrived, he had succeeded in getting his guns into position, and just opened fire. As his position commanded that of the enemy and enfiladed their line, his fire was very effective, and with that of Ames (G, First New York, six 12-pounders) and Clark (B, First New Jersey, six 10-pounders) in front, soon silenced that battery. In the meantime the enemy had established his new batteries to the north of the road, and Smith turned his guns upon them. I now moved along the line and examined the condition of the different batteries. Winslow (D, First New York, six 12-pounders) had not yet been attacked, his position facing a wood at short range that the enemy had not yet occupied. Bigelow, Phillips, and Hart were hotly engaged, and the battle soon raged along the lines.

In the meantime the additional batteries ordered from the reserve —Thompson's (C and F, Pennsylvania, six 3-inch) and Sterling's (Second Connecticut, four James and two howitzers), and Ransom's brigade, consisting of Thomas' (C, Fourth United States, six 12-pounders), Weir's (C, Fifth United States, six 12-pounders), and Turnbull's (F and K, Third United States, six 12-pounders) batteries —were brought up by General Tyler in person. Ransom's brigade was formed on the crest, above general headquarters, and soon after Turnbull's, Weir's, and Thomas' batteries were ordered forward to join Humphreys' division, taking position on the right of Seeley.

Some time after, two batteries of the Fifth Corps—Watson's (I, Fifth United States, four 3-inch) and Walcott's (C, Massachusetts Artillery, six 12-pounders)—were brought upon the ground by some staff officer of General Sickles; but for this there seemed to be no necessity, abundant provision having been made to supply all needs from the Artillery Reserve. The effect was to deprive the Fifth Corps of its batteries, without the knowledge and to the inconvenience of the commander of the corps. The batteries were exposed to heavy front and enfilading fires, and suffered terribly, but as rapidly as any were disabled they were retired and replaced by others. Watson (I, Fifth United States, four 3-inch) relieved Ames' battery (G, First New York, six 12-pounders); Thompson's (Pennsylvania, six 3-inch) took position near it, relieving Hart (Fifteenth New York, four 12-pounders). Turnbull's (F and K, Third United States, six 12-pounders) was posted near the Emmitsburg road. The officers and men performed their duties with great gallantry and success, notwithstanding the unfavorable nature of the ground, which gave the enemy all the advantages of position, driving off several of the enemy's batteries, silencing others, and doing good execution on his infantry, until about 5.30 or 6 P.M., when the line was forced back, and the batteries were compelled to withdraw.

So great had been the loss in men and horses, that many of the carriages had to be withdrawn by hand and others left on the field, which, with the exception of four, were afterward brought off. Three of these belonged to Smith's battery (Fourth New York, six 10-pounders), on our extreme left. The guns were stationed on the brow of a very precipitous and rocky height, beyond a ravine in front of our line. The difficulty of getting these guns up the height had caused the delay in Smith's opening his fire. He fought them to the last moment in hopes of keeping the enemy off, and in the belief that the ground would be in our possession again before the guns could be carried off by the enemy. He got off one of the four guns he had placed on the height, but was compelled to abandon the other three. The fourth of the guns lost belonged to Thompson's battery, the horses being all killed, the men engaged in hauling off the other pieces by hand, and his infantry supports having left him. In withdrawing, many acts of gallantry were performed, the enemy in several instances being driven out from the batteries by the cannoneers and such assistance as they could procure from the infantry near them. The line reformed on the crest, which constituted our original line, and repulsed all further attacks.

The batteries of the Second Corps were posted on the morning of the 2d by its chief of artillery, Captain Hazard, First Rhode Island Artillery, as follows, from left to right, connecting with the batteries of the Third Corps on the left, and those on Cemetery Hill on the right: Rorty's (B, First New York, four 10-pounders), Brown's (B, First Rhode Island, six 12-pounders), Cushing's (A, Fourth United States, six 3-inch), Arnold's (A, First Rhode Island, six 3-inch), and Woodruff's (I, First United States, six 12-pounders). The enemy opened upon them several times during the morning, but were always silenced by their concentrated fire.

When the Third Corps fell back, about 6 P.M., their batteries opened a vigorous fire, and the two left batteries (Rorty's and Brown's) conformed their movements to those of the infantry. When the crest of the hill occupied by our lines was reached, it gave the batteries a commanding position; a rapid fire was opened, and the enemy gradually driven back. Brown's battery suffered so severely in men and horses that it became necessary to send two guns to the rear.

The artillery of the Fifth Corps arrived on the field between 4 and 5 P.M. Hazlett's (D, Fifth United States, six 10-pounders), Walcott's (C, Massachusetts Artillery, six 12-pounders), and Watson's (I, Fifth United States, four 3-inch) batteries, with the First Division of the corps; Gibbs' (L, First Ohio, six 12-pounders), and Barnes' (C, First New York, four 3-inch), with Second Division. I have already stated that Watson's and Walcott's were taken from their positions by order of Major-General Sickles, and noted their services. Walcott's was not engaged, but was under fire; 6 men wounded, and 6 horses killed and wounded.

About 4.30 P.M. Hazlett's battery was moved to the extreme left, placed in position on Round Top, and immediately opened upon that portion of the enemy's force which attacked the First Division, and continued it until night with marked effect, as its fire enfiladed the enemy's line. Guthrie's section of Gibbs' battery was posted on the same hill on the right of Hazlett, and Walworth's section at the base of the hill, commanding the ravine in front of Round Top, the remaining section being held in reserve. These sections did excellent service, especially Guthrie's. On this afternoon, Lieut. Charles E. Hazlett, Fifth U.S. Artillery, a young officer, who had gained an enviable reputation for gallantry, skill, and devotion to his country and the service, received a mortal wound, and died the same evening.

For more detailed reports of the services of the artillery in the action on our left, I respectfully refer to the reports of General Tyler, commanding Artillery Reserve, and to the reports of the chiefs of artillery of the Second, Third, and Fifth Corps, transmitted herewith. It will be perceived that the batteries suffered severely in officers, men, and horses, losing a large proportionate number of officers—3 killed (Lieut. Charles E. Hazlett, Fifth Artillery, commanding Battery B; Lieut. M. Livingston, Third Artillery, commanding Turnbull's battery; Lieut. C. Erickson, Bigelow's battery); and 12 wounded (Capt. D. R. Ransom, Third Artillery, commanding Regular Brigade, Artillery Reserve; Capt. J. Thompson, C, Pennsylvania Artillery; Capt. N. Irish, D, Pennsylvania Artillery; Capt. Patrick Hart, Fifteenth New York Battery; Lieut. T. F. Brown, Hazard's battery; Lieut. Samuel Canby, Fourth Artillery, Cushing's battery; Lieut. J. K. Bucklyn, First Rhode Island, Randolph's battery; Lieut. F. W. Seeley, Fourth U.S. Artillery, commanding Battery K; Lieut. M. F. Watson, Fifth U.S. Artillery, commanding Battery I; Lieut. J. L. Miller, Thompson's battery, mortally; Lieut. E. M. Knox, Fifteenth New York Battery; Lieut. E. Spence, Ricketts' battery).

The night of the 2d was devoted in great part to repairing damages, replenishing the ammunition chests, and reducing and reorganizing such batteries as had lost so many men and horses as to be unable efficiently to work the full number of guns.

By daylight next morning this duty had been performed so far as possible, and, when it was found impossible to reorganize in time, the batteries were withdrawn, replaced by others from the Artillery Reserve, and finished their work during the next morning.

On the evening of July 2, a portion of Slocum's corps (the Second) [Twelfth], which formed the right of our line, was sent to re-enforce the left. During its absence, the enemy took possession of a portion of the line in the woods, and it was resolved to drive him out at daylight. Knap's battery (E, Pennsylvania, six 10-pounders) was placed on the hill known as Slocum's headquarters, and near the Baltimore pike, and Winegar's battery (M, First New York, four 10-pounders) at a short distance east of it. These batteries overlooked and commanded the ground vacated by the corps.

At 1 A.M. of the 3d, Muhlenberg's (F, Fourth United States, six 12-pounders) and Kinzie's (K, Fifth United States, four 12-pounders) batteries were posted opposite the center of the line of the Twelfth Corps, so as to command the ravine formed by Rock Creek.

At 4.30 A.M. these batteries opened, and fired without intermission for fifteen minutes into the wood, at a range of from 600 to 800 yards. Soon after daylight, Rigby's battery (A, Maryland, six 3-inch) was also placed on the hill, and at 5.30 A.M. all the batteries opened, and continued firing at intervals until 10 A.M., when the infantry succeeded in driving out the enemy and reoccupied their position of the day before. In this work the artillery rendered good service.

At our center, on and near Cemetery Hill, the batteries were in position very nearly the same as on the previous day. Those outside of the cemetery gate and north of the Baltimore pike, under the command of Colonel Wainwright, First New York Artillery, were, from right to left: Stevens' (Fifth Maine, six 12-pounders), Reynolds' (L, First New York, four 3-inch), Ricketts' (F, First Pennsylvania, six 3-inch)—which had relieved Cooper's (B, First Pennsylvania, four 3-inch) the night before—Wiedrich's (I, First New York, four 3-inch), and Stewart's (B, Fourth United States, four 12-pounders). The batteries south of the pike, and under command of Major Osborn, First New York Artillery, were: Dilger's (I, First Ohio, six 12-pounders), Bancroft's (G, Fourth United States, six 12-pounders), Eakin's (H, First United States, six 12-pounders), Wheeler's (Thirteenth New York, three 3-inch), Hill's (C, First West Virginia, four 10-pounders), and Taft's (Fifth New York, six 20-pounders).

On the left of the cemetery the batteries of the Second Corps were in line on the crest occupied by their corps in the following order, from right to left: Woodruff's (I, First United States, six 12-pounders), Arnold's (A, First Rhode Island, six 3-inch), Cushing's (A, Fourth United States, six 3-inch), Brown's (B, First Rhode Island, four 12-pounders), and Rorty's (B, First New York, four 10-pounders), all under command of Captain Hazard, chief of artillery.

Next on the left of the artillery of the Second Corps were stationed Thomas' battery (C, Fourth United States, six 12-pounders), and on his left Major McGilvery's command, consisting of Thompson's (C and F, Pennsylvania, five 3-inch), Phillips' (Fifth Massachusetts, six 3-inch), Hart's (Fifteenth New York, four 12-pounders), Sterling's (Second Connecticut, four James and two howitzers), Rank's section (two 3-inch), Dow's (Sixth Maine, four 12-pounders), and Ames' (G, First New York, six 12-pounders), all of the Artillery Reserve, to which was added, soon after the cannonade commenced, Cooper's battery (B, First Pennsylvania, four 3-inch), of the First Corps.

On our extreme left, occupying the position of the day before, were Gibbs' (L, First Ohio, six 12-pounders) and Rittenhouse's (late Hazlett's, D, Fifth United States, six 10-pounders) batteries. Gibbs' was, however, too distant from the enemy's position for 12-pounders, and was not used during the day, although under fire. Rittenhouse was in an excellent position for the service of his rifled guns, on the top of Round Top. We had thus on the western crest line seventy-five guns, which could be aided by a few of those on Cemetery Hill. There was but little firing during the morning.

At 10 A.M. I made an inspection of the whole line, ascertaining that all the batteries—only those of our right serving with the Twelfth Corps being engaged at the time—were in good condition and well supplied with ammunition. As the enemy was evidently increasing his artillery force in front of our left, I gave instructions to the batteries and to the chiefs of artillery not to fire at small bodies, nor to allow their fire to be drawn without promise of adequate results; to watch the enemy closely, and when he opened to concentrate the fire of their guns on one battery at a time until it was silenced; under all circumstances to fire deliberately, and to husband their ammunition as much as possible.

I had just finished my inspection, and was with Lieutenant Rittenhouse on the top of Round Top, when the enemy opened, at about 1 P.M., along his whole right, a furious cannonade on the left of our line. I estimated the number of his guns bearing on our west front at from one hundred to one hundred and twenty. I have since seen it stated by the enemy's correspondents that there were sixty guns from Longstreet's, and fifty-five from Hill's corps, making one hundred and fifteen in all. To oppose these we could not, from our restricted position, bring more than eighty to reply effectively. Our fire was well withheld until the first burst was over, excepting from the extreme right and left of our positions. It was then opened deliberately and with excellent effect. As soon as the nature of the enemy's attack was made clear, and I could form an opinion as to the number of his guns, for which my position afforded great facility, I went to the park of the Artillery Reserve, and ordered all the batteries to be ready to move at a moment's notice, and hastened to report to the commanding general, but found he had left his headquarters. I then proceeded along the line, to observe the effects of the cannonade and to replace such batteries as should become disabled.

About 2.30 P.M., finding our ammunition running low and that it was very unsafe to bring up loads of it, a number of caissons and limbers having been exploded, I directed that the fire should be gradually stopped, which was done, and the enemy soon slackened his fire also. I then sent orders for such batteries as were necessary to replace exhausted ones, and all that were disposable were sent me.

About 3 P.M., and soon after the enemy's fire had ceased, he formed a column of attack in the edge of the woods in front of the Second Corps. At this time Fitzhugh's (K, First New York, six 3-inch), Parsons' (A, First New Jersey, six 10-pounders), Weir's (C, Fifth United States, six 12-pounders), and Cowan's (First New York Independent, six 3-inch) batteries reached this point, and were put in position in front of the advancing enemy. I rode down to McGilvery's batteries, and directed them to take the enemy in flank as they approached. The enemy advanced magnificently, unshaken by the shot and shell which tore through his ranks from his front and from our left. The batteries of the Second Corps on our right, having nearly exhausted their supply of ammunition, except canister, were compelled to withhold their fire until the enemy, who approached in three lines, came within its range. When our canister fire and musketry were opened upon them, it occasioned disorder, but still they advanced gallantly until they reached the stone wall behind which our troops lay. Here ensued a desperate conflict, the enemy succeeding in passing the wall and entering our lines, causing great destruction of life, especially among the batteries. Infantry troops were, however, advanced from our right; the rear line of the enemy broke, and the others, who had fought with a gallantry that excited the admiration of our troops, found themselves cut off and compelled to surrender. As soon as their fate was evident, the enemy opened his batteries upon the masses of our troops at this point without regard to the presence of his own. Toward the close of this struggle, Rorty's (B, First New York, four 10-pounders), Arnold's (A, First Rhode Island, six 3-inch), and Cushing's (A, Fourth United States, six 3-inch) batteries, which had lost heavily in men and horses, were withdrawn, and as soon as the affair was over their places were filled with fresh ones.

Soon the necessary measures had been taken to restore this portion of the line to an efficient condition. It required but a few minutes, as the batteries, as fast as withdrawn from any point, were sent to the Artillery Reserve, replenished with ammunition, reorganized, returned to the rear of the lines, and there awaited assignment. I then went to the left, to see that proper measures had been taken there for the same object. On my way, I saw that the enemy was forming a second column of attack to his right of the point where the first was formed, and in front of the position of the First Corps (Newton's). I gave instructions to the artillery, under command of Major McGilvery, to be ready to meet the first movements of the enemy in front, and, returning to the position of the Second Corps, directed the batteries there, mostly belonging to the Artillery Reserve, to take the enemy in flank as he advanced. When the enemy moved, these orders were well executed, and before he reached our line he was brought to a stand. The appearance of a body of our infantry moving down in front of our lines from the direction of the Second Corps caused the enemy to move off by his right flank, under cover of the woods and undergrowth, and, a few minutes after, the column had broken up, and in the utmost confusion the men of which it was composed fled across the ground over which they had just before advanced, and took refuge behind their batteries. The attacks on the part of the enemy were not well managed. Their artillery fire was too much dispersed, and failed to produce the intended effect. It was, however, so severe and so well sustained that it put to the test, and fully proved, the discipline and excellence of our troops. The two assaults, had they been simultaneous, would have divided our artillery fire. As it was, each attack was met by a heavy front and flank fire of our artillery, the batteries which met the enemy directly in front in one assault taking him in flank in the other.

The losses of the artillery on this day, and especially in the assault on the Second Corps, were very large. The loss in officers was 3 killed, 2 mortally and 9 severely wounded. Killed: Capt. J. M. Rorty, B, First New York; Lieut. A. H. Cushing, Fourth United States; Lieut. G. A. Woodruff, First United States (mortally wounded); Lieut. J. S. Milne, First Rhode Island; Lieut. A. H. Whitaker, Ninth Massachusetts (wounded severely); Capt. J. Bigelow, Ninth Massachusetts; Lieut. A. S. Sheldon, B, First New York; Lieut. H. H. Baldwin, Fifth United States; Lieut. J. McGilvray, Fourth United States; Lieut. R. C. Hazlett, Fourth Pennsylvania Battery; Lieut. J. Stephenson, Fourth Pennsylvania Battery; Lieut. H. D. Scott, Battery E, Massachusetts; Lieut. W. P. Wright, First New York Battery; Lieut. W. H. Johnson, First New York Battery. Captain Rorty, who had taken command of his battery but three days before, fell, fighting, at his guns. Lieutenants Cushing and Woodruff belonged to a class of young officers who, although of the lowest commissioned rank, have gained distinguished army reputation. The destruction of *matériel* was large. The enemy's cannonade, in which he must have almost exhausted his ammunition, was well sustained, and cost us a great many horses and the explosion of an unusually large number of caissons and limbers. The whole slope behind our crest, although concealed from the enemy, was swept by his shot, and offered no protection to horses or carriages. The enemy's superiority in the number of guns was fully matched by the superior accuracy of ours, and a personal inspection of the line he occupied, made on the 5th, enables me to state with certainty that his losses in *matériel* in this artillery combat were equal to ours, while the marks of the shot in the trees on both crests bear conclusive evidence of the superiority of our practice.

This struggle closed the battle, and the night of the 3d, like the previous one, was devoted to repairs and reorganization. A large number of batteries had been so reduced in men and horses that many guns and carriages, after completing the outfit of those which remained with the army, were sent to the rear and turned in to the ordnance department.

Our losses in the three days' operations, as reported, were as follows:

Casualties, July 1, 2, and 3.

Organizations.	Number of guns.	Killed.		Wounded.		Missing.	Horses.
		Officers.	Men.	Officers.	Men.		
In the corps.............	212	5	57	18	361	52	565
Artillery Reserve..........	108	2	41	15	171	15	316
Total................	320	7	98	33	532	67	881

Of these 320 guns, 142 were light 12-pounders, 106 3-inch guns, 6 20-pounders, 60 10-pounder Parrott guns, and a battery of 4 James rifles and 2 12-pounder howitzers, which joined the army on the march to Gettysburg. This table excludes the Horse Artillery, 44 3-inch guns, serving with the cavalry. It will be seen that the Artillery Reserve, every gun of which was brought into requisition, bore, as in all the campaigns of the Army of the Potomac, its full share, and more, of the losses.

The expenditure of ammunition in the three days amounted to 32,781 rounds, averaging over 100 rounds per gun. Many rounds were lost in the caissons and limbers by explosions and otherwise. The supply carried with the army being 270 rounds per gun, left sufficient to fill the ammunition chests and enable the army to fight another battle. There was for a short time during the battle a fear that the ammunition would give out. This fear was caused by the large and unreasonable demands made by corps commanders who had left their own trains or a portion of them behind, contrary to the orders of the commanding general. In this emergency, the train of the Artillery Reserve, as on so many other occasions, supplied all demands, and proved its great usefulness to the army.

For a more particular account of the operations of the artillery and of their relations to those of the other arms of service, I respectfully refer to the report of the commander of the Artillery Reserve, and to those of the chiefs of artillery of the army corps, transmitted herewith, to which reports I also refer for the names of those who distinguished themselves by their conduct and courage.

I have to acknowledge my indebtedness to these officers: Brig. Gen. R. O. Tyler, commanding Artillery Reserve; Col. C. S. Wainwright, First New York Artillery, First Corps; Capt. J. G. Hazard, First Rhode Island Artillery, Second Corps; Capt. G. E. Randolph, First Rhode Island Artillery, Third Corps; Capt. A. P. Martin, Third Massachusetts Battery, Fifth Corps; Col. C. H. Tompkins, First Rhode Island Artillery, Sixth Corps; Maj. T. W. Osborn, First New York Artillery, Eleventh Corps; Lieut. E. D. Muhlenberg, Fourth U.S. Artillery, Twelfth Corps, for the zealous co-operation in all the administrative labors that devolved upon me, and for the efficiency with which they discharged their duties in the field.

My staff—Lieut. Col. E. R. Warner, First New York Artillery, inspector of artillery; Capt. J. N. Craig, assistant adjutant-general, and Lieut. C. E. Bissell, aide-de-camp—performed the duties devolving upon them with intelligence and gallantry.

Upon Lieutenant-Colonel Warner fell much of the labor required in the reorganization of batteries withdrawn from the field and in replacing them. These duties and others which devolved upon him were discharged with his accustomed energy and thoroughness. Lieutenant Bissell was my only aide, and was, therefore, busily employed. He was much exposed, his duties keeping him more or less under fire at every point at which attacks were made.

In my report of the battle of Chancellorsville, I took occasion to call attention to the great evils arising from the want of field officers for the artillery. The operations of this campaign, and especially the battle of Gettysburg, afford further proofs, if such were necessary, of the mistaken policy of depriving so important an arm of the officers necessary for managing it. In this campaign, for the command of 67 batteries (372 guns), with over 8,000 men and 7,000 horses, and all the *matériel*, and large ammunition trains, I had one general officer commanding the reserve, and but four field officers (Brig. Gen. R. O. Tyler, U.S. Volunteers, commanding Artillery Reserve; Lieut. Col. F. McGilvery, First Maine Artillery, commanding brigade Artillery Reserve; Col. C. H. Tompkins, First Rhode Island Artillery, Sixth Corps; Col. C. S. Wainwright, First New York Artillery, First Corps; Maj. T. W. Osborn, First New York Artillery, Eleventh Corps; Capt. J. M. Robertson, Second U.S. Artillery, commanding First Brigade Horse Artillery; Capt. J. C. Tidball, Second U.S. Artillery, commanding Second Brigade Horse Artillery).

In the seven corps, the artillery of two were commanded by colonels, of one by a major, of three by captains, and of one by a lieutenant, taken from their batteries for the purpose. The two brigades of horse artillery attached to the cavalry were commanded by captains, and there was one field officer in the reserve. The most of these commands in any other army would have been considered proper ones for a general officer. In no army would the command of the artillery of a corps be considered of less importance, to say the least, than that of a brigade of infantry. In none of our corps ought the artillery commander to have been of less rank than a colonel, and in all there should have been a proper proportion of field officers, with the necessary staffs. The defects of our organization were made palpable at Gettysburg, not only on the field, but in the necessary and important duties of reorganizing the batteries, repairing damages, and getting the artillery in condition to renew the battle, or take the road in efficient condition on the morning after a conflict.

I respectfully and urgently call the attention of the commanding general, and through him of the War Department, to this subject.

Not only does the service suffer, necessarily, from the great deficiency of officers of rank, but a policy which closes the door of promotion to battery officers, and places them and the arm itself under a ban, and degrades them in comparison with other arms of service, induces discontent, and has caused many of our best officers to seek positions, wherever they can find them, which will remove them from this branch of the service. We have lost many such officers, and unless something is done to cure the evil we will lose more.

The reports of the horse artillery were rendered to the cavalry officers under whose orders they served, and I have not yet received all of them. As their operations were detached from those of the main body of the army, and do not naturally connect with them, I reserve them as the subject of a separate report.

Very respectfully, your obedient servant,

HENRY J. HUNT,
Brigadier-General and Chief of Artillery, Commanding.

Brig. Gen. S. WILLIAMS,
Assistant Adjutant-General, Army of the Potomac.

ARTILLERY HDQRS. ARMY OF THE POTOMAC,
October 4, 1863.

GENERAL: In compliance with your directions, I have the honor to state that the following were the captures from the army in the recent operations:

First Corps lost one gun, 3-inch, from Reynolds' battery (L, First New York), July 1; Eleventh Corps, one light 12-pounder, Heckman's battery (K, First Ohio), July 1; Third Corps, three 10-pounder Parrotts, Smith's Fourth Independent New York Battery, July 2; Artillery Reserve, one 3-inch, Thompson's battery, Third and Fourth Pennsylvania, July 2; six lost.

I received no report of captures from the enemy in an official form, although I heard that the cavalry had picked up several on the road, and that two were taken at Falling Waters.

Respectfully, your obedient servant,

HENRY J. HUNT,
Major-General, Chief of Artillery.

Brig. Gen. S. WILLIAMS,
Assistant Adjutant-General.

Appendix D

Report of Brig. Gen. William N. Pendleton, C. S. Army, Chief of Artillery.

HDQRS. ARTILLERY CORPS, ARMY OF NORTHERN VIRGINIA,
September 12, 1863.

GENERAL: A report of artillery operations during the late campaign I have now the honor to submit. It has been somewhat retarded by delays on the part of battalion commanders.

The severe contests near Fredericksburg early in May having resulted disastrously to the enemy, opportunity was allowed us of repairing losses and getting ready for subsequent operations. To this end my energies were directed throughout the month of May. What has been the general reserve was distributed, and the three corps, into which the army was now divided, had assigned to each five artillery battalions, averaging four four-gun batteries, each battalion being satisfactorily equipped and well commanded, and the group for each corps being under charge of a suitable chief.

On June 5, when preparations were in progress for a removal of general headquarters on the new campaign, the First and Second Corps having already marched toward Culpeper, the enemy appeared in some force opposite Fredericksburg, and in the afternoon opened a heavy artillery fire near the mouth of Deep Run, under cover of which they established, as some months before, a pontoon bridge, and pushed across a body of infantry. That evening and the following morning were employed in adjusting the artillery and other troops of the Third Corps left on the Fredericksburg Heights for this very contingency. But indications being satisfactory that the movement was only a feint, the commanding general soon after mid-day moved forward. According to instructions, my own course was also directed toward Culpeper, where, after a bivouac for the night, we arrived early on Sunday morning, June 7.

On the afternoon of June 13, the Second Corps, Lieutenant-General Ewell commanding, which had a day or two before marched from Culpeper, approached Winchester, and Lieutenant-Colonel [R. S.] Andrews' artillery battalion operated with effect in driving back the enemy's advance on the Front Royal road. In the attack upon the enemy's fortifications next day, resulting in his hasty retreat and the capture of his guns and stores, most valuable service was rendered by the artillery under the immediate command of Lieutenant-Colonel [H. P.] Jones, and the general charge of the acting chief of artillery for the corps, Col. J. T. Brown. The works and their armament were alike formidable, and that they were thus rendered untenable by the enemy evinces at once the skill with which our batteries were composed and the resolution with which they were served. The death of Captain [C.] Thompson, of the Louisiana Guard Artillery, a most gallant and esteemed officer, was part of the price of this victory.

Retreating toward Charlestown, the enemy, near Jordan Springs, on the morning of the 15th, encountered, with Johnson's division, which had marched to intercept him, Lieutenant-Colonel Andrews' artillery battalion. The sharp action ensuing, which resulted in the rout of the enemy and capture of most of his men, was especially remarkable for the unexampled steadiness with which artillery fought infantry skirmishers at close quarters. Lieutenant [Charles S.] Contee, who commanded a section, in a contest of this kind dis-tinguished himself by cool and persistent daring, and several non-commissioned officers are mentioned by their commanders as evincing like gallantry. Lieutenant-Colonel Andrews and Lieutenant Contee were in this affair painfully, though not very dangerously, wounded. While these events were transpiring at and near Win-chester, General Rodes' division, accompanied by Lieutenant-

Colonel Carter's artillery battalion, having marched by Berryville, approached Martinsburg, where was an additional force of the enemy. Under the well-directed fire of Colonel Carter's batteries, that force speedily abandoned the town, leaving, in addition to twenty-three captured in Winchester, five superior field guns.

In these several engagements our batteries lost 6 men killed and 15 wounded.

The Second Corps, in its subsequent advance across the Potomac into Maryland and Pennsylvania, was attended by its five battalions, Lieutenant-Colonel Carter's, Lieutenant-Colonel Andrews', Lieutenant-Colonel Jones', Colonel Brown's, and Lieutenant-Colonel [William] Nelson's, the three former marching with Rodes', Johnson's, and Early's divisions, the two latter constituting a corps reserve. Simultaneously with these movements of the Second Corps, the First and Third were put in motion, each accompanied by its own artillery force.

The First Corps, Lieutenant-General Longstreet commanding, left Culpeper June 15, attended by Major [M. W.] Henry's, Colonel [H. C.] Cabell's, Major [James] Dearing's, Colonel [E. Porter] Alexander's, and Major [B. F.] Eshleman's artillery battalions, the three former marching with Hood's, McLaws', and Pickett's divisions, and the two latter constituting a corps reserve. As the route of this corps lay along the eastern slope of the Blue Ridge, to guard the several passes of that barrier against incursions of the enemy, its artillery was subjected to serious trial from roads frequently difficult and generally rough, and marches, under extreme heat, more than usually long. Additional labor was also imposed on some of the battalions by the necessity of meeting certain demonstrations of the enemy. Actual contest beyond cavalry skirmishing he declined.

The Third Corps, on June 15, left Fredericksburg *en route* for Culpeper and the Shenandoah Valley, via Front Royal, accompanied by its artillery battalions, viz.: Lieutenant-Colonel [John J.] Garnett's, Major [W. T.] Poague's, and Lieutenant-Colonel [A. S.] Cutts', attending the divisions of Generals Heth, Pender, and Anderson, and Majors [D. G.] McIntosh's and [W. J.] Pegram's battalions as a corps reserve. In this advance, general headquarters being with the First Corps, my own were thereby also chiefly regulated.

On June 16, after a week at Culpeper of such artillery preparation and supervision as were requisite and practicable, I marched toward the Valley, attending near the commanding general, to be ready for such service as might be required.

On the 25th, the army, having sufficiently rested in camp near Millwood and Berryville, crossed the Potomac, the Third Corps at Shepherdstown, the First at Williamsport, the commanding general being with the latter, and my duties lying near him.

On Wednesday, July 1, Chambersburg, Pa., having been reached by easy marches and passed, after a rest of one or two days, and the army being in motion toward Gettysburg, occasional cannon-shots in that direction were heard by myself and others with the main body, as before noon we crossed the mountain. Two divisions of the Third Corps (Heth's and Pender's, the former with Pegram's artillery battalion, the latter with McIntosh's) were in advance on this road; while of the Second Corps, Early's division, attended by Jones' artillery battalion, was approaching from the direction of York, and Rodes' from that of Carlisle, accompanied by Carter's battalion. The advance of the Third Corps had encountered at Gettysburg a force of the enemy, and the firing heard was the beginning of a battle. Its significance, however, was not then fully understood. It might be only a passing skirmish; it might be more serious. After a brief pause near Cashtown, to see how it would prove, the commanding general, finding the cannonade to continue and increase, moved rapidly forward. I did the same, and, at his request, rode near him for instructions. Arriving near the crest of an eminence more than a mile west of the town, dismounting and leaving horses under cover, on foot we took position overlooking the field. It was, perhaps, 2 o'clock, and the battle was raging with considerable violence. The troops of the Second Corps having reached the field some time after the engagement was opened by those of the Third, Carter's and Jones' batteries were at the time of our arrival plied on the left with freshness and vigor upon the batteries and infantry that had been pressing the Third Corps, and, when these turned upon their new assailants, they were handsomely enfiladed by the batteries of McIntosh and Pegram, posted in front of our lookout on the left and right of the road. To counteract this damaging double attack, the enemy made, especially with his artillery, such effort as he could. Observing the course of events, the commanding general suggested whether positions on the right could not be found to enfilade the valley between our position and the town and the enemy's batteries next the town. My services were immediately tendered, and the endeavor made. Where the Fairfield road crosses one range of hills was the farthest to the right admissible, as there was no infantry support near, and a wooded height a few hundred yards beyond seemed occupied by the enemy. Here some guns that had been sent for from McIntosh's battalion were posted, under Capt. M. Johnson; but to advance them and open fire was not deemed proper till some infantry should arrive, the need of which had been promptly reported. They were more or less under fire from the first.

Meanwhile the enemy yielded ground on the left. Our batteries as well as infantry were advanced, and additional troops came up. Garnett's battalion moved to the front, slightly participating in the fight, and then, under cover of a hill near the brick seminary, awaited orders. Poague's battalion also arrived, and moved to Garnett's right into line under cover across the Fairfield road, between Captain Johnson's position and the town.

Having sent members of my staff to reconnoiter the woods on the right, and explore, as well as they might be able, a road observed along a ravine back of those woods, I now pushed forward on the Fairfield road to the ridge adjoining the town, intending to put there Garnett's and other guns which had been previously ordered forward. The position was within range of the hill beyond the town, to which the enemy was retreating, and where he was massing his batteries. General Ramseur coming up from the town, which his command had just occupied, met me at this point, and requested that our batteries might not then open, as they would draw a concentrated fire upon his men, much exposed. Unless as part of a combined assault, I at once saw it would be worse than useless to open fire there. Captain [V.] Maurin, of Garnett's battalion, in command of several batteries, was therefore directed to post his guns, and be ready, but to keep his horses under cover, and not to fire till further orders. Having further examined this ridge, and communicated with Colonel Walker, chief of artillery Third Corps, I returned across the battlefield, and sent to inform the commanding general of the state of facts, especially of the road to the right, believed to be important toward a flank movement against the enemy in his new position. While these operations occurred, Andrews' battalion and the two reserve battalions, Second Corps, came up with Johnson's division on the Cashtown road, and proceeded to join the other troops of their corps on the left, and Colonel Brown, acting chief of artillery for that corps, sent to find, if practicable, an artillery route toward a wooded height commanding the enemy's right. No further attack, however, was made, and night closed upon the scene.

Early on the morning of the 2d, the enemy being now strongly posted on the heights to which he had retired the previous evening, the artillery of the Second Corps occupied positions from the Seminary Hill, around to the left, the gallant Major [J. W.] Latimer, commanding Andrews' battalion, being on the extreme left, and Colonel Brown's battalion, under Captain [W. J.] Dance, on the right, near the seminary. Farther to the right, on the Seminary Ridge, Colonel [R. L.] Walker posted the artillery of the Third Corps, excepting Poague's battalion and a portion of Garnett's, held for a season in reserve. From the farthest occupied point on the right and front, in company with Colonels [A. L.] Long and Walker and Captain [S. R.] Johnston (engineer), soon after sunrise, I surveyed the enemy's position toward some estimate of the ground and the best mode of attack. So far as judgment could be formed from such a view, assault on the enemy's left by our extreme right might succeed, should the mountain there offer no insuperable obstacle. To attack on that side, if practicable, I understood to be the purpose of the commanding general. Returning from this position more to the right and rear, for the sake of tracing more exactly the mode of approach, I proceeded some distance along the ravine road noticed the previous evening, and was made aware of having entered the enemy's lines by meeting two armed dismounted cavalrymen. Apparently surprised, they immediately surrendered, and were disarmed and sent to the rear with two of the three members of my staff present.

Having satisfied myself of the course and character of this road, I returned to an elevated point on the Fairfield road, which furnished a very extensive view, and dispatched messengers to General Longstreet and the commanding general. Between this point and the Emmitsburg road, the enemy's cavalry were seen in considerable force, and, moving up along that road toward the enemy's main position, bodies of infantry and artillery, accompanied by their trains. This front was, after some time, examined by Colonel [William P.] Smith and Captain Johnston (engineers), and about midday General Longstreet arrived and viewed the ground. He desired Colonel [E. P.] Alexander to obtain the best view he then could of the front. I therefore conducted the colonel to the advanced point of observation previously visited. Its approach was now more hazardous, from the fire of the enemy's sharpshooters, so that special caution was necessary in making the desired observation. Just then a sharp contest occurred in the woods to the right and rear of this forward point. Anderson's division, Third Corps, had moved up, and was driving the enemy from these woods. Poague's artillery battalion was soon after sent to co-operate with that division, and also a battery from Lane's battalion. These woods having been thus cleared of the enemy, some view of the ground beyond them, and much farther to the right than had yet been examined, seemed practicable. I therefore rode in that direction, and, when about to enter the woods, met the commanding general, *en route* himself for a survey of the ground.

There being here still a good deal of sharpshooting, the front had to be examined with caution. General Wilcox, commanding on the right of Anderson's division, had already seen beyond the farther edge of these woods, and, under his guidance, I accompanied Colonel

Long to the farm-house at the summit, where the cross-road from Fairfield, &c., emerges. Having noticed the field and the enemy's batteries, &c., I returned to General Longstreet, for the purpose of conducting his column to this point, and supervising, as might be necessary, the disposition of his artillery. He was advancing by the ravine road (as most out of view), time having been already lost in attempting another, which proved objectionable, because exposed to observation. On learning the state of facts ahead, the general halted, and sent back to hasten his artillery. Members of my staff were also dispatched to remedy, as far as practicable, the delay. Cabell's, Alexander's, and Henry's battalions at length arrived, and the whole column moved toward the enemy's left. Colonel Alexander, by General Longstreet's direction, proceeded to explore the ground still farther to the right, and Henry's battalion, accompanying Hood's division, was thrown in that direction. Upon these, as soon as observed, the enemy opened a furious cannonade, the course of which rendered necessary a change in the main artillery column. Cabell's battalion deflected to the right, while Alexander's was mainly parked for a season, somewhat under cover, till it could advance to better purpose. The fire on the cross-road through the woods having, after some time, slackened, I reconnoitered that front again. As before, the enemy was only a few hundred yards off, awaiting attack.

Soon after, at about 4 P.M., the general assault was made. Alexander's battalion moved into position, fronting the peach orchard near the Emmitsburg road, and opened with vigor, as did the battalions to its right. The enemy obstinately resisted, and our batteries suffered severely. Within an hour, however, his guns were silenced and his position was carried. Alexander then ran forward his pieces, which did effectual service in hastening and confining the enemy to his rear position on the mountain. Between his guns in that position and our batteries a cannonade was kept up, more or less briskly, till dark.

While the First Corps thus advanced into position and operated on the right, the batteries of the Third Corps from the advanced position in the center, early taken, occupied the attention of the enemy by a deliberate fire during the whole afternoon. Opportunity was once or twice taken by myself to observe the progress and effect of this fire. It elicited a spirited reply, and was useful in preventing full concentration by the enemy on either flank. On the left, attack was also delayed till the afternoon.

About 4 P.M. the guns of the Second Corps, in position on that front, generally opened with a well-directed and effective fire. This also (although the right seemed to claim my chief attention) was partially observed by me from the central ridge in rear of the Third Corps. Massed as were the enemy's batteries on the Cemetery Hill, fronting our left, and commanding as was their position, our artillery, admirably served as it was, operated there under serious disadvantage and with considerable loss. It still, however, for the most part, maintained its ground, and prepared the way for infantry operations. Here the gallant Major Latimer, so young and yet so exemplary, received the wound which eventuated in his death.

Thus stood affairs at nightfall, the 2d: On the left and in the center, nothing gained; on the right, batteries and lines well advanced, the enemy meanwhile strengthening himself in a position naturally formidable and everywhere difficult of approach.

By direction of the commanding general, the artillery along our entire line was to be prepared for opening, as early as possible on the morning of the 3d, a concentrated and destructive fire, consequent upon which a general advance was to be made. The right, especially, was, if practicable, to sweep the enemy from his stronghold on that flank. Visiting the lines at a very early hour toward securing readiness for this great attempt, I found much (by Colonel Alexander's energy) already accomplished on the right. Henry's battalion held about its original position on the flank. Alexander's was next, in front of the peach orchard. Then came the Washington Artillery Battalion, under Major Eshleman, and Dearing's battalion on his left, these two having arrived since dusk of the day before; and beyond Dearing, Cabell's battalion had been arranged, making nearly sixty guns for that wing, all well advanced in a sweeping curve of about a mile. In the posting of these there appeared little room for improvement, so judiciously had they been adjusted. To Colonel Alexander, placed here in charge by General Longstreet, the wishes of the commanding general were repeated. The battalion and battery commanders were also cautioned how to fire so as to waste as little ammunition as possible. To the Third Corps artillery attention was also given. Major Poague's battalion had been advanced to the line of the right wing, and was not far from its left. His guns also were well posted. Proper directions were also given to him and his officers. The other battalions of this corps, a portion of Garnett's, under Major [Charles] Richardson, being in reserve, held their positions of the day before, as did those of the Second Corps, each group having specific instructions from its chief. Care was also given to the convenient posting of ordnance trains, especially for the right, as most distant from the main depot, and due notice given of their position.

From some cause, the expected attack was delayed several hours. Meanwhile the enemy threw against our extreme right a considerable force, which was met with energy, Henry's battalion rendering, in its repulse, efficient service.

At length, about 1 P.M., on the concerted signal, our guns in position, nearly one hundred and fifty, opened fire along the entire line from right to left, salvos by battery being much practiced, as directed, to secure greater deliberation and power. The enemy replied with their full force. So mighty an artillery contest has perhaps never been waged, estimating together the number and character of guns and the duration of the conflict. The average distance between contestants was about 1,400 yards, and the effect was necessarily serious on both sides. With the enemy, there was advantage of elevation and protection from earthworks; but his fire was unavoidably more or less divergent, while ours was convergent. His troops were massed, ours diffused. We, therefore, suffered apparently much less. Great commotion was produced in his ranks, and his batteries were to such extent driven off or silenced as to have insured his defeat but for the extraordinary strength of his position.

Proceeding again to the right, to see about the anticipated advance of the artillery, delayed beyond expectation, I found, among other difficulties, many batteries getting out of or low in ammunition, and the all-important question of supply received my earnest attention. Frequent shell endangering the First Corps ordnance train in the convenient locality I had assigned it, it had been removed farther back. This necessitated longer time for refilling caissons. What was worse, the train itself was very limited, so that its stock was soon exhausted, rendering requisite demand upon the reserve train, farther off. The whole amount was thus being rapidly reduced. With our means, to keep up supply at the rate required for such a conflict proved practically impossible. There had to be, therefore, some relaxation of the protracted fire, and some lack of support for the deferred and attempted advance. But if this and other causes prevented our sweeping the enemy from his position, he was so crippled as to be incapable of any formidable movement. Night closed upon our guns in their advanced position. And had our resources allowed ammunition for the artillery to play another day, the tremendous part it had performed on this his stronghold could scarcely have sufficed to save the enemy from rout and ruin.

In the defensive measures directed for the 4th, my care was given to the whole line. The batteries on the right and left were drawn back and kept ready for emergencies. Two batteries of Garnett's battalion, Third Corps, two of Eshleman's, First Corps, and one of Jones', Second Corps, were detailed to report to General Imboden, at Cashtown, and aid in guarding the main wagon train back to Williamsport. The battalions generally remained in position most of the day. Nothing, however, was attempted by the enemy. That night artillery and infantry all moved to the rear.

After some casualties incident in part to the progress of such a train in an enemy's country, through mountains infested by cavalry attachments, the batteries accompanying General Imboden arrived with the train at Williamsport late on the 5th, and, on the 6th, did excellent service in repelling an attack of the enemy.

On the 7th, the artillery, with the body of the army, encamped near Hagerstown, without material incident since leaving Gettysburg. Men and animals were, however, much fatigued, and the latter greatly worn down by the hard service they had endured with light fare, and by heavy draught in roads rendered deep by continued rain, with numbers reduced by losses in battle.

On the 10th, attack being threatened by the enemy, the artillery, partaking the hopeful expectations of the whole army, earnestly participated in forming an extended and fortified line of battle, whose left rested on heights west of Hagerstown, and right on the Potomac, some miles below Williamsport. In full expectation of a decisive battle here, the army was, by the commanding general, called upon for its utmost efforts, and I was specially directed to see that everything possible was accomplished by the artillery. Accordingly, for three days, during which the enemy was waited for, my best energies were given, with those of others, to the work of arrangement and preparation. The enemy, however, prudently forbore, and, it being undesirable to await him longer, our army was, on the night of the 13th, withdrawn to the south bank of the Potomac. In this movement, necessarily involving much labor, greatly increased difficulty was imposed upon those responsible for artillery operations by the enfeebled condition of horses drawing through roads saturated with rain, and by the swollen state of the river, which confined the whole army, train and all, to one route across the pontoon bridge at Falling Waters. Still, the task was cheerfully undertaken, and in the main successfully accomplished. With the exception of a few caissons abandoned by some officers because teams could draw them no longer, and two guns left by those in charge for like reason, the battalions were entirely across by noon of the 14th. After crossing, Carter's guns were placed in position on the hill just below the bridge, and some of Garnett's on that just above. Lane's 20-pounder Parrotts were also posted some distance farther down, and [W. B.] Hurt's Whitworths higher up, all to repel an expected advance of the enemy. A few only of his guns, however, approached, and threw a shell or two, though they took care to keep out of view. A small body of skirmishers, besides, ventured rather nearer, but they were speedily dispersed by some well-directed shots, and cannon were there needed no longer.

In this Pennsylvania expedition our artillery lost:

Command.	Killed.	Wounded.	Missing.	Total.
First Corps:				
Officers	2	9	......	11
Enlisted men	45	215	42	302
Second Corps:				
Officers	2	8	......	10
Enlisted men	28	94	5	127
Third Corps:				
Officers	1	9	2	12
Enlisted men	16	102	28	146
Total	94	437	77	.608

Of the officers lost, Captain [J. C.] Fraser, Cabell's battalion, First Corps, claims the tribute of grateful honor. No soldier of more unflinching nerve and efficient energy has served the Confederacy in its struggle for existence. He fell, severely wounded, at Gettysburg, and has since yielded his life for his country.

Besides the two serviceable guns mentioned as lost from failure of teams near the Potomac, the enemy got three of our disabled pieces, of which two were left on the field as worthless, and one sent to the rear was captured by his cavalry, with a few wagons from the train. We wrested from him, on the battlefield at Gettysburg, three 10-pounder Parrotts, one 3-inch rifle, and three Napoleons, all ready for use against himself.

In the operations thus imperfectly reported, officers and men, almost without exception, evinced in high degree the important virtues of courage, fortitude, and patience. Shrinking from no danger at the call of duty, they accepted with equal fidelity the hardships incident to just forbearance and stern service in an enemy's country. Alternating heat and protracted storms aggravated other trials. The arid hills of Gettysburg afford no springs, and wells are there speedily exhausted. Many, therefore, were the sufferers from thirst in this long midsummer conflict. Subsequently, on the march, scarcely less was endurance taxed by pouring rain day and night. Yet all this, and whatever else occurred, was borne with ready acquiescence and steady resolution.

Where great merit is so prevalent, individual instances can scarcely be distinguished without danger of injustice to others. Certain cases of special heroism are, however, mentioned by several commanders, whose reports present the facts. On all such details, and all the *minutiæ* of operations, more exact information is contained in the several reports of corps chiefs of artillery and battalion commanders, herewith submitted, than can be presented in a general statement.

Regretting that no more could be achieved in the campaign, yet grateful for what has been accomplished, and for the still-increasing strength with which we are enabled to wield this great arm of defense, I have the honor to be, general, respectfully, your obedient servant,

W. N. PENDLETON,
Brigadier-General, and Chief of Artillery.

General R. E. LEE,
    Commanding.

Appendix E

THE LIGHT ARTILLERY

Anonymous. *Southern Historical Society Papers,* xxxi, 97.

On the unstained sward of the gentle slope,
Full of valor and nerved by hope,
The infantry sways like a coming sea;
Why lingers the light artillery?
   "Action front!"

Whirling the Parrotts like children's toys,
The horses strain to the rushing noise;
To right and to left, so fast and free,
They carry the light artillery.
   "Drive on!"

The gunner cries with a tug and a jerk.
The limbers fly, and we bend to our work;
The handspike in, and the implements out—
We wait for the word, and it comes with a shout—
   "Load!"

The foes pour on their billowy line;
Can nothing check their bold design?
With yells and oaths of fiendish glee,
They rush for the light artillery.
   "Commence firing!"

Hurrah! Hurrah! our bulldogs bark,
And the enemy's line is a glorious mark;
Hundreds fall like grain on the lea,
Mowed down by the light artillery.

"Fire!" and "Load!" are the only cries,
Thundered and rolled to the vaulted skies;
Aha! they falter, they halt, they flee
From the hail of the light artillery.
    "Cease firing!"

The battle is over, the victory won,
Ere the dew is dried by the rising sun;
While the shout bursts out, like a full-voiced sea,
"Hurrah for the light artillery!"

Appendix F

The Cannoneer

Air: "Happy Land of Canaan."

Words by A. G. Knight, First Sergeant, Second Company

We will sing of the boys who make the loudest noise,
And from fighting you can scarcely restrain them. *Aha!*
They have "guns," "howitzers," "rifles," and other sorts of trifles
To send soldiers past the "Happy land of Canaan."

> *Chorus:*
> Oh! ho ho! Ah, ha ha!
> The good times, boys, are a-coming,
> Oh, never mind the weather, but get over double trouble,
> When you're bound for the "Happy land of Canaan."

We will sing of number *one,* he comes first upon the gun,
And works like a horse without complaining. *Aha!*
He will let you know that he is not too *slow,*
In sending soldiers past the "Happy land of Canaan."

Next comes number *two.* He has as much as he can do
To make the enemy think 'tis iron raining. *Aha!*
He will let you know that he is not too *slow,*
At sending soldiers past the "Happy land of Canaan."

Then comes number *three,* who, as brisk as he can be,
His thumb upon the vent he's retaining. *Aha!*
He will let you know that he is not too *slow,*
At sending soldiers to the "Happy land of Canaan."

Next comes number *four,* who, to make the matter sure,
Pulls the lanyard with a steady sort of straining. *Aha!*
And then, with loud report, King Death cries out, "Come into court,"
If you're going to the "Happy land of Canaan."

Next comes number *five,* who, to keep the game alive,
Proves his legs must have the right sort of training. *Aha!*
For, with cartridge in his pouch, you can see he's no slouch,
At sending soldiers past the "Happy land of Canaan."

Then comes number *six,* who works hard his little tricks
For fear the others he'll be detaining. *Aha!*
And he knows—to help the fight—he must cut the fuses right,
So as to send them to the "Happy land of Canaan."

Next comes number *seven,* to whom important place is given;
Like five, his legs must have right sort of training. *Aha!*
For both of them must run 'tween the limber and the gun,
If they're going to the "Happy land of Canaan."

And here's to number *eight,* who with patience has to wait,
Though in this he's slightly given to complaining. *Aha!*
So he helps our number *six,* with all his little tricks,
At sending soldiers past the "Happy land of Canaan."

Now it never would be right, if the *Corporal* we should slight,
For he's the bully boy that does the aiming. *Aha!*
With his screw and with his trail, we hope he'll never fail,
At sending soldiers past the "Happy land of Canaan."

But what are we about? we have left the sergeant out;
No doubt of this slight he'll be complaining. *Aha!*
But he's a sort of *Boss,* you know, and we keep him more for show,
Than sending soldiers to the "Happy land of Canaan."

NOTE: These words were first sung and composed by Sergeant Knight at Camp Taylor, near Orange, C. H., Virginia, March, 1862. Text is from Owen, *In Camp and Battle with the Washington Artillery of New Orleans,* pp. 433 f.

Appendix G

MANUAL OF THE PIECE

(Field Artillery Tactics, 1864)

93. The instructor should bear in mind that, in every change of numbers at the gun, each recruit has to learn different duties, and to handle different implements from those he was previously engaged with; and these, again, vary with the several natures of ordnance and machines which an artilleryman must use. It is impossible that such a variety of exercises can be well executed, or even remembered, unless the recruit is made to comprehend the object of the various duties he is called upon to perform.

For the purpose of instructing the recruit, each detachment is to be formed in front of the piece, unlimbered, and the different numbers are to be called upon, successively, to perform their respective duties *in detail;* while the rest of the detachment look on and observe their motions. When it is found difficult to make the recruit sensible of the defect of his position, etc., the instructor will place himself, or another recruit, in the correct position.

94. Nine men, including the gunner, are necessary for the service of a field-piece. When, from necessity, the detachment consists of less than nine, the higher numbers are struck out, and additional duties are imposed upon those remaining.

POSTS OF THE CANNONEERS—PIECE UNLIMBERED

95. The gunner is at the end of the trail handspike; Nos. 1 and 2 are about 2 feet outside the wheels, No. 1 on the right, and No. 2 on

the left; with howitzers, rather in rear of the muzzle; with guns, in line with the front part of the wheels; Nos. 3 and 4 are in line with the knob of the cascabel, covering Nos. 1 and 2; No. 5 is 5 yards in rear of the left wheel; No. 6 in rear of the limber, and No. 7 on his left, covering No. 5; No. 8, the chief of the caisson, is 4 yards in rear of the limber, and on its left; all face to the front.

The chief of the piece is opposite the middle of the trail handspike, outside and near the left cannoneers. In actual firing he takes his place on the right or left, where he can best observe the effect of the shot.

LOADING AND FIRING

96. The piece is taken at the drill ground, unlimbered, and prepared for action; the limber in position behind the piece, and facing towards it; the end of the pole 6 yards from the end of the trail handspike.

97. COMMANDING AND POINTING.—The gunner gives all executive commands in action. He is answerable that all the numbers perform their duties correctly. He communicates the orders which he receives for the kind of ammunition to be fired; sending to No. 6 the time or distance for each round, when firing shells or spherical case shot. He should, when the firing is slow, see that each fuze is properly prepared, and make such corrections as are necessary; for this purpose he, as well as No. 6, should be provided with a fuze-gouge.

On receiving the command or signal to commence firing, he gives the command LOAD; takes hold of the handspike at the end with his right hand, and at the centre with his left; places his left knee against the left hand, bending over it, the right knee being slightly bent; looks over the top of the piece, and gives the direction. He then steps to the breech to give the elevation, which he does by placing the hausse on its seat; taking hold of a handle of the elevating screw, drawing back his right foot, bending over his left knee, and sighting through the slit in the hausse. In the drill of recruits, the gunner should be made to name the elevation and range before stepping up to the breech.

When the piece is loaded and pointed, he removes the hausse, gives the command READY, and, stepping clear of the wheel to that side where he can best observe the effect of his shot, gives the command FIRE. As soon as the piece has been fired, he causes it to be run up to its former place, if necessary.

When the instructor, instead of giving the command COMMENCE FIRING, gives that of LOAD, the gunner repeats it, and performs the same duties as before, except that he does not command FIRE until the firing is ordered to commence. After the command COMMENCE FIRING is given, the action is continued by the gunner, without further commands from the instructor, until the firing is ordered to cease. When the commands are all given by the instructor, as in *loading by detail,* the gunner performs the same duties, but without repeating the commands.

98. The detachment being formed in front of and facing the piece, the instructor commences by giving the following explanations:

The term CANNON embraces all kinds of heavy ordnance, GUNS, HOWITZERS, MORTARS; each is mounted on a *carriage,* and each field carriage has a *limber.*

The term PIECE is applied to the *cannon,* and is also used to designate it in union with its carriage, with or without the limber attached.

The *front* of a piece, when *limbered,* or prepared for moving, is the direction in which the pole points; when *unlimbered,* or prepared for action, it is the direction in which the gun points; the *right* and *left* are in each case determined accordingly.

He then repeats the names of the following objects, indicating each of them.

The LIMBER: *ammunition chest, lid, handles;* POLE: *pole-yoke, branches, sliding ring, pole-prop,* and *chain;* WHEEL: *spokes, felloes, nave, tire;* PINTLE-HOOK, and *key.*

The GUN-CARRIAGE: *handspike, pointing rings, elevating screw, handles, sponge-hook.*

The GUN or HOWITZER, giving explanations of the parts:

The *bore* is the interior hollow cylinder, which receives the charge.

The *muzzle* is the entrance of the bore.

The *face* is the front plane terminating the piece.

The *vent* is the hole through which fire is communicated to the charge.

The *trunnions* are the projecting cylinders which support the gun.

The instructor then calls No. 1 to the right side of the piece, and indicates the following parts with his hand, after naming them. The SPONGE and RAMMER: *staff, sponge, rammer-head, ferrules.* GUN: *bore, muzzle, face, vent.* He then commands:

TO YOUR POSTS

99. SPONGING AND RAMMING.—Under the command LOAD, No. 1 stands square to the front, in line with the front part of the wheels, holding the sponge about the middle of the staff in his right hand, and trailing it an angle of 45°, sponge-head up. The instructor commands:

By detail—LOAD

3 pauses; 4 motions

At this command No. 1 faces to the left, steps obliquely to the right with his right foot, without moving his left, and at the same time brings the sponge smartly to a perpendicular position by drawing his right hand up in line with the elbow. The sponge is grasped firmly in the hand, and the rammer-head kept just over the right toe, the elbow close to the side.

TWO. He steps obliquely to the left with his left foot, planting it about half-way between the piece and the wheel, and opposite the muzzle; bringing the sponge at the same time across his body to the left, so that his right hand may be opposite the middle of the body, the sponge-staff being inclined at an angle of 45° across the front of it.

THREE. He takes a side step to the right of 30 inches, and bending his right knee, brings the sponge to a horizontal position, extending the hands to the ends of the staff, the sponge-head to the left, the back of his right hand up, and that of his left down, the sponge-head against the face of the piece.

Four. He inserts the sponge-head, drops his left hand behind his thigh, shoulders square, feet equally turned out, straightens the right knee, and, bending over the left, forces the sponge home.

SPONGE
3 pauses; 4 motions

100. At this command No. 1 fixes his eye on the vent to see that it is closed, gives two turns to the sponge, taking great care to press it at the same time against the bottom of the bore.

Two. He draws out the sponge, at the same time straightening his left knee, and bending his right; seizes the staff near the sponge-head with his left hand, back of the hand down, and places the sponge against the face of the piece.

Three. He turns the sponge by bringing his hands together in the middle of the staff, giving it a cant with each hand, throwing the sponge-head over, at the same time turning his wrist, which brings the staff horizontal, and extending his hands to the ends of the staff, back of the left up, that of the other down.

During the whole time of sponging, No. 1 keeps his eye on the vent. If at any time it is not closed, he will discontinue the manœuvre, and command STOP VENT.

Four. He introduces the rammer-head into the muzzle as soon as No. 2 has inserted the charge, and joins his left hand to his right, casting his eyes to the front.

RAM
2 pauses; 3 motions

101. At this command No. 1 rams home, throwing the weight of his body with the rammer; bending over his left knee, and passing his left arm, with the elbow slightly bent, and back of the hand up, in a horizontal position over the piece, until it points in the direction of the left trunnion; the right shoulder thrown back, and the eyes cast toward the front until the cartridge is home.

Two. He jerks the sponge out with his right hand, allowing it to slide through the hand as far as the middle of the staff, when he grasps it firmly, and seizing it close to the rammer-head with the left hand, back of the hand up, places the rammer-head against the face of the piece; both knees straight; eyes to his own front.

THREE. He then draws the sponge close to his body, and immediately steps back outside the wheel, first with the right, then with the left foot, so that when the right foot is brought to it, the right hip may be on a line with the front of the wheel. In drawing the right foot to the left, he gives the sponge a cant with his left hand, at the same time quitting it, and brings the sponge to a perpendicular position in the right hand, the rammer-head resting on the right toe.

102. READY.—At this command, which is given as soon as the piece is loaded, or the firing about to commence, No. 1 breaks well off to his left with the left foot, bending the left knee, and straightening the right leg, drops the end of the sponge-staff into the left hand, back of the hand down, and fixes his eyes on the muzzle.

The heels should be parallel to the wheel, the body erect on the haunches, and the sponge and rammer held in both hands in a horizontal position, sponge-head to the left.

The piece having been fired, No. 1 rises on his right knee, and returns to his position, as in the third motion of RAM.

At the command LOAD, he steps in and performs his duties in the same manner as before.

103. When the loading is not *by detail*, No. 1 goes through all his duties at the command LOAD; returns to his position outside the wheel, as given in the third motion of RAM; breaks off at the command READY, and at the flash of the gun rises, steps in and performs his duties in the same manner as before. This he continues until the command CEASE FIRING is given, at which command he resumes the position: TO YOUR POSTS. If the sponging has been commenced when the command CEASE FIRING is given, it is completed before No. 1 resumes his post.

In sponging and ramming, if the length of the piece requires it, the sponge and rammer are to be pressed home in two motions, No. 1 extending his right hand to the end of the staff as soon as it reaches the muzzle.

In sponging *howitzers*, No. 1 presses the sponge to the bottom of the chamber, which should be well sponged out. He wipes the bore by rubbing its whole surface, without allowing the sponge to turn in his hands.

REMARKS ON THE DUTIES OF NO. 1

104. The position of the left foot will not be considered as absolute; it is given as the usual one, and may be modified according to the caliber of the piece and height of the man. The same remarks will apply to the distance between the feet. They will be placed in such position, and at such distance from each other, as will enable the man to perform his duties with the most ease and steadiness, and at the same time exert his full strength, which will always be required after firing a few rounds, especially when a new sponge is used.

One object of joining the left hand to the right, and casting the eyes to the front whilst ramming, is to refuse the right shoulder, and to secure this object the left hand, when it passes over the piece, is not carried further back than the direction indicated. This will keep the shoulders in a line parallel with their position at the commencement of the movement, until the cartridge is set home, and thus guard against fatal results in case of a premature discharge.

106. LOADING. The instructor places No. 2 on the left of the piece, repeats the nomenclature as for No. 1, indicates the following named objects, and explains their uses: STRAPPED SHOT: *cartridge, ball, sabot;* CANISTER SHOT: *cartridge, canister;* SHELL, or SPHERICAL CASE SHOT: *cartridge, case shot,* or *shell, fuze.* He then commands:

TO YOUR POSTS

Until the command LOAD is given, as for No. 1, No. 2 remains in his position. On this command being given, he faces to his right, and by two oblique steps, corresponding to those of No. 1, the first with the left, the second at the command TWO, with the right foot, he places himself near the muzzle of the piece. At the command THREE, he brings up his left foot to the side of the right, and faces to his right, bringing his hands together to receive the ammunition from No. 5, the cartridge in the right, the shot in the left hand. As soon as the sponge is withdrawn, he faces to his left, and puts the ammunition into the muzzle, taking care that the seam of the cartridge does not come under the vent, and then steps back, commencing with his left foot, to his position outside the wheel, in the same manner that No. 1 does.

At the command READY, he breaks well off to his right with the right foot, bending the right knee, and straightening the left leg, the body erect on the haunches, and fixes his eyes on the muzzle.

The piece having been fired, No. 2 rises on his left leg, remains facing the piece until he hears the command LOAD, or observes the flash of the gun, then steps in and performs his duty as before. At the command CEASE FIRING he takes his position outside the wheel and faces to the front.

With the *howitzer*, No. 2 puts in the charge so that the fuze may rest against the rammer-head, and No. 1 sets it home carefully.

106. SERVING THE VENT.—The instructor places No. 3 on the right of the piece, indicates the following objects, and explains their uses:

TUBE-POUCH; THUMBSTALL; PRIMING WIRE; GUNNER'S GIMLET; FRICTION PRIMER; LANYARD; *lanyard hook;* VENT; *vent field;* BREECH: *cascabel, knob,* and *neck of cascabel.* He then commands:

TO YOUR POSTS

No. 3 stands in line with the knob of the cascabel, covering No. 1, the priming wire in his right hand, thumb through the ring, the thumbstall on the left thumb, the tube-pouch fastened to the waist.

LOAD.—At this command he steps to his left, wipes the vent-field with the thumbstall, which he then holds pressed upon the vent, keeping his elbow raised; his fingers on the left side of the piece, so as to allow the gunner to point over his thumb; the right hand on the tube-pouch. When the piece is sponged, and the charge inserted by No. 2, he jumps to the end of the trail handspike, and, seizing it with both hands, prepares to move it to the right or left, on a signal from the gunner, who taps the right of the trail for a movement to the left, and the left of the trail for a movement to the right. As soon as the piece is pointed, the gunner raises both hands as a signal to No. 3, who then resumes the position To your posts.

READY.—At this command, he steps in to the piece, pricks the cartridge, taking care not to move the charge, and covers the vent with his left hand as soon as the tube is inserted. At the command FIRE, he steps to his right, clear of the wheel, and at the flash of the gun, or at the command LOAD, serves vent as before.

No. 3 should be careful to keep the vent closed from the time the sponge enters the muzzle until the charge is inserted by No. 2.

107. FIRING.—The instructor places No. 4 on the left of the piece, equips him with a tube-pouch, and repeats the nomenclature as for No. 3. He then commands:

TO YOUR POSTS

No. 4 stands in line with the knob of the cascabel, and covering No. 2.

LOAD.—At this command, No. 4 inserts the lanyard hook into the ring of a primer, and stands fast.

READY.—At this command, he steps in with the right foot, drops the tube in the vent, takes the lanyard in his right hand, moves to the rear so far as to keep the lanyard slack, but capable of being stretched, without altering his position, which should be clear of the wheel, left foot broken to the left and rear.

FIRE.—As soon as No. 3 is clear of the wheel, No. 4 pulls the lanyard briskly and firmly, passing the hand, back up, in a downward direction to the rear, so as to keep the lanyard hook from flying back in the direction of the face. Should the tube fail to explode the charge, the gunner immediately commands, *Don't advance, the primer has failed.* Upon which No. 2 steps inside the wheel, close to the axletree, receives from No. 3 over the wheel a priming wire, and from No. 4 a prepared primer, pricks, primes, and resumes his post. At the command CEASE FIRING, No. 4 secures his lanyards.

108. No. 3, as well as No. 4, should be equipped with a tube-

pouch, furnished with friction primers and lanyards. In the absence of No. 4, immediately after pricking the cartridge, he prepares and inserts a tube, steps to his post, faces the vent, breaks to his rear with the left foot, and at the command FIRE, discharges the piece. He then resumes his post, and tends the vent as before.

109. SERVING AMMUNITION.—The instructor stations No. 5, covering the left wheel, 5 yards in rear of it, and No. 7 in rear of and near the left limber wheel; No. 6 is stationed in rear of the limber chest, and issues the ammunition. He is provided with a fuze-gouge, and prepares the shell and spherical case shot according to the distance or time ordered, before delivering it to No. 5.

To CUT THE FUZE.—Place the projectile between the knees, fuze uppermost, and support it with the left hand. Holding the fuze-gouge in the right hand, place the left corner of its edge close to, and on the right of, the graduated mark indicating the time desired; then cut away gradually until the composition is exposed for a length about equal to the width of the gouge. Great care must be taken not to expose the composition to the left of the proper graduation mark, and, to this end, particularly avoid *commencing to cut* too close to the desired mark; for after the composition is once exposed it is very easy to pare away to the left, if the time has not been accurately cut. When time permits, it is well to expose the composition fully, either by cutting the opening larger, *towards the right,* or (with shells only) by cutting another opening to the right of the first. It is in all cases better to enlarge the first opening, and always by extending it towards the right.

Care must be taken not to cut the fuzes more rapidly than the demand for shells and shrapnel shot requires.

At the command LOAD, No. 5 runs to the ammunition chest, receives from No. 7 or No. 6 a single round, the shot in the right hand, the cartridge in his left; takes it to the piece and delivers it to No. 2; returns immediately for another round, and then halts at his post until the piece is fired. In firing shells or spherical case, he exhibits the fuze to the gunner before delivering the charge to No. 2.

When ammunition pouches are used they are worn by Nos. 5

and 7, hung from the left shoulder to the right side; the round is placed in the pouch by No. 6 or No. 7, so that the cartridge will be to the front. When it is brought up No. 5 holds open the pouch, and No. 2 takes out the round with both hands. In rapid firing with round shot and canister, Nos. 5 and 7 may alternate in delivering the charges to No. 2, especially when the ammunition is issued direct from the caisson. At the command CEASE FIRING, No. 5 carries the round back to No. 6.

No. 6 will be careful not to raise the lid unnecessarily. It should be kept closed when possible. In firing shells and spherical case, he prepares each fuze as directed, assisted, when necessary, by No. 7. He gives No. 5 the *time* or *distance* of the fuze with each round issued, who reports to the gunner before delivering it to No. 2. At the command CEASE FIRING, he carefully replaces the ammunition in the chest and secures the lid.

110. LOADING BY DETAIL.—For the instruction of recruits united for the service of the gun, the exercise is conducted by detail, the instructor giving all the commands. His commands are: *Load by detail*—LOAD; TWO, THREE, FOUR: SPONGE; TWO, THREE, FOUR: RAM; TWO, THREE: READY; FIRE; CEASE FIRING.

When the men are sufficiently instructed to go through the manual without detail, the commands of the instructor for that purpose are: LOAD; COMMENCE FIRING; CEASE FIRING; or simply COMMENCE FIRING and CEASE FIRING. After the command COMMENCE FIRING, the action is continued as laid down for loading without detail, until the command CEASE FIRING is given, which is repeated by the chief of the piece and the gunner.

Notes and References

CHAPTER 1

1. The guns used to mark positions at Gettysburg are of the same caliber and type as those employed during the battle. After the war the guns were assembled in various arsenals, and beginning about twenty-five years later selected pieces were shipped to the battlefield. In some cases where the proper types were not available dummies were constructed. Only one of the guns, a 3-inch rifle mounted at the foot of Buford's statue, can be definitely identified as having been in action at Gettysburg through a marking made at the time. It is, however, probable that others of the guns now on the field were present in July, 1863. —Information from Frederick Tilberg, Historian, Gettysburg National Military Park.

2. For a list of guns on the battlefield see Appendix A.

3. For location of markers see Appendix B.

4. Alexander, *Military Memoirs of a Confederate*, pp. 368–70. Figures are based on Confederate and Federal strength returns before the battle.

5. *Ibid.*, 434. An estimated 22,000 rounds were fired by the Confederates, including expenditure by the horse artillery. General Hunt's report in *War of the Rebellion: Official Records* (hereinafter referred to as *O.R.*) states that the Federal expenditure of ammunition, exclusive of the horse artillery which had not yet reported, was 32,781 rounds. For Hunt's Gettysburg report see Appendix C.

6. All the shells fired at Gettysburg would have lasted only a few minutes of the tremendous bombardments on the battlefields of Flanders. Farrow, *American Guns in the War with Germany*, p. 3.

7. Buell, *The Cannoneer*, p. 70.

8. Wooden carriages have been replaced by cast iron, made in a local foundry. Tubes of the bronze guns require no maintenance; those of iron are painted every three or four years.

9. For the artillery organization of the Union and Confederate armies at Gettysburg see Appendix B. In several cases, because of depletion by

battle casualties or sickness, two batteries were combined as one. Figures given in paragraph, referred to by this note, enumerate such attached batteries separately.

CHAPTER 2

10. *Field Artillery Tactics, 1864,* gives the war strength and equipment of a 12-pounder 6-gun battery as follows: 1 captain and 4 lieutenants; 150 enlisted men (2 staff sergeants, 6 sergeants, 12 corporals, 6 artificers, 2 buglers, 52 drivers, 70 cannoneers, with 2 men and 12 horses per piece added for a battery of horse artillery where all cannoneers are mounted) ; 20 carriages; from 1,218 to 1,344 rounds of shot, spherical case (shrapnel), shells, and canister.

11. The forge and its limber chest carried 430 pounds of tools, oils, and other supplies; the battery wagon and its limber chest another 1,451 pounds, including forage for the horses.

12. Calef retired as a lieutenant colonel in 1900.

13. Tidball, *Field Artillery during the Civil War.* "...At this period the law permitted officers appointed from the line to Adjutant General's, Quartermaster, and Commissary departments to retain their positions in the line; thus taking from batteries a large number of valuable officers, especially captains. Throughout the war this was a most serious drawback, one depriving batteries of their captains, and lieutenants of justly entitled promotion."

14. Catton, *Glory Road,* p. 221. "Griffin was an old artillerist, one of the numerous excellent generals contributed to the Union Army by the regular artillery." Tidball, *op. cit.,* p. 18 f. "As the war progressed, quite a number, in fact a large percentage of the artillery officers who won the coveted star gained it while commanding batteries; but as soon as they were promoted they were transferred to infantry commands and thus became lost to the artillery service—all except Barry and Hunt who continued with the artillery to the end."

15. Tidball, *op. cit.,* p. 21. "... Artillery, in fact every branch of the regular service, suffered greatly by the workings of the bounty system during the Civil War. As this system applied only to Volunteers the consequence was that it became almost, if not quite, impossible to secure men by enlistment for any branch of the regular service. To overcome this difficulty so far as the artillery was concerned, authority was granted to make details of men from volunteer infantry regiments to serve with regular batteries. Men thus detailed soon became familiar with their duties, and becoming fond of their new surroundings took advantage of another privilege permitting them to make permanent transfer to regular batteries. But even

under this arrangement batteries were maintained with difficulty and many of them were merged together, making one battery out of two."

16. *O. R.*, XXVII, Part I, 1031; also Meade, *Life and Letters*, II, 32.

17. Wise, *The Long Arm of Lee*, I, 253–54. For a full account of Pegram's life see the sketch by his adjutant, W. Gordon McCabe, in *The University Memorial* by the Rev. John L. Johnson.

18. Tidball, *op. cit.*, pp. 19 f. "In this extensive command [the Union artillery] there was but one general officer and four field officers—two colonels, one lieutenant colonel, and one major. In the seven corps of which the army then consisted the artillery of two was commanded by colonels, and of one by a major; of three by captains, and one by a lieutenant, taken from their batteries for that purpose. The two brigades of horse batteries attached to the cavalry corps were commanded by captains, and there was one field officer with the Artillery Reserve."

19. *Southern Historical Society Papers* (hereinafter *S. H. S. P.*), XXXI, 275–98.

20. *Freemantle Diary*, p. 191.

21. Such patriotic contributions became rare in subsequent wars when they were replaced by more impersonal war bond subscriptions. However, *cf.* the Astor Battery of the Spanish-American War. Its guns, ammunition, and equipment were imported from abroad and presented by John Jacob Astor.

22. Dawson, *Reminiscences of Confederate Service*.

23. *S. H. S. P.*, XXXII, 241.

24. Wise, *op. cit.*, II, 616.

25. *O. R.*, XXVII, Part I, 927.

26. *Battles and Leaders* (hereinafter *B. & L.*), III, 276.

27. Stine, *History of the Army of the Potomac*, pp. 253 f.

CHAPTER 3

28. To the "ifs" of Gettysburg may be added: What if Lee had turned over the cavalry to Wade Hampton, for instance, and given Stuart command of one of his corps instead of Ewell, Hill, or even Longstreet? Stuart had ably led Jackson's Corps at Chancellorsville after Stonewall's mortal wounding.

29. Freeman, *Lee's Lieutenants*, III, 80.

30. Catton, *Glory Road*, p. 56, and Small, *The Road to Richmond*, p. 65.

31. Stine, *op. cit.*, p. 463, quoting J. V. Pierce, then a captain in the 147th New York Regiment.

32. The Whitworth bolts were solid shot. Armor-piercing and explosive

shell also were made for them, but the latter were not effective since the shape of the projectile did not permit a large enough powder cavity. Bolts were manufactured in the Tredegar Works, Richmond. The North bought a battery of Whitworth guns from England and took them on the Peninsular Campaign but did not put them in action; they remained in the Washington defenses for the remainder of the war. Although Hurt's Confederate battery at Gettysburg was equipped with only two Whitworths, four of them stand on the battlefield today, two in their position of July 2 and the other pair in that of July 3. Information from Jac Weller, firearms consultant.

33. For this little-known poem, which embodies the dashing action of the light artillery and its commands, see Appendix E.

34. Freeman, *op. cit.*, III, 81.

35. Downey, *Sound of the Guns*, p. 121.

36. Gatlings and another early make of machine gun had been invented and used in the Civil War, though not extensively. See Wise, *op. cit.*, I, 32 f.; *Confederate Veteran* (1908), p. 581, and (1909), p. 65.

37. Battery E of the same regiment, much depleted by sickness during the Peninsula Campaign, had been amalgamated with L.

38. Buell, *The Cannoneer*, 62 f. The last phrase is not exactly quoted but altered from literary language to more likely soldier talk.

39. Not "A little more grape, Captain Bragg," as textbooks have it. See Chamberlain's *Diary* and Buell, *op. cit.*, p. 15.

40. Buell, *op. cit.*, one of the best battery histories.

41. For the exploit of O'Brien and B Battery and the recovery of the captured "Bulldogs" later in the war see Downey, *Sound of the Guns*, 101 ff., 110 f.

42. Gibbon, *Personal Recollections of the Civil War*. When a lieutenant, 4th U. S. Artillery, Gibbon compiled *The Artillerist's Manual* (1860), standard text for that era.

43. Weapons for close defense of the guns would develop from Colt automatic pistols and light machine guns issued World War I batteries to the pistols, M-1 and automatic rifles, grenades, and machine guns (including four of .50 caliber mounted on the half-tracks called Quad-50's) that became imperative in Korea to repulse enemy infiltration of a battery position.

44. Buell, *op. cit.*, p. 70.

45. *O. R.*, XXVII, Part I, 356. Wainwright's report.

CHAPTER 4

46. For Pendleton's Gettysburg report see Appendix D.

47. Freeman, *Lee's Lieutenants*, I, 614 f.

48. Wise, *The Long Arm of Lee*, I, 326.

49. See Wise, "Field Artillery in Rearguard Actions." *Field Artillery Journal*, XIII, 1923.

Dilger and his battery later fought at Chattanooga and then through Sherman's campaign in Georgia and the Carolinas. "He was known throughout the entire Union Army as one of its most brilliant officers. It was said that 'the infantry always went into battle in better spirit when it knew that Dilger's battery was with them.' Dozens of officers held that Dilger was the best artillerist of the entire Union Army. It is rather difficult to understand why so obviously able a man remained only a captain despite his many acknowledged deeds." Lonn, *Foreigners in the Union Army and Navy.*

50. The Richmond Howitzers, enjoying a similar feast of cherries en route to Gettysburg, were angrily ordered by a farm woman to "leave them cherries be." They grinned at her and picked more. She shouted after them, "Those are Union cherries, and I hope they'll choke you!" *Contributions to a History of the Richmond Howitzers.*

51. *B. & L.,* editorial note, III, 281.

52. *Ibid.*

53. For General Hunt's Gettysburg report see Appendix C.

54. Osborn, *Trials and Triumphs,* p. 96.

55. "Almost every military historian has now agreed that this decision was a mistake, that the position could have been carried that evening." Mitchell, *Decisive Battles of the Civil War,* p. 153.

56. It was Hunt who was chosen by the *Century* editors to write the series of three articles on the Battle of Gettysburg in *Battles and Leaders.*

57. *B. & L.,* III, 300.

CHAPTER 5

58. For the song in full see Appendix F.

59. Owen, *In Camp and Battle with the Washington Artillery of New Orleans,* p. 91.

60. Figg, *"Where Only Men Dare Go!"* p. 68.

61. Catton, *Glory Road,* p. 310.

62. Two poetic tributes, one by Captain Jack Crawford, "the Poet-

Scout," are included in the 4th New York's history: Smith, *A Famous Battery and Its Campaigns.*

63. Each caisson normally carried a spare limber pole in addition to a spare wheel.

64. Shrapnel (spherical case) contained 76 musket balls for a 12-pounder round. Hanifen here confuses that load with that of canister, which held 27 shot for a gun and 48 for a howitzer.

65. Hanifen, *History of Battery B, First New Jersey Light Artillery,* pp. 71–78.

66. *B. & L.,* III, 305 f.

67. *History of the Corn Exchange Regiment,* p. 267.

68. Bigelow, *The Peach Orchard.* He was also the author of a two-volume work on the Battle of Chancellorsville. His *Peach Orchard* was written as an appeal for renaming United States Avenue, Gettysburg National Military Park, Hunt Avenue in honor of his idol, the Union Chief of Artillery. The appeal failed. Later, however, an avenue was given Hunt's name; it is generally in the area of the Artillery Reserve between the Taneytown Road and Baltimore Pike. While there is a headquarters marker for General Hunt, an upturned cannon sited on Taneytown Road just south of Meade's headquarters house, singularly no monument to the Chief of Artillery, in commemoration of his distinguished service, stands on the field.

69. The explosion probably was due to improper or insufficient tow packing between rounds in the chest. *Field Artillery Tactics* (1861), p. 14, prescribes the placing of "rounds in proper position and then to secure them from movement by filling all void spaces closely with packing.... The tow should be inserted in small portions and packed down with a straight, smooth stick, prepared for the purpose." Every gun limber was supplied with a tow hook for pulling out that material, and each caisson with two such tools. They were iron, 13 inches long, with a small claw hammer head at one end and a right-angle hook at the other.

70. Bigelow, *op. cit.,* p. 53.

71. *Ibid.,* pp. 57 f.

72. Wise, *The Long Arm of Lee,* II, 647.

CHAPTER 6

73. Swinton, *Campaigns of the Army of the Potomac,* pp. 346 f.

74. Accounts of the battle often fail to distinguish between the two hills, calling them both simply Round Top. It is Little Round Top, the scene of action, that is referred to usually, as the context makes clear.

75. *B. & L.*, III, 322.

76. *Ibid.*, 307 n.

77. This celebrated unit is now designated Battery D, 5th Field Artillery Battalion. Because of the United States Army's regained consciousness of the value of tradition to *esprit de corps*, in 1957 the battery was flown from Fort Riley, Kansas, to New York City to take part in the bicentennial observance of its founder's birth in the city where he organized it.

78. Hunt in *B. & L.*, III, 309, ironically observes: "Weed had served with much distinction as an artillerist in the Peninsular, Second Bull Run, and Antietam campaigns, had become chief of artillery of his army corps, and at Chancellorsville showed such special aptitude and fitness for large artillery commands that he was immediately promoted from captain to brigadier general and transferred to the infantry."

79. *Ibid.*, 309.

80. Author of *The Corps* was Bishop Herbert S. Shipman, Chaplain, U.S. Military Academy, 1896–1905.

81. Smith, *Richard Snowden Andrews*, p. 43.

82. Andrews, *Mounted Artillery Drill*.

83. *Names and Records of All the Members Who Served in the First New Hampshire Battery of Light Artillery.*

84. For the battle order of the artillery on the Federal right see Hunt's report, Appendix C.

85. Buell, *The Cannoneer*, pp. 81 f.

86. Stine, *History of the Army of the Potomac*, p. 512. Long, *Gettysburg*, p. 38.

87. Catton, *Glory Road*, p. 325.

88. Whittier, *Civil War Papers*, V. 1.

89. Haskell, *The Battle of Gettysburg*, in *Harvard Classics*, XLIII, 354 f.

90. Wise, *The Long Arm of Lee, passim*.

91. Wise in *Field Artillery Journal*, XIII, (November, December, 1923), 495.

92. Wise, *The Long Arm of Lee*, II, 656.

93. *B. & L.*, III, 313.

94. *Ibid.*, 386 f.

95. *Ibid.*, 314.

CHAPTER 7

96. *O. R.*, XXVII, Part II, 544. Freeman, *Lee's Lieutenants*, III, 142.

97. *The 20th Connecticut: A Regimental History*, pp. 104 f. Catton, *Glory Road*, p. 329.

98. Catton, *op. cit.*, pp. 331 f.

99. Wise, *The Long Arm of Lee,* II, 665 f. "As the Chief of Artillery [General Pendleton] had since daybreak on the 3rd been busily engaged visiting every portion of the Confederate position from left to right he must have known of the absence of many of these guns from the line. Specific orders were personally given by him to the various group and even battery commanders. His aim was to secure a concentrated and destructive fire, under cover of which the infantry might advance. The problem now seems to be a simple one so far as the posting of the batteries was concerned, for even had it been impracticable to place them all actually in position, they might have all been held in readiness under cover. Most careful instructions were given by Pendleton on this point, and while he did actually supervise the placing of the ordnance trains, he seems to have failed for some reason to verify personally the posting of the batteries. Subordinate artillery commanders are, of course, responsible for such neglects as the actual failure to bring their own guns into action, and in this respect, Col. Brown, of the 2d Corps, was undoubtedly remiss, subject, however, to the limitations imposed upon him by the orders of his corps commander, and those orders, it would seem, were responsible for the elimination of Nelson's, Jones', and Raine's battalions. Walker's failure to engage his 15 howitzers was due solely to the ineffectiveness of their range, so no fault is to be found with the artillery dispositions of the 3d Corps, and Alexander brought every piece of the 1st Corps into action.

"Viewing the disposition of the Confederate Artillery before the attack, a grave error should have been detected, and for this error the Chief of Artillery, subject also to the orders from the Commander-in-Chief, was responsible. Since Lee assumed no direct control of his artillery, only informing himself of its general situation through Col. Long of his staff, Pendleton must receive the blame. Not only did he permit 56 of his guns to remain idle as pointed out before, but he allowed 80 of the 84 guns of the 2d and 3d Corps, which were engaged, to be brought into action on a mathematically straight line, parallel to the position of the enemy and constantly increasing in range therefrom to the left and north! It was indeed a phenomenal oversight on his part, as declared by Col. Alexander, not to place a part of the Artillery, at least, north of the town and east of the prolongation of his line of guns at the center to enfilade the shank of the fish-hook, and crossfire with the guns on Seminary Ridge."

100. For the order of battle of the Federal artillery see Hunt's report, Appendix C.

101. In praise of Hunt, Birkhimer, *Historical Sketch of the Artillery, U. S. A.,* pp. 82 f, quotes McClellan's report of August 4, 1862, that he

"had commanded the artillery reserve with marked skill, and brought to his duties as chief of artillery the highest qualifications. The services of this distinguished officer in reorganizing and refitting the batteries prior to and after the battle of Antietam, and his gallant and skillful conduct on that field, merit the highest encomiums in my power to bestow." Birkhimer adds: "General Hunt continued in this position during the rest of the war, stamping on the service of which he was the head the impress of a cultivated mind stored with knowledge of the uses and capabilities of the artillery arm, the result of extensive experience, profound study, and reflection."

102. *O. R.*, I, Part I, 827 f.

103. *Military Historical Society of Massachusetts. Papers,* XIII, 94 f.

104. *Ibid.,* p. 95, quoting a speech at a Gettysburg reunion.

105. *Ibid.*

106. "This special ammunition train was organized by Brigadier-General Henry J. Hunt, chief of artillery of the army, upon his own motion, and without special orders to that effect. Upon his requesting it, the quartermaster of the Army of the Potomac furnished the wagons. General Meade knew nothing about it until some time afterwards. The intelligent foresight evinced in the formation of this train becomes apparent when we contemplate the situation at Gettysburg, where, owing to the fact that much ammunition with some of the commands was left behind in the hurry to arrive on the field, its absence might have led to serious embarrassment, not to say disastrous results." Birkhimer, *op. cit.,* p. 102 n.

107. *Ibid.,* pp. 101 f.

108. All the shells fired at Gettysburg would have lasted only a few minutes of the tremendous bombardments on the battlefields of Flanders in World War I. Farrow, *American Guns in the War with Germany.*

109. Buell, *The Cannoneer,* pp. 92 f.

110. *B. & L.,* III, 37 f.

111. *Ibid.,* p. 372. Such tactics, Hunt continued, were provided for in army regulations, but they had been condensed in successive editions into a few short lines, "so obscure as to be virtually worthless, because, like the rudimentary toe of the dog's paw, they had become, from lack of use, mere survivals, unintelligible except to the specialist." General Meade subsequently clarified those instructions by specifying the position of the Chief of Artillery in General Orders No. 82, Headquarters Army of the Potomac, August 21, 1863:

"The duties of the chief of artillery of this army are both administrative and executive. He is responsible for the condition of the artillery wherever serving, respecting which he will keep the commanding general fully informed. Through him the commanding general of the army will take the proper steps to insure the efficiency of the artillery for movement and action and its proper employment in battle. All artillery not attached to other troops will be commanded by the chief of artillery. He will, both personally and through his staff, maintain supervision and inspection of the personnel and material of the artillery to insure the instruction of the former and completeness of the latter, as well as the discipline of the artillery not attached to other troops. In battle he will, under the instructions of the major-general commanding, distribute and place in position the reserve artillery, and, when so directed, select the positions for the batteries attached to troops, conveying to the commander of the troops the directions of the commanding general. He will give such directions as may be necessary to secure the supply of ammunition and to furnish it promptly to the batteries when in action. He will give no orders that will interfere with the military control exercised by the commanders of a corps or division over the batteries attached to their troops, nor will he withdraw batteries from a corps, or transfer them from one corps to another, unless directed to do so by the general commanding the army. Commandants of the artillery attached to troops will be responsible to the chief of artillery for the condition and efficiency of their batteries so far as relates to equipments, supplies, and instructions, and will be governed with respect to orders received from him by paragraph 489, Revised Army Regulations of 1861."

The order, comments Birkhimer, *op. cit.*, p. 217, "very nicely balances the various parts of a delicate machinery, the disjointing of which had caused serious inconvenience. It continued in force until the close of the Civil War, and deserves to be preserved among the valuable contributions to our code of regulations resulting from experience then acquired."

112. Downey, *Sound of the Guns*, p. 133.

113. Cullum, *Biographical Register of the Officers and Graduates of the U.S. Military Academy*, II, 11-13. Cf. Wise, Freeman, Catton, *op. cit.*

The bill (HR 78) to place Henry Hunt on the retired list of major generals, U.S. Army, was introduced in 1883 in the 48th Congress. Its text runs:

"Whereas Col. and Bvt. Maj. Gen. Henry J. Hunt was, on the 14th of September, 1883, retired from active service as Colonel of the Fifth Regiment of Artillery, by due operation of law, after more than forty-four years of continuous active, honorable, and distinguished service in the Army of the United States; and

"Whereas the said Henry J. Hunt exercised the appropriate command of a major-general in the field during the greater portion of the late war, and at the date of his retirement he was in command of a geographical military department, held the command of a major-general of the United States Army by brevet, dating March 13, 1865, conferred upon him for 'gallant and meritorious services in the field during the rebellion:' Therefore,

"Be it enacted &c., That the President be, and he is hereby, authorized to place Col. and Bvt. Maj. Gen. Henry J. Hunt on the retired-list of major-generals, with the rank, pay, and emoluments of a major-general of the United States Army on the retired-list, to date from September 14, 1883."

The Senate did not act on the bill until the second session of the 48th Congress. On March 3, 1885, the Senate passed the bill without further amendment. This was next to the last day of the session, and of the administration of President Arthur. Apparently, the bill was killed by a pocket veto. I find no record of a veto message.

The debate in the House gives some indication of the objections which were advanced against the bill. The opponents of the bill felt that it was a bad precedent to single out one officer for higher rank and pay when there might be many others who were also deserving of such recognition. (Information from Philip A. Hazleton, Law Librarian, New Hampshire State Library.)

114. Mitchell in *Decisive Battles of the Civil War*, pp. 156 f, sums up concisely. "The first day's battle had been favorable to the Confederates and, furthermore, they should have taken Cemetery Hill that evening. As for the results of the second day, General Lee knew that the attacks had not been coordinated and apparently believed that they had failed for that reason. It is certainly probable that if they had been delivered simultaneously, and early in the morning, as Lee had originally planned, the Confederates might have won the battle.

"He therefore resolved to deliver a concentrated, fully coordinated assault on the Union center. As we look back on this decision with all the advantages of hindsight we cannot help but wonder if General Lee had not become overly infected with the supreme confidence of his men in their ability to accomplish anything. Certainly, by now, the Union position was well organized. It was quite a different situation from that which prevailed on the evening of the first day, or on the second day when Little Round Top was entirely unprotected."

115. Before the war Long had served in Hunt's battery expressly to receive instruction in the use of field artillery. When the two men met at Appomattox, Hunt scolded his former subordinate for his part in the direction of the Gettysburg cannonade. The Confederate artilleryman, the Union chief observed, had not done justice to his teaching. The "fire, instead of being concentrated on the point of attack, as it ought to have been, and as I expected it would be, was scattered over the whole field. He was amused at the criticism and said: 'I remembered my lessons at the time, and when the fire became so scattered, wondered what you would think about it!'" *B & L.*, III, 373 f. The Comte de Paris in his *History of the Civil War in America*, III, 655, declares that Long, replying to Hunt's strictures, blamed the dispersion of the fire on "the interference of the generals" (commanding the army corps and divisions).

116. Records do not state whether the second gun was reprimed and fired or whether the third piece took over the signal duty, as would be the case in firing salutes when a misfire occurred.

117. Wise, *op. cit.*, II, 677.

CHAPTER 8

118. *B. & L.*, III, 327.

119. Buell, *The Cannoneer*, p. 94.

120. *Philadelphia Weekly Times*, May 31, 1877.

121. Wise, *The Long Arm of Lee*, II, 667.

122. Bishop, *Field Artillery, the King of Battles*, pp. 137 f. Bishop, who as a young officer served under the Gettysburg veteran quoted, subsequently became Chief of Field Artillery.

123. Gibbon, *Personal Recollections of the Civil War*, p. 148.

124. Haskell, *The Battle of Gettysburg* (reprint in *Harvard Classics*, XLIII, 326–414). Then a first lieutenant, Haskell wrote this extraordinarily vivid account a week after the battle as a letter to his brother. He rose to a colonelcy and was killed leading his regiment in a charge at the Battle of Cold Harbor.

125. Another Union officer, Jesse Bowman Young, recalled in *The Battle of Gettysburg*, pp. 295 f, "the fiendish wailing of certain oblong, convoluted, heavy projectiles which came from a few Whitworth pieces on the Confederate side, which broke now and then into the horrible discord, sounding like the predatory howls of demons in search of their prey." Veterans of World War I similarly remember the distinctive sound of shells from high-velocity Austrian 88's; almost simultaneously with the shrieking onrush came their burst. However, as has been noted, the Whit-

worth bolts were solid shot because of insufficient space for an adequate bursting charge.

126. *B. & L.*, III, 385 ff. On controversial points it was the policy of the editors of this work to permit the presentation of both sides. Hunt's statement on the cease-fire affair in his article, "The Third Day at Gettysburg" (p. 375), was rebutted by an officer who had served under the late General Hancock, Bvt. Brig.-Gen. Francis A. Walker, U.S.V. Thereto Hunt made the rejoinder, part of which is quoted in the text.

127. See Note 111.

128. Wise, *op. cit.*, p. 677.

129. *Ibid.*, p. 684. *Cf.* Pendleton's report, Appendix D.

130. *B. & L.*, III, 364

131. Harbord, *The American Army in France*, p. 296.

132. *B. & L.*, III, 345.

CHAPTER 9

133. Freeman, *R. E. Lee*, III, 122; *Lee's Lieutenants*, III, 158. By Pickett's orders all other officers in the charge were afoot.

134. Lewis, *Recollections from 1860 to 1865*, pp. 81 f.

135. Confederate Major McIntosh in *S. H. S. P.*, XXXVII, 136 f., wrote: "The impression that any very serious effect had been produced upon the enemy's lines by the artillery fire proved to be a delusion. The aim of the Confederate guns was accurate, and they did their work as well as could be, but the distance was too great to produce the results which they sanguinely hoped for. Previous experience should have taught them better. It is not a little surprising that General Lee should have reckoned so largely upon the result. Both sides had been pretty well taught that sheltered lines of infantry cannot be shattered or dislodged when behind breastworks by field artillery at the distance of a thousand yards or upwards.

"The soldier who has been taught by experience to hang tight to his breastworks, and who knows it is more dangerous to run than to lie still, comes to regard with stoical indifference the bursting missiles which are mostly above or behind."

Manucy in *Artillery Through the Ages*, p. 19, sums up the situation: "On the battlefield, Napoleon's artillery tactics were no longer practical. The infantry, armed with its own comparatively long-range firearms, was usually able to keep artillery beyond case-shot range, and cannon had to stand off at such long distances that their primitive ammunition was relatively ineffective. The result was that when the attacking infantry moved in, the defending infantry and artillery were still fresh and unshaken, ready to pour a devastating point-blank fire into the assaulting lines. Thus, in spite of an intensive 2-hour bombardment by 138 Confederate guns at the crisis at Gettysburg, as the gray-clad troops advanced across the field to close range, double canister and concentrated infantry volleys cut them down in masses."

136. Wise, *The Long Arm of Lee*, II, 684 f.

137. Tully McCrea, Battery I, 1st U.S. Artillery, in *Journal of the Military Service Institution of the United States*, XXII, 532.

138. *B & L.*, III, 387.

139. *Ibid.*, p. 366.

140. Benét, *John Brown's Body*, p. 312.

141. To mention "ifs" from the artillery angle, one may speculate whether the charge might have succeeded if the Confederate artillery had been better positioned and its preparation of fire really effective. "Division and corps commanders view with alarm any attempts to take from them their batteries in time of action—witness Fredericksburg!—while to the practical impossibility of withdrawing artillery from the corps, and bringing it to bear upon the decisive point of attack, was attributed by some of the ablest generals of the Confederacy the failure of Pickett's charge at Gettysburg." Birkhimer, *Historical Sketch of the Artillery, U.S. Army*, pp. 104 f.

Or could the charge have been driven home, if McGilvery's and the Little Round Top batteries, by reason of premature expenditure of their long-range ammunition, had been unable to shatter the right of the assault with their devastating enfilade? Birkhimer (p. 104) quotes in comment: "'After a defensive army has developed its strength, and the weak parts of its line have been ascertained, a powerful reserve artillery will have little difficulty in bringing about a preponderating cross or enfilade fire upon an exposed flank already engaged in front, . . . that will inevitably cause disaster.'"

142. Freeman, *Lee's Lieutenants*, III, 162.

CHAPTER 10

143. David Cardwell, quoted in Brooks' *Stories of the Confederacy*, pp. 380 f.

144. Bellah, *The Valiant Virginians*.

145. Development of the Union horse artillery is noted by Birkhimer, *Historical Sketch of the Artillery, U.S.A.*, pp. 70 f. "Horse artillery was early recognized as the associate of properly organized cavalry. Accordingly, some time in the fall of 1861, Tidball's company, (A) of the Second, was

equipped for that service at Washington, D.C., forming the first company of horse artillery in the army since Bragg's company was dismounted at Santa Fé after the Mexican war. This was soon followed by the similar equipment of (M), Second, and March, 1862, by (B-L), Second (consolidated for want of men), and (C), Third Artillery. These companies were formed into a horse artillery brigade; and so efficient did they prove that by the date of the battle of Chancellorsville (May 2–4, 1863) their number had been doubled. After this battle the horse batteries of that army were organized into two brigades, that they might alternate campaigning and recuperating, in their arduous service with the cavalry."

146. Brooks, *Stories of the Confederacy*, p. 7.

147. *B. & L.*, III, 393.

148. *O. R.*, XXVII, Part I, 993—Kilpatrick's report. "I am of the opinion that, had our infantry on my right, advanced at once when relieved from the enemy's attack on the front, the enemy could not have recovered from the confusion into which Generals Farnsworth and Merritt had thrown them, but would have been rushed back, one division after another, until, instead of defeat, a total rout would have ensued."

149. H. C. Parsons in *B. & L.*, III, 394.

150. Owen, *In Camp and Battle with the Washington Artillery of New Orleans*, p. 255.

151. *B. & L.*, III, 376.

152. Figures are from revised returns, noted in *B. & L.*, III, 384, and Pendleton's and Hunt's reports. The Confederate casualty list is stated to be incomplete.

153. Drake, *The Battle of Gettysburg, 1863*. Although Hunt defends Meade's conduct of the pursuit, he does so far less effectively than in the case of the withheld counterattack. Catton in *Glory Road*, p. 351, writes of Meade: "He had been one of the few men who could have lost the war irretrievably in one day, and he had managed to avoid the mistakes which would have lost it. He would continue to avoid mistakes, even if he had to miss opportunity."

154. Battery B, 4th U.S. Artillery. Because of its heavy losses at Gettysburg it was known as "Bloody B."

155. Haskell, *The Battle of Gettysburg, Harvard Classics*, pp. 408, 411 f.

Bibliography

ABBOT, BREVET-BRIGADIER GENERAL HENRY L. *Siege Artillery in the Campaigns against Richmond, with notes on the 15-inch Gun.* New York: 1868.

ALDRICH, THOMAS M. *The History of Battery A, First Regiment Rhode Island Light Artillery, in the War to Preserve the Union, 1861–1865.* Providence: Snow & Farnam, 1904.

ALEXANDER, GENERAL EDWARD PORTER. *Military Memoirs of a Confederate.* New York: Charles Scribner's Sons, 1907.

AMERICAN HISTORICAL ASSOCIATION. *Annual Reports.* Washington: 1885–1954.

ANDERSON, CAPT. ROBERT. *Instruction for Field Artillery, Horse and Foot.* Translated from the French. Philadelphia: 1839.

———. *Evolutions of Field Batteries of Artillery.* New York: 1860.

ANDREWS, R. SNOWDEN. *Andrews' Mounted Artillery Drill.* Charleston: Evans & Cogswell, 1863.

BACHELDER, JOHN B. *Descriptive Key to the Painting of the Repulse of Longstreet's Assault at the Battle of Gettysburg.* New York: John B. Bachelder, 1870.

BAKER, L. W. *History of the Ninth Massachusetts Battery.* South Framingham, Massachusetts: Lakeview Press, 1888.

BATTINE, CECIL. *The Crisis of the Confederacy.* London and New York: Longmans, Green & Co., 1905.

Battles and Leaders of the Civil War. Robert Underwood Johnson, ed. 4 vols. New York: The Century Co., 1884–87.

BELCHER, HENRY. *The First American Civil War.* 2 vols. London: The Macmillan Co., 1911.

BENÉT, STEPHEN VINCENT. *John Brown's Body*. Garden City, New York: Doubleday, Doran & Co., 1927.

BENNETT, A. J. *The Story of the First Massachusetts Light Battery*. Boston: Press of Deland & Barta, 1886.

BIGELOW, MAJOR JOHN, JR. *The Peach Orchard, Gettysburg, July 2, 1863*. Minneapolis: Kimball-Storer Co., 1910.

BILLINGS, JOHN D. *Hard Tack and Coffee*. Boston: 1888.

――――. *The History of the Tenth Massachusetts Battery of Light Artillery in the War of the Rebellion*. Boston: 1881.

BIRKHIMER, WILLIAM E. *Historical Sketch of the Organization, Administration, Matériel, and Tactics of the Artillery, United States Army*. Washington: 1884.

BISHOP, MAJOR GENERAL HARRY G. *Elements of Modern Field Artillery, U. S. Service*. Menasha, Wisconsin: G. Banta Publishing Co., 1914.

BLACKFORD, LIEUTENANT COLONEL WILLIAM WILLIS. *War Years with Jeb Stuart*. New York: Charles Scribner's Sons, 1945.

BOATNER, MAJOR MARK M., III. *Army Lore*. Tokyo, Japan: 1954.

――――. *Military Customs and Traditions*. New York: David McKay Company, Inc., 1956.

BROOKS, U. R., ed. *Stories of the Confederacy*. Columbia, South Carolina: The State Co., 1912.

BRUSH, LIEUTENANT JAMES G. *A Short History of the Fifth Regiment, U.S. Artillery*. New York: 1895.

BUELL, AUGUSTUS. *The Cannoneer; Recollections of Service in the Army of the Potomac*. Washington: National Tribune, 1890.

BURCHARD, JOHN ELY, ed. *Rockets, Guns and Targets*. Boston: Little, Brown & Company, 1948.

CASTLE, HENRY A. *The Army Mule*. Indianapolis: Bobbs-Merrill Company, 1897.

CATTON, BRUCE. *Mr. Lincoln's Army*. New York: Doubleday & Company, Inc., 1951.

――――. *Glory Road*. New York: Doubleday & Company, Inc., 1952.

――――. *A Stillness at Appomattox*. New York: Doubleday & Company, Inc., 1953.

CATTON, BRUCE. *This Hallowed Ground*. New York: Doubleday & Company, Inc., 1956.

CHAMBERLAIN, BREVET MAJOR GENERAL JOSHUA LAWRENCE. *Five Forks*. Portland, Maine: 1902.

———. *The Passing of the Armies*. New York: G. P. Putnam's Sons, 1915.

CHAMBERLAYNE, E. H. *War History and Roll of the Richmond Fayette Artillery, 38th Virginia Battalion Artillery, Confederate States Army, 1861–1865*. Richmond, Virginia: Everett Waddey, 1883.

CHAMBERLAYNE, JOHN HAMPDEN. *Ham Chamberlayne, Virginian; Letters and Papers of an Artillery Officer in the War for Southern Independence*. Richmond, Virginia: Dietz Printing Company, 1932.

CHILD, B. H. *From Fredericksburg to Gettysburg*. Providence: 1895.

Civil War Papers Read Before the Commandery of the State of Massachusetts, Military Order of the Loyal Legion of the United States. Boston: Printed for the Commandery, 1900.

CLARK, WALTER, ed. *Histories of the Several Regiments and Battalions from North Carolina in the Great War, 1861–65*. 5 vols. Raleigh, North Carolina: E. M. Uzzell, 1901.

COMMAGER, HENRY STEELE, ed. *The Blue and the Gray*. 2 vols. Indianapolis: Bobbs-Merrill Company, 1950.

Confederate Veteran, The. 40 vols. Nashville, Tennessee: 1893–1932.

Contributions to a History of the Richmond Howitzer Battalion. Pamphlets 1–4. Richmond, Virginia: Carlton McCarthy & Co., 1883-86.

COOKE, JOHN ESTEN. *Wearing of the Gray*. New York: 1867.

CROTTY, D. G. *Four Years Campaigning in the Army of the Potomac*. Grand Rapids, Michigan: 1874.

CULLUM, GEORGE W. *Biographical Register of the Officers and Graduates of the U. S. Military Academy*. 7 vols. Boston: 1891–1930.

DANIEL, FREDERICK S. *Richmond Howitzers in the War*. Richmond: 1891.

DAWSON, F. W. *Reminiscences of the Confederate Service*. Charleston, South Carolina: News and Courier Book Press, 1882.

DE TOBRIAND REGIS. *Four Years with the Army of the Potomac*. Boston: 1889.

Dictionary of American Biography. James T. Adams, ed. 21 vols. New York: 1928–44.

Dictionary of American History. James T. Adams, ed. 5 vols. New York: 1940.

DOUBLEDAY, ABNER. *Chancellorsville and Gettysburg*. New York: Charles Scribner's Sons, 1882.

DOWNEY, FAIRFAX. *Sound of the Guns*. New York: David McKay Company, Inc., 1956.

DRAKE, SAMUEL ADAMS. *The Battle of Gettysburg, 1863*. Boston: Lothrop, Lee & Shepard Co., 1892.

DYER, ALEXANDER BRYDIE. *Handbook of Light Artillery*. New York: John Wiley & Sons, 1896.

DYER, FREDERICK H. *A Compendium of the War of the Rebellion*. Des Moines, Iowa: The Dyer Publishing Co., 1908.

ELIOT, ELLSWORTH, JR. *Yale in the Civil War*. New Haven: Yale University Press, 1932.

EVANS, GENERAL CLEMENT A., ed. *Confederate Military History*. 12 vols. Atlanta, Georgia: Confederate Publishing Co., 1899.

FARROW, EDWARD S. *American Guns in the War with Germany*. New York: 1920.

FIEBEGER, COLONEL GUSTAVE JOSEPH. *The Campaign and Battle of Gettysburg*. West Point, New York: Military Academy Printing Office, 1910.

Field Artillery Journal. Washington: 1911–45.

FIGG, R. W. *"Where Only Men Dare Go!" or The Story of a Boy Company*. Richmond, Virginia: Whiltet and Shepperson, 1885.

FITZGERALD, DAVID. *In Memoriam. Gen. Henry J. Hunt, 1819–1889*. N.d.

FONDERDEN, C. A. *A Brief History of the Military Career of Carpenter's Battery*. New Market, Virginia: 1911.

FORBES, EDWIN. *Life Studies of the Great Army*. New York: 1899.

FOSTER, JOHN Y. *New Jersey and the Rebellion*. Newark, New Jersey: Martin R. Dennis and Co., 1868.

FOX, WILLIAM F. *Regimental Losses in the American Civil War*. Albany: 1889.

FREEMAN, DOUGLAS SOUTHALL. *Lee's Lieutenants, a Study in Command*. 3 vols. New York: Charles Scribner's Sons, 1942-44.

———. *R. E. Lee, A Biography*. 4 vols. New York: Charles Scribner's Sons, 1934-35.

FREEMANTLE, LIEUTENANT COLONEL ARTHUR J. L. *The Freemantle Diary*. Boston: Little, Brown & Company, 1954.

FULLER, J. F. C. *Decisive Battles of the U.S.A.* New York: The Beechhurst Press, 1953.

GANOE, WILLIAM ADDLEMAN. *The History of the United States Army*. New York: D. Appleton-Century Company, Inc., 1942.

GIBBON, BRIGADIER GENERAL JOHN. *The Artillerist's Manual*. Washington: 1863.

———. *Personal Recollections of the Civil War*. New York: G. P. Putnam's Sons, 1928.

GREER, ALLEN J. "The Roaring Guns from the Seven Days to Cold Harbor," *Field Artillery Journal*, XXVI (1935), 5-26.

HAIGHT, THERON WILBER. *Three Wisconsin Cushings*. Madison, Wisconsin: 1910.

HANCOCK, MRS. WINFIELD S. *Reminiscences of Winfield Scott Hancock*. New York: 1887.

HANIFEN, MICHAEL. *History of Battery B, 1st New Jersey Artillery*. Ottawa, Illinois: Republican Times, 1905.

HARBORD, MAJOR GENERAL JAMES G. *The American Army in France, 1917-1919*. Boston: Little, Brown & Company, 1936.

HARRIS, FIRST LIEUTENANT SAMUEL. *Michigan Brigade of Cavalry at the Battle of Gettysburg, July 3, 1863*. Chicago: Samuel Harris & Co., 1894.

HASKELL, COLONEL FRANKLIN ARETAS. *The Battle of Gettysburg*. Harvard Classics. Vol. 43. New York: P. F. Collier & Son Co., 1910.

HASKIN, BREVET MAJOR W. L. *History of the First Regiment of Artillery*. Portland, Maine: 1879.

HEITMAN, FRANCIS B. *Historical Register of Officers of the Continental Army*. Washington: 1914.

――――. *Historical Register and Dictionary of the United States Army*. 2 vols. Washington: 1900.

HENRY, ROBERT SELPH. *The Story of the Confederacy*. Indianapolis: Bobbs-Merrill Company, 1931.

History of the Corn Exchange Regiment, 118th Pennsylvania Volunteers, by the Survivors' Association. Philadelphia: 1888.

History of the Fifth Massachusetts Battery. Boston: Luther E. Cowles, 1902.

History of the Third Pennsylvania Cavalry. Philadelphia: Franklin Printing Co., 1905.

HOKE, JACOB. *Gettysburg, the Great Invasion of 1863*. Dayton, Ohio: 1887.

JACOBS, M. *Notes on the Rebel Invasion and the Battle of Gettysburg*. Philadelphia: Lippincott & Co., 1864.

JOHNSON, BRIGADIER GENERAL RICHARD W. *A Soldier's Reminiscences in Peace and War*. Philadelphia: 1886.

JONES, JENKIN L. *An Artilleryman's Diary*. Madison, Wisconsin: Wisconsin History Commission, 1914.

JONES, REV. J. WILLIAM. *Army of Northern Virginia*. Richmond, Virginia: J. W. Randolph & English, 1880.

Journal of the Military Service Institution of the United States. Vols. 1–61. New York: 1880–1917.

Journal of the U. S. Artillery and Coast Artillery Journal. Files. Fortress Monroe, Virginia.

KILMER, G. S. *Bigelow's Battery, the Ninth Massachusetts at the Gettysburg Peach Orchard*. Washington: War Department Library Pamphlet No. 270.

KREDEL, FRITZ, and TODD, FREDERICK P. *Soldiers of the American Army, 1775–1954*. Chicago: Henry Regnery Co., 1954.

KUSHNER, ERVAN F. *The Campaign at Gettysburg* (typescript ms. in New York Public Library). N.d.

LANG, T. F. *Loyal West Virginia*.

LEE, ROBERT E., JR. *Recollections and Letters of General Robert E. Lee.* New York: Doubleday, Doran & Company, Inc., 1924.

LEWIS, GEORGE. *The History of Battery E, First Regiment Rhode Island Light Artillery in the War of 1861 to 1865 to Preserve the Union.* Providence: 1892.

LEWIS, JOHN H. *Recollections from 1860 to 1865.* Washington: Peake & Co., 1895.

LONG, CAPTAIN JAMES F. *How the Battle Was Fought.* Harrisburg, Pennsylvania: Meyers Printing House, 1891.

LONGSTREET, HELEN D. *Lee and Longstreet at the High Tide; Gettysburg in the Light of Official Records.* Gainesville, Georgia: 1904.

LONGSTREET, JAMES. *From Manassas to Appomattox.* Philadelphia: 1896.

LONN, ELLA. *Foreigners in the Union Army and Navy.* Baton Rouge, Louisiana: Louisiana State Press, 1951.

————. *Foreigners in the Confederacy.* Chapel Hill, North Carolina: University of North Carolina Press, 1940.

McCARTHY, CARLTON. *Detailed Minutiae of a Soldier's Life in the Army of Northern Virginia.* Richmond, Virginia: Carlton McCarthy & Co., 1882.

McCLELLAN, H. B. *The Life and Campaigns of Major General J. E. B. Stuart.* Boston and New York: Houghton, Mifflin & Co., 1885.

McCREA, TULLY. "Light Artillery: Its Use and Misuse," *Journal of the Military Service Institution* (New York), XXII (1898), 519–23.

McDONALD, CAPTAIN WILLIAM N. *A History of the Laurel Brigade.* Baltimore, Maryland: Sun Job Printing Office, 1907.

MACON, T. J. *Reminiscences of the First Company of Richmond Howitzers.* Richmond, Virginia: 1909.

MANUCY, ALBERT. *Artillery through the Ages.* National Park Service Interpretive Series, History No. 3. Washington: 1949.

MEADE, GEORGE GORDON. *With Meade at Gettysburg.* Philadelphia: Winston Co., 1930.

MERCER, PHILIP. *The Life of the Gallant Pelham.* Macon, Georgia: J. W. Burke Company, 1929.

MEREDITH, ROY. *The American Wars: A Pictorial History from Quebec to Korea, 1755–1953.* Cleveland and New York: The World Publishing Company, 1955.

MIERS, EARL SCHENCK, and BROWN, RICHARD A., eds. *Gettysburg.* New Brunswick, New Jersey: Rutgers University Press, 1948.

Military Affairs. "Guide to the Writing of American Military History." Appendix, Vol. XIV [No. 4].

Military Collector and Historian Journal. Files.

MILITARY HISTORICAL SOCIETY OF MASSACHUSETTS. *Papers.* XIII, Chapter III: "Artillery" by Brevet Major General Henry J. Hunt. Boston: 1918.

MILLIS, WALTER. *Arms and Men.* New York: G. P. Putnam's Sons, 1956.

MITCHELL, LIEUTENANT COLONEL JOSEPH B. *Decisive Battles of the Civil War.* New York: G. P. Putnam's Sons, 1955.

MOORE, EDWARD A. *The Story of a Cannoneer under Stonewall Jackson.* Lynchburg, Virginia: J. P. Bell Co., 1910.

MORRIS, RICHARD B., ed. *Encyclopedia of American History.* New York: Harper & Brothers, 1953.

MOSBY, JOHN S. *Stuart's Cavalry in the Gettysburg Campaign.* New York: Moffat, Yard & Co., 1908.

Names and Records of All the Members Who Served in the First New Hampshire Battery of Light Artillery. Manchester, New Hampshire: Budget Job Print, 1891.

National Tribune. Files. Washington.

NEESE, GEORGE M. *Three Years in the Confederate Horse Artillery.* New York and Washington: Neale Publishing Co., 1911.

NEW YORK MONUMENTS COMMISSION FOR THE BATTLEFIELDS OF GETTYSBURG AND CHATTANOOGA. *Final Report on the Battlefield of Gettysburg.* 3 vols. Albany, New York: J. B. Lyon Co., 1900.

New York Times. Files.

NORTON, OLIVER WILLCOX. *The Attack and Defense of Little Round Top, Gettysburg, July 2, 1863.* New York: Neale Publishing Co., 1913.

Ohio Memorials at Gettysburg. Columbus, Ohio: Nitschke Bros., 1887.

OSBORN, CAPTAIN HARTWELL. *Trials and Triumphs, the Record of the Fifty-fifth Illinois Volunteer Infantry.* Chicago: A. C. McClurg and Co., 1904.

OWEN, W. M. *In Camp and Battle with the Washington Artillery of New Orleans.* Boston: Ticknor & Co., 1885.

PAGE, R. C. M. *Sketch of Page's Battery or Morris Artillery, 2d Corps, Army Northern Virginia.* New York: Thomas Smeltzer, 1885.

PAGE, THOMAS NELSON. *The Burial of the Guns.* New York: Charles Scribner's Sons, 1894.

PARIS, LOUIS PHILIPPE ALBERT D'ORLEANS, COMTE DE. *History of the Civil War in America.* 4 vols. Philadelphia: Porter and Coates, 1875–88.

PHILLIPS, MAJOR THOMAS R., ed. *Roots of Strategy.* Harrisburg, Pennsylvania: Military Service Publishing Company, 1940.

Photographic History of the Civil War. Francis Trevelyan Miller, ed. 10 vols. New York: Review of Reviews Co., 1911.

POAGUE, WILLIAM THOMAS. *Gunner with Stonewall Jackson.* Tennessee: McCowat-Mercer Press, 1957.

PRATT, FLETCHER. *Eleven Generals; Studies in American Command.* New York: William Sloane, Associates, Inc., 1949.

———. *Ordeal by Fire.* New York: Harrison Smith & Robert Haas, Inc., 1935.

RAMSDELL, CHARLES M. "General Robert E. Lee's Horse Supply, 1862–1865." *American Historical Review,* XXXV (1931), 758–77.

RAWLE, WILLIAM B. *The Right Flank at Gettysburg.* Philadelphia: 1878.

RAY, FREDERIC, JR. *Gettysburg Sketches.* Gettysburg, Pennsylvania: Times and News Publishing Co., 1939.

REICHARDT, THEODORE. *Diary of Battery A, First Regiment Rhode Island Light Artillery.* Providence, Rhode Island: 1865.

REMINGTON, CYRUS K. *A Record of Battery I, First New York Light Artillery Vols., Otherwise Known as Wiedrich's Battery during the War of the Rebellion.* Buffalo, New York: 1901.

RHODES, JAMES FORD. *History of the Civil War.* New York: The Macmillan Company, 1917.

RHODES, J. H. *The History of Battery B, First Rhode Island Light Artillery in the War to Preserve the Union, 1861–1865.* Providence, Rhode Island: Snow & Farnham, 1894.

RODENBOUGH, THEOPHILUS F., and HASKINS, WILLIAM L., eds. *The Army of the United States, Historical Sketches of Staff and Line.* New York: Charles E. Merrill Co., 1896.

ROE, ALFRED SEELYE. *The Ninth New York Heavy Artillery.* Worcester, Massachusetts: A. S. Roe, 1899.

ROPES, JOHN CODMAN. *The Story of the Civil War,* 4 vols. New York: 1894–1913.

ROSKE, RALPH J., and VAN DOREN, CHARLES. *Lincoln's Commando, a Biography of Commander W. B. Cushing, U.S.N.* New York: Harper and Brothers, 1957.

SCHAFF, MORRIS. *The Spirit of Old West Point.* Boston and New York: Houghton, Mifflin & Co., 1907.

SCOTT, JAMES K. R. *The Story of the Battles at Gettysburg.* Harrisburg, Pennsylvania: The Telegraph Press, 1927.

SHANNON, FRED ALBERT. *The Organization and Administration of The Union Army, 1861–1865.* 2 vols. Glendale, California: Arthur H. Clark Company, 1928.

SHOEMAKER, J. J. *Shoemaker's Battery, Stuart Horse Artillery Battalion, Afterward Commanded by Col. R. P. Chew, Army of Northern Virginia.* Memphis, Tennessee: S. C. Toof & Co., n.d.

Sketch of Page's Battery or Morris Artillery, 2nd Corps, Army of Northern Virginia, by One of the Company. New York: Thomas Smeltzer, 1885.

SMALL, MAJOR ABNER RALPH. *The Road to Richmond.* Berkeley, California: University of California Press, 1939.

SMITH, CAPTAIN JAMES E. *A Famous Battery and Its Campaigns, 1861–64.* Washington: W. H. Lowdermilk & Co., 1892.

SMITH, TUNSTALL, ed. *Richard Snowden Andrews. Lieutenant-Colonel Commanding the First Maryland Artillery, C.S.A.* Baltimore, Maryland: Press of the Sun, 1910.

A Soldier's Story of the War: Including the Marches and Battles of the Washington Artillery and of Other Louisiana Troops. New Orleans: Clark & Hofeline, 1874.

Southern Historical Society Papers, vols. 1–50. Richmond, Virginia: 1914–53.

SPAULDING, COLONEL OLIVER LYMAN, JR. *The United States Army in War and Peace.* New York: G. P. Putnam's Sons, 1937.

———. *Notes on Field Artillery for Officers of All Arms.* Leavenworth, Kansas: U.S. Cavalry Association, 1914.

———. NICKERSON, HOFFMAN, and WRIGHT, COLONEL JOHN W. *Warfare.* New York: Harcourt, Brace & Company, 1925.

STACKPOLE, EDWARD J. *They Met at Gettysburg.* Harrisburg, Pennsylvania: Eagle Books, 1956.

STEELE, MAJOR MATTHEW FORNEY. *American Campaigns.* 2 vols. Washington: War Department Document No. 324, 1943.

STILES, ROBERT. *Four Years under Marse Robert.* New York: 1903.

STINE, J. H. *History of the Army of the Potomac.* Philadelphia: 1892.

STORRICK, W. C. *Gettysburg, the Place, the Battle, the Outcome.* Harrisburg, Pennsylvania: J. Horace McFarland Co., 1932.

STREET, JAMES. *The Civil War.* New York: Dial Press, 1953.

SWINTON, WILLIAM. *Campaigns of the Army of the Potomac.* New York: Charles B. Richardson, 1866.

THOMASON, JOHN W. *Jeb Stuart.* New York: Charles Scribner's Sons, 1934.

TIDBALL, GENERAL JOHN C. *Manual of Heavy Artillery Service.* Washington: 1891.

———. *Remarks upon the Organization, Command, and Employment of Field Artillery during War; Based on Experiences of the Civil War, 1861–5.* Typescript ms. in Library, Artillery and Guided Missile Center, Fort Sill, Oklahoma: c. 1907.

TILBERG, FREDERICK. *Gettysburg National Military Park,* National Park Service Historical Handbook Series, No. 9. Washington: Government Printing Office, 1950.

TOOMBS, SAMUEL. *New Jersey Troops in the Gettysburg Campaign.* Orange, New Jersey: Evening Mail Publishing House, 1888.

U.S. DEPARTMENT OF THE ARMY, THE ARTILLERY AND GUIDED MISSILE CENTER. *Artillery Unit Histories.* Special Bibliography, No. 6. Fort Sill, Oklahoma: 1955.

———. *Famous Artillery Quotations.* Fort Sill, Oklahoma: n. d.

———. *History of the Development of Field Artillery Matériel.* Fort Sill, Oklahoma: 1941.

U.S. DEPARTMENT OF THE ARMY, THE FIELD ARTILLERY SCHOOL. *Instruction Memorandum; History of the Development of Field Artillery Matériel.* Fort Sill, Oklahoma: 1941.

U.S. DEPARTMENT OF THE ARMY, THE INFANTRY SCHOOL. *Selected Readings in American Military History.* 3 vols. Fort Benning, Georgia: 1953.

U.S. DEPARTMENT OF THE ARMY, OFFICE OF THE CHIEF OF MILITARY HISTORY. *Army Lineage Books.* Washington: 1954.

———. *The History of Military Mobilization in the United States.* Washington: 1953.

U.S. DEPARTMENT OF THE ARMY, U.S. MILITARY ACADEMY. *Summaries of Selected Military Campaigns.* West Point, New York: 1953.

U.S. GETTYSBURG NATIONAL PARK COMMISSION. *Locations of the Monuments, Markers, and Tablets on the Battlefield of Gettysburg.* Washington: Government Printing Office, 1932.

U.S. WAR DEPARTMENT. *Bibliography of State Participation in the Civil War, 1861–1866.* Washington: 1913.

———. *Instructions for Field Artillery, 1861;* also *1864.*

———. *The War of the Rebellion: Official Records.* 130 vols. Washington: 1880–1901.

UPTON, EMERY. *The Military Policy of the United States.* 64th Congress, first session, Senate Document No. 379. Washington: Superintendent of Documents, 1917.

VANDERSLICE, JOHN M. *Gettysburg, Then and Now.* New York: G. W. Dillingham Co., 1897.

WAGNER, CAPTAIN ARTHUR L., ed. *Cavalry Studies from Two Great Wars: The Operation of the Cavalry in the Gettysburg Campaign,* by Lt. Col. George B. Davis. Kansas City, Missouri: Hudson-Kimberly Publishing Co., 1896.

WALTON, WILLIAM. *The Army and Navy of the United States from the Period of the Revolution to the Present Day.* Part 4, Sec. 5. "Artillery." Boston: 1889–96.

WHITMAN, WILLIAM E. S., and TRUE, CHARLES H. *Maine in the War for the Union.* Lewiston, Maine: Nelson Dingley, Jr., and Co., 1865.

WILEY, BELL IRWIN. *The Life of Johnny Reb.* Indianapolis: Bobbs-Merrill Company, Inc., 1943.

———. *The Life of Billy Yank.* Indianapolis: Bobbs-Merrill Company, Inc., 1943.

WILKESON, FRANK. *Recollections of a Private Soldier in the Army of the Potomac.* New York: 1887.

WILSON, LIEUTENANT A. W. *The Story of the Gun.* Woolwich, England: 1944.

WILSON, JAMES H. *Under the Old Flag: Recollections of Military Operations in the War for the Union, the Spanish War, the Boxer Rebellion, etc.* 2 vols. New York: Daniel Appleton Co., 1912.

WISE, JENNINGS CROPPER. *The Long Arm of Lee.* 2 vols. Lynchburg, Virginia: J. P. Bell Co., 1915.

YOUNG, JESSE BOWMAN. *The Battle of Gettysburg.* New York: Harper & Brothers, 1913.

Index

Batteries and other units are indexed under Military Units. Battery assignments and their commanders at Gettysburg are specified in Appendix B.

Weapons, ammunition, and equipment are cross-indexed. They are described in detail in Appendix A, with diagrams included in the illustrations.

Ranks of officers here given are generally the highest they attained in the war. The ranks they held at Gettysburg are used in the text.

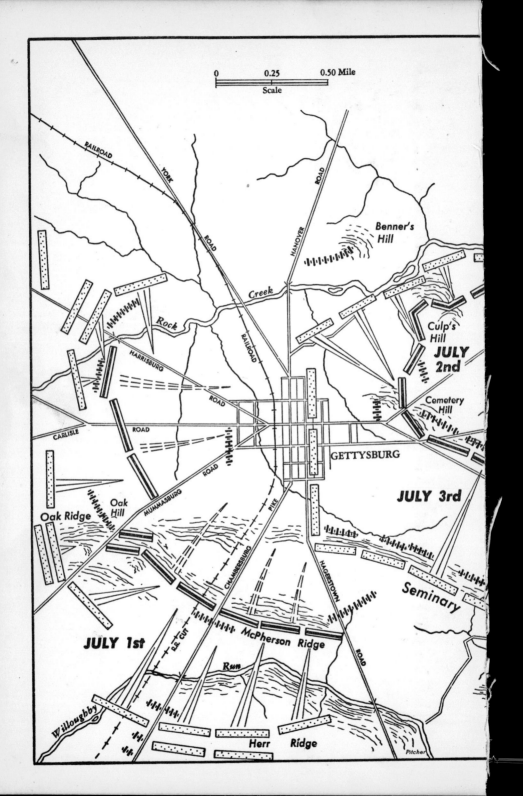

Scale
0   0.25   0.50 Mile

RAILROAD

YORK

ROAD

Benner's
Hill

HANOVER ROAD

Creek

Culp's
Hill

Rock

JULY
2nd

HARRISBURG

RAILROAD

ROAD

Cemetery
Hill

CARLISLE

ROAD

GETTYSBURG

JULY 3rd

Oak
Hill

MUMMASBURG

PIKE

ROAD

Oak Ridge

Seminary

CHAMBERSBURG

HAGERSTOWN

ROAD

JULY 1st

R.R. Cut

McPherson Ridge

Run

Willoughby

Herr   Ridge

Pitcher